DEVELOPMENT AND EXTERNAL DEBT IN LATIN AMERICA

Development and External Debt in Latin America

Bases for a New Consensus

Edited by Richard E. Feinberg
and Ricardo Ffrench-Davis

UNIVERSITY OF NOTRE DAME PRESS
NOTRE DAME, INDIANA 46556

Library of Congress Cataloging-in-Publication Data

Development and external debt in Latin America.

Contains material prepared for the Working Group on
Economics of the Inter-American Dialogue and presented
in a seminar held Mar. 17-19, 1986 at the headquarters
of the Latin American Economic Research Corporation
in Santiago, Chile.
  1. Debts, External—Latin America—Congresses.
2. Debt relief—Latin America—Congresses. 3. Latin
America—Economic policy—Congresses. I. Feinberg,
Richard E. II. Ffrench-Davis, Ricardo. III. Inter-
American Dialogue (Organization). Working Group on
Economics. IV. Corporación de Investigaciones
Económicas para Latinoamérica.
HJ8514.5.D49 1987   336.3'435'098   86-40584
ISBN 0-268-00862-0
ISBN 0-268-00863-9 (pbk.)

Contents

III. COUNTRY STUDIES: PERSPECTIVES ON EXTERNAL INDEBTEDNESS AND INTERNAL DEVELOPMENT

IV. PANEL ON STRATEGIES FOR CONFRONTING THE CRISIS

Preface

This book contains material prepared for the Working Group on Economics of the Inter-American Dialogue. The Group began its work in June 1985, in a meeting held at the headquarters of the Latin American Economic Research Corporation (Corporación de Investigaciones Económicas para América Latina — CIEPLAN) in Santiago, Chile, followed by sessions at the Kellogg Institute of the University of Notre Dame in September and at the Wye Plantation in November. Most of the papers comprising this volume were presented and discussed in a seminar held March 17–19, 1986, at CIEPLAN.

The versions of the articles, comments, and panel discussions appearing in this book were subsequently revised and updated by the authors.

Throughout the organization and development of this work, Peter Hakim (Staff Director) provided ongoing support for coordination of the Group. José María Dagnino-Pastore and Alejandro Foxley (members of the Dialogue) also assisted with various aspects of the work. With respect to the final seminar, we would like to express our gratitude for the generous cooperation of ECLA, RIAL, and SELA, and for the support of specialists from the Inter-American Development Bank and the World Bank. José De Gregorio at CIEPLAN and Mary L. Williamson at the Overseas Development Council very ably assisted in reviewing the contents and preparing the final manuscript, Cornelio González edited draft comments, and María de la Luz Castillo provided valuable secretarial support.

The contents of each paper are the sole responsibility of the respective authors.

Overview

RICHARD E. FEINBERG AND RICARDO FFRENCH-DAVIS

Despite several years of costly adjustments, Latin America remains mired in the twin crises of debt and development. Per capita output is substantially lower than in the early 1980s in most countries. Investment is notoriously weak, and unemployment and social conditions have worsened. Country after country is experiencing sharp obstacles to servicing debt. Responding to this deterioration commercial banks are cutting back lending wherever they can—thereby deepening the crisis.

Creditors have managed the debt problem so as to successfully avoid a breakdown of the international financial system, but have postponed more lasting solutions. In the meantime, countries are being pushed away from the road to development. There is need for a change in strategy.

This volume presents a frank assessment of the past errors of national governments in developed and developing countries, and of international creditors, public and private, that contributed to the downturn. This volume does not pretend to provide a uniform perspective, but the individual contributions do amount to a cogent indictment of the international financial system for its failure to reduce the costs of adjustment and of many Latin American governments for their slowness to adjust to the destructive impact of repeated shocks from the global economy. The separate essays offer numerous recommendations for altering the shape of the international economy and improving the future performance of Latin American economies.

Some of the papers discuss global trends in trade, finance, and investment, and offer a sense of the overarching problems faced by the whole continent, while other papers discuss specific country

1

circumstances to illustrate how differentiated Latin America has become. Overall, negative financial transfers, lower export prices, and reduced domestic output, employment, and investment have troubled the region since the early 1980s, but the authors convey the sharp variations in national conditions, illustrated by the country cases of Brazil, Costa Rica, and Peru.

THE IMPORTANCE OF THE GLOBAL ENVIRONMENT AND THE NEED FOR NEGOTIATIONS

Massive and largely unforeseen swings in commodities markets, exchange rates, capital flows, and interest rates were key causes of the current crisis. Few prognosticators, whether official or private, anticipated the crisis, and many proceeded to underestimate its seriousness and persistence. Until 1982 debtor countries were generally encouraged to borrow, and commercial banks were praised for lending by industrial-country governments and the most influential multilateral institutions who considered the boom in private international capital markets to be conducive to Third World development. Even though the crisis became apparent in 1982, the tendency to provide optimistic assessments of future trends has continued (Ffrench-Davis, Ossa). It has been repeatedly assumed that a rapid and sustained recovery of international trade and of voluntary lending would occur. Influential projections by the International Monetary Fund have caused some public and private actors to adopt incorrect policies. Dagnino-Pastore in this volume notes that debtor nations have had to suffer the consequences and laments the absence of mechanisms to correct such mistakes.

Eventual recovery in Latin America will depend heavily on improving the global economic environment, especially with regard to industrial-country growth rates, net resource transfers (capital flows minus interest and profit payments), trading opportunities, interest rates, exchange rates, and, in the best of worlds, commodity prices (Dornbusch, Ffrench-Davis). Latin American nations will have to make major adjustments in their own economic policies in response to changing international circumstances, but they cannot resume steady growth if repeatedly subject to adverse external shocks.

Many Latin American nations have made a substantial effort to increase exports, a large proportion of which have been absorbed by a buoyant U.S. market for imports. However, a large rise in the volume of sales has been offset by a drastic fall in export prices, and the prospects for a revival of commodity prices are not good for the coming years (Ibarra). A stagnant international trade together with the simultaneous export drive of most debtor nations has contributed to this drop in prices. Similarly, White argues that foreign investment flows are contingent upon an improved global environment and its impact on Latin American growth — even more than on national policies targeted to attract direct foreign investment. Uncertainty in world markets depresses direct foreign investment as well as bank lending. National policies toward foreign investment also play a minor role compared to the growth prospects and macroeconomic policies of host countries. Economic recession is a strong deterrent to direct foreign investment and is not overridden by more generous national policies. But even though foreign investment may not contribute a great deal in terms of capital inflows, it can potentially bring technology and access to external markets (White, Bitar). An active policy of host countries may contribute in attracting foreign investment that will effectively improve the countries' access to new technologies and export markets.

A persistent theme of the volume is that efforts at international cooperation should be revived to reduce growing North-South tensions and to produce a better international economic environment. Authors advocate negotiations on debt (Dornbusch, Feinberg, Ffrench-Davis, Foxley), direct investment (White, Bitar), and trade (Ibarra). Additional negotiations are proposed for country-specific problems (Castillo, Rodriguez). Given their weakened bargaining position, it seems unlikely that the Latin American nations would adopt strongly confrontational postures in the event that negotiations were convened. However, several authors warn that the persistence of the financial crisis into the 1990s represents potentially strong factors that could push the Latin American nations toward unilateral measures if the industrial nations maintain uncompromising positions.

THE ROLE OF INTERNATIONAL AGENCIES

The contributors generally consider the Bretton Woods institutions to be important and vital, but in need of "adjustment." The authors' attitudes range from fear and distrust to condescension. Some authors and commentators paint a picture of the IMF as rigid, ideological, dominated by the North—and as inducing unnecessarily costly stabilization programs. Others note that national governments house economists at least as competent—and more grounded in local realities—as those employed by the IMF. The Costa Rican government designed its stabilization program largely on its own (Castillo, Rodríguez). The Brazilian government has often followed its own path (Carneiro). For its part Peru has a bitter history of confrontation with the IMF (Webb). All three country studies are highly critical of the quality of the prescriptions of the Fund.

The World Bank is hardly mentioned, which is symptomatic of a widespread feeling that it has failed to play a significant role during the debt crisis. Some authors welcome the enhanced role for the Bank as outlined in the Baker Plan, seeing the Bank as a potential source of capital and advice (Feinberg), while others fear that the Bank might join forces with the Fund to impose a strongly ideological conditionality. Some view the Baker Plan with serious concern and criticize it for failing to give Latin America adequate credit for the costly adjustment efforts already undertaken, and for signaling an intention to limit further the capacity of countries to choose their own development strategies (Foxley).

Even the more critical authors have not given up on the Bretton Woods agencies. On the contrary, they generally advocate increasing the agencies' resources while altering their programs to make them more sensitive to the policy preferences of national authorities. These authors seek a better balance between the desire for national sovereignty and the requirements of international markets and lending agencies from whom countries seek credit. Several authors stress that it is not the multilateral institutions' conditional funding that is in question, but rather the content of conditionality. In this respect, several authors recommend that a systematic effort be undertaken to design a new form of conditionality, a process in which the view from debtor nations should play a major role.

LESSONS FROM STABILIZATION EXPERIENCES

There is a broad and clear recognition that although the main cause of the crisis is external shocks, Latin American governments have made mistakes, including overborrowing and postponing inevitable austerity measures. Contributors emphasize the need for consistent development strategies and sensible economic policies. But it is also stressed that these goals cannot be achieved by sudden and across-the-board market liberalization, as illustrated by the costly experiences in the southern cone. Indeed, ill-timed and extreme liberalization of financial markets, including the decontrol of private foreign borrowing, contributed to the crisis in several countries by encouraging exchange rate appreciation, capital flight, and nonproductive indebtedness.

Several authors stress that countries such as Brazil and Colombia, which made moderate and pragmatic reforms, have performed better with respect to economic development. However, the Costa Rican example suggests that "shock" treatment is sometimes appropriate. Bold and decisive policies can win popular support after a period of drift, decline, and soaring inflation—as presidents Alfonsín, Garcia, and Sarney have demonstrated. In particular, it is argued that shock treatment may be the right response to soaring inflation rates; the precise response ought to depend on whether high inflation was short-lived (Costa Rica) or long-standing (Argentina and Brazil).

Many of these examples of decisive action to combat financial disequilibrium have diverged from orthodox, free-market formulas and have included a heavy dose of government intervention to regulate wages and prices, to control foreign exchange markets, and to try to minimize the damage to the more vulnerable social groups. The three country studies illustrate the great differences among Latin American nations, and the corresponding need for policies designed to take into account the peculiarities of each country.

GROWTH AND DEBT

Latin American nations are feeling "debt fatigue" (Foxley). Authors emphasize the instability of a situation where a recession-ridden continent has had to disburse 5 percent of its GNP in interest payments to banks no longer willing to lend. The promise of a resumption of "voluntary lending" to well-behaved debtors has proved illusionary. The consequence of large negative transfers is that debtor nations have had to restrict their aggregate demand drastically, causing substantial increases in unemployment and drops in economic activity and investment. The decline in domestic investment dangerously impairs future growth prospects and nations' capacity to service debt in the long run.

Some countries may be able to combine growth and debt service under the current rules of the game, but others have a debt profile and export potential that preclude a resumption of growth without major debt relief. Articles in this volume suggest that Brazil fits in the former category and Peru in the latter, while Costa Rica might be able to live within current rules only if it received favorable treatment by creditors and better commodity prices. However, several authors stress that the situation of each country is extremely sensitive to changes both in the domestic and in the world economy.

ADJUSTMENT—THE TASKS AHEAD

Latin American economists have been working to forge a new consensus, what some have dubbed a "pragmatic neo-structuralism." Attitudes have become more sophisticated regarding the role of the state, the private sector, and foreign investment, and more positive concerning the value of trade and economic efficiency. The new approach is more policy-oriented, concerned with how to achieve more efficiently a set of conflicting goals. Extreme forms of socialization—and of liberalization—are rejected. Economists have reconsidered their ideas regarding macroeconomic policies, adjusting them to the specific circumstances of semi-industrialized countries. While there are wide areas of agreement, some important differences remain that should be hammered out on a country-by-country basis.

No major school of thought, and certainly no contributor to this volume, favors autarchy, although fear does exist that a rigid international system might push some nations in that direction. Rather, there is broad agreement on the need for international trade and financing and the strong link between them. Several authors are alarmed at the threats that current global economic crises pose to a mutually fair interdependence—the contraction of trade and the negative direction of net resource transfers. Reforms are required that reverse these adverse trends, provide for more stable and open markets, and reduce the resource drain that is inhibiting Latin American growth.

Several authors are concerned that while Latin Americans have become more pragmatic, some governments and creditors are becoming more demanding and ideological. This trend is seen as a serious setback in progress toward understanding the forces behind economic development, and as an obstacle to more efficient adjustment and an improved international economic system. It forfeits an historic opportunity to improve North-South relations in the economic and the diplomatic spheres.

There is a challenge to combine growth with equity, at both the international and the national levels, to protect vulnerable groups during a period of rapid dislocation and change. The costs of global adjustment should be equitably shared between creditors and debtors, between North and South. And as Latin American countries undertake the necessary structural adjustments in their own economies, their macroeconomic and social policies should seek to offset harm done to the poorer sectors and to establish programs that directly attack poverty. Economic development strategies should be consistent with the enhancement of democratic institutions.

The next decade will be a decisive one for Latin American economic and political development and for the region's relations with the global economy. These essays seek to provide insights and recommendations that enhance the prospects for success.

PART I

Adjustment Processes and the Framework of External Debt Negotiations

World Economic Issues of Interest to Latin America

RUDIGER DORNBUSCH*

At the 1984 Economic Summit and the Annual Meeting of the IMF, industrial countries could compliment themselves and above all the IMF's managing director for their approach to the Latin debt issue. By avoiding a liquidity crisis and putting in place adjustment programs, they had placed debtor nations in a position to service their debts rather than simply default. The recovery of the industrialized countries, notably the U.S. boom, had fulfilled the promise that a favorable external environment would lighten the debtor countries adjustment burden. But by 1986 it had become clear that the process of debt collection—while successful on the surface—was in fact taking place at the extreme case: the non-interest surpluses required for debt service were achieved by a matching decline in investment. The indecency of forced debt collection at all costs is thus matched by outright imprudence. The same shortsightedness that presided over lending is now applied to collection.

The outstanding fact of 1983–84, much to the embarrassment of pessimists, was the apparent ease and overkill with which external targets were met. Brazil managed to generate a surplus nearly equal to the full interest bill, and Mexico's external performance was strong enough to support a multiyear rescheduling. Argentina went into a stabilization program with renewed commitment to debt service. Latin America was therefore successfully transferring resources to the advanced countries. But this success is illusory because

*Department of Economics, Massachusetts Institute of Technology, Cambridge.

in fact it is coming at the expense of expansion and steady maintenance of the productive capacity in debtor countries. Whereas
debtor countries are hoping to increase standards of living, the very
low rates of investment in conjunction with high rates of productivity growth offer the more likely prospect of little growth beyond
mere recovery.

The achievement in external debt service in the past few years
occurred against a background of very poor domestic performance.
Income per capita today in Latin America is more than 10 percent
lower than in 1980, and the sharp decline in investment has reduced
the rate at which employment could even potentially expand. Table
1 shows the extent of deterioration by comparing recent growth
rates with the long-term trend. The inflation rate over the past few
years has increased sharply, and in 1984–85 hyperinflation conditions arose in some countries.

THE RESOURCE TRANSFER REVERSAL

Following the 1982 debt crisis, the debt issue almost disap-
peared from the media and LDC debt problems became primarily
technical issues of adjustment programs between bank committees
and debtor country treasuries. The need for fiscal correction in
debtor countries became the chief issue since budget deficits were
seen as the case for the remaining problem of high inflation. Indeed, budget deficits were also singled out as the major source of
the debt crisis.[1] A senior IMF official states:

TABLE 1

*Per Capita Output Growth, Inflation, and Gross Capital Formation
in Latin America (Annual Average Rates)*

	1962–80	1977–82	1983–85
Per Capita Growth	3.3	−2.7	−0.9
Inflation	29.4	91.0	171
Gross Capital Formation (% of GDP)	21.5	23.3	17.5

Source: IMF

> No other set of factors explains more of the debt crisis than the fiscal deficits incurred by most of the major countries in Latin America. Although there were other factors which were relevant, I have no doubt that the main problem was excessive public (and private) spending that was financed by both easy domestic credit policies and by ample resources from abroad. The world recession and high real rates of interest in international markets aggravated the crisis, but I do not believe they created it. (Wiesner, 1984, p. 191)

Needless to say, this is an extravagant interpretation. A more balanced account would assign equal responsibility to domestic mismanagement, world economic conditions and imprudent lending by the creditor banks.[2]

Figure 1 shows Latin America's external balance, distinguishing

FIGURE 1
Latin America's Trade and Debt Service
(Billion $U.S.)

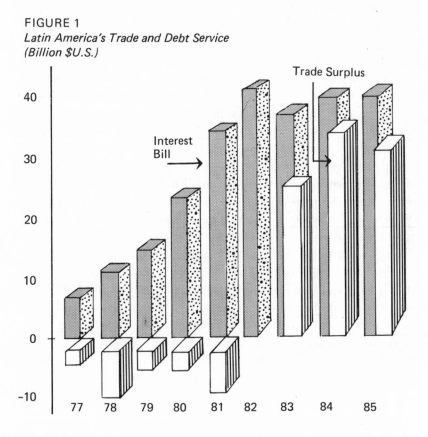

between the non-interest current account and interest payments. The striped bars represent the non-interest surplus (or deficit) on goods and services account and the dotted bars show total interest liabilities. The non-interest deficits represent the net transfers of goods and services toward Latin America in the 1977–82 period. Since then, resources have been transferred out of Latin America to the creditor countries.

The diagram also shows trends in debt. The increase in debt is equal to the current account deficit, which can be split into the non-interest current account deficit plus net-interest liabilities. With these definitions in mind we note that up to 1982 the debt increased because the entire interest bill was financed by borrowing or "new money." In addition, borrowing financed the non-interest current account deficits. Since 1982 credit rationing has forced Latin America to transfer resources abroad to earn rather than borrow the foreign exchange with which to pay interest. In 1984–85 interest payments were almost entirely met by non-interest surpluses rather than new money.

Figure 1 is important to bear in mind in the policy discussion. In this context "new money" and "return of voluntary lending" mean, for all practical purposes, that LDCs will gain access to larger amounts of credit to finance their interest charges. Given the magnitude of their interest bill at present, it is difficult to believe that Latin America will in the next five years gain financing for non-interest surpluses. That means the net flow of resources will be from poor to rich countries. The only discussion in terms of figure 1 is the size of these net transfers. The 1984–85 experiences encouraged creditors to take the view that more is not enough since the debtors seem to be able to marshal surpluses with so much ease.

But the belief that LDCs' problems are of their own making and that the solution is mostly domestic is overshadowed by a basic worry. Even in the industrialized countries it is felt that unless the world economic environment is outright favorable, the debt problem is far from solved. This is clear from the September 22, 1985 statement of the Group of Five, finance ministers of leading industrial countries, as reported in the New York Times:

> Sustained growth in world trade, lower interest rates, open markets, and continued financing in amounts and on terms appropriate to

each individual case are essential to enable developing countries to achieve sound growth and overcome their economic and financial difficulties.

The qualifications "continued," "sound," and "their" make it clear that any expectation of debt relief is unwarranted. That raises the question of whether the world economy will make a significant contribution toward solving the debt problem or whether most of the work will have to be done by the debtor countries themselves. If the latter were the case one must ask whether debt service fatigue will become a live issue.

EXTERNAL LINKAGES

Latin America is linked to world economic developments through four partly overlapping channels:

- The terms of trade, that is, the prices of exports relative to those of imports.
- The level of foreign demand for a country's exports and hence export volume.
- Market access, which influences export volume for commodities, semimanufactures, and manufactures.
- Interest rates prevailing in world markets, which determine debt service applying to all debt other than concessional loans.

Credit rationing and conditionality appear as additional aspects of the external environment, while the creation of foreign tax havens is a further issue in respect to capital flight.

The external environment can either favor debtor countries through favorable terms of trade and negative real interest rates or set them back, as in 1980–82, through a collapse of commodity prices and sharply positive real interest rates. Table 2 compares some recent episodes. The 1970–73 period stands out as particularly favorable. (The next section reviews two alternative frameworks to assess the impact of the external environment on domestic performance and welfare.)

There are two very different approaches to studying the impact of external macroeconomic events on debtor LDCs. The cash-

flow approach uses economic theory to assess the welfare effects
of external shocks. Another, the welfare approach, asks how these
shocks affect a country's near-term quality as a debtor.

The cash-flow model

A country's debt-to-export ratio is routinely taken as a measure
of creditworthiness.[3] High debt-export ratios such as 300 or 400
percent are thought to represent excessive indebtedness, while
numbers in the range of 100 to 200 percent would be characteristic
of countries in good standing.

The debt-export ratio grows when debt service is not met by
trade surpluses but rather by extra borrowing. Debt is growing even
more strongly when in addition to the interest bill, a country runs
a deficit financed by borrowing. By contrast, growth in export
revenue because of higher export prices or volume reduces the debt-
export ratio.

These factors can be reduced to a simple equation focusing
on three factors:

i the interest rate, usually LIBOR
x the growth rate of export earnings in dollars
v the non-interest current account surplus expressed as a frac-
   tion of debt outstanding.

Using these definitions, the percentage increase in the debt-export
ratio is given by the following relation:

$$\text{Growth of Debt-Export Ratio} = i - x - v \qquad (1)$$

TABLE 2

Key Macroeconomic Variables of the World Economy
(Average Annual Percentage Rates)

		INFLATION		
	LIBOR	Manufactures	Commodities	OECD GROWTH
1970–73	7.6	12.4	14.4	4.5
1980–82	14.7	–2.4	–13.3	0.7
1983–85	9.7	–2.0	–0.5	3.4

Source: IMF

The relation can be used for two purposes. Looking backward, it can be used to identify the proximate causes of a deterioration in the debt-export ratio. The deterioration can be attributed to three possible sources: high interest rates, low growth of export revenue or even declining export earnings, and a fall in non-interest surpluses. Looking forward, the model can be used to ask whether the predicted level of interest rates exceeds the projected growth of export revenues so that the debt-export ratio will decline even if all the interest bill were borrowed so that $v = 0$. Or one might ask how much of the non-interest surplus must be achieved to bring about a specified reduction in the debt-export ratio.

Table 3 shows the data for two periods. For the 1970–79 period the interest rate fell significantly short of growth in export revenue and, for this reason, the debt-export ratio was declining. But since 1978 interest rates have exceeded growth rates of export earnings, thus adding to debt problems.

Cline (1985) in reviewing his predictions using the cash-flow approach offered the following conclusions:

> My estimates in mid-1983 indicated that the debt problem was indeed one of illiquidity rather than insolvency. Under central critical expectations for international economic variables (and politically acceptable growth rates in debtor countries), the projections showed that most major debtor countries in balance of payments and relative debt burden, and that by the late 1980s debt-export ratios would be back to levels previously associated with creditworthiness. A return to higher OECD growth rates would increase export volume and prices, an eventual easing of interest rates would moderate

TABLE 3

Determinants of Debt Dynamics for Latin America
(Annual Average Percentage Rate)

	1978–82	1983–85
LIBOR	13.0	9.7
Growth of Export Earnings	11.9	0.5
Non-Interest Current Account Surplus[a]	–11.1	22.3

[a] Percent of Exports of Goods and Services
    Source: IMF

interest payments, and a decline of the dollar from its seriously over-
valued level would raise the dollar value of the export base. However,
the analysis also indicated that a critical threshold of 2.5 to 3 percent was required for OECD growth to avoid stagnation or severe
deterioration in external deficits and debt-export ratios for debtor
countries. (p. 186)

As noted above, the external balance of Latin America did,
indeed, improve substantially and even outdid the Cline projections.
Moreover, these improvements occurred even though interest rates
did not decline rapidly and the dollar remained strong (until 1985).
Much of the external balance performance came from export volume growth and cuts in import levels and much less from improved
terms of trade or inflationary erosion of debt burdens.

In judging the prospects for the debt problem from this cash-
flow and solvency perspective, one asks whether the next few years
will look like 1970–79 or more nearly like 1980–85. In the former
case strong export growth erodes overindebtedness, already without
any significant non-interest surpluses. But if conditions of low export and poor terms of trade continue, then persistent, large non-
interest surpluses are required to maintain creditworthiness. (Of
course it is essential here to distinguish between oil importers and
exporters. Where Mexico and Venezuela are hurt by lower oil prices,
Brazil benefits significantly.) These non-interest surpluses of course
impair the growth potential of Latin America since they involve
transferring savings to the creditors rather than investing in an expansion of productive capacity.

The framework does not tell us as yet how rapidly a country
should work down its debt-export ratio. The pace is in fact determined by another set of considerations, namely the amount of new
credit banks are willing to make available. By keeping down the
growth rate of LDC loans relative to those of other loans, the share
of LDC debt in total bank loans can be worked down over time.
The size of debtors' non-interest surpluses is therefore determined
by credit rationing. Banks (in collaboration with the IMF) set the
growth in LDC exposure that they are willing to accept. With the
growth of debt or "new money" thus determined, the required non-
interest surplus is equal to the interest bill less the permitted increase
in exposure. Letting b stand for the debt-export ratio and y for the

permitted increase in exposure, the required non-interest surplus, v^*, is given by

$$v^* = (i-y)b \tag{2}$$

Thus the higher the interest rate relative to the permitted exposure growth, and the higher the debt-export ratio, the higher must be the non-interest surplus. Considering a country paying a 10 percent interest rate, having a debt-export ratio of 3.5 and an exposure growth of 2 percent implies that the non-interest surplus will have to equal nearly one-third of exports.

The framework we have looked at so far highlights three sets of variables determined by world macroeconomic developments: the short-term interest rate that determines debt service for a given debt-export ratio, the rate of inflation of LDC export prices, and the growth rate of export revenue. The last two combine to yield the growth rate of export revenue. The outlook for the world debt problem, from this perspective, focuses on alternative scenarios for interest rates and growth in export revenue by identifying the factors that most decisively influence these key variables. Before looking at these factors in the next section, we turn now to an alternative framework.

The welfare approach

The preceding model looks at cash flow to judge whether the debt problem is being worked down over time or whether a deterioration is likely. It is a (narrow) creditor's perspective in that it focuses on the quality of loans, not on the economic and social welfare in the debtor countries. Although some of the factors already mentioned above will enter the welfare calculations, the role and weighting are quite different.

In the welfare perspective it can be shown that a country benefits if the terms of trade improve or if, in the case of a debtor country, the real interest rate declines:

- The terms of trade improvement imply that a unit of exports commands increased purchasing power in terms of imports. The measure of the welfare improvement is the level of imports times the gain in the terms of trade.

- A real interest rate decline raises welfare by the initial level of the debt times the fall in the real interest rate.
- An increase in export volume does *not*, except in special circumstances, represent a welfare gain. Increased export volume enhances welfare only when imperfect competition causes export prices to exceed their costs or when resources are not fungible between alternative activities. In these special cases, which are not implausible, the gain in welfare does not correspond one-for-one to the gain in export volume, but rather depends on the size of the distortion.

Note that the welfare approach emphasizes the advantage of increased foreign demand, but it spreads benefits to debtor LDCs through improved terms of trade, not trade volume. The proper reckoning of export volume and non-interest surpluses is what sets the two alternative approaches most clearly apart. In the cash flow model an increased non-interest surplus is viewed as a good thing because it reduces indebtedness. But of course from a welfare point of view, reducing indebtedness means foregoing current consumption or investment (and perhaps even output through a recession) and therefore may be a bad idea. In fact, non-interest surpluses may be primarily a reflection of credit rationing as in equation (2) rather than the outcome of optimal resource allocation.[4]

Export volume, too, appears very different in this perspective. An increase in export volume that reflects a domestic recession is viewed positively in the cash-flow model since it helps reduce indebtedness. Not so in the welfare approach, where it means hard work or foregone consumption. Moreover, the welfare approach singles out another determinant that does not appear at all in the cash-flow model, namely credit rationing. The relaxation of an effective credit constraint such as emerged in 1983–4 in the course of involuntary debt service enhances welfare. This is the case because the productivity of investment or the valuation of increased current consumption exceeds the world rate of interest. This is, of course, highly plausible when one views the premature debt service now under way as a tour de force in cutting down the absorption of current resources.

The welfare approach has a very strong implication. It shows that the flow of resources from debtor to creditor countries or "success at correcting external imbalances" cannot be interpreted as a welfare improvement.

ADJUSTMENT IN LATIN AMERICA

In 1946 the Foreign Bond Holders Protective Council reported that of the outstanding publicly offered or guaranteed dollar bonds of Latin America 53.2 percent were in default as to interest and sinking fund, 44.8 percent were receiving *adjusted* debt service, and only 2 percent were serviced in full.[5] Against this historical record which is typical for the past 150 years, the current experience is completely new and, for that reason, untried. It means that developing countries, rather than receiving resource transfers to foster capital accumulation and growth in their standard of living, will be servicing their debts by transferring resources toward the creditors. But the creditors are also reluctant to receive debt service in the only way it can come, namely in kind. Just as in the 1930s prior to default, they are erecting trade obstacles to debt service.

There is now a confusion of priorities: banks practice credit rationing, seeking a dramatically accelerated path of reduction in the debt-export ratio. The pace is entirely unwarranted by any consideration of debt stability. Its primary purpose is to reduce the cost of capital for banks and enhance their own balance sheets. The benefits to LDCs from reductions in the cost of capital to banks may be present, but surely not sufficient to warrant the debt retirement strategy. The question, then, is why LDCs would collaborate in the strategy.

Debt service, as is remembered from the discussion of German reparations in the interwar period, involves a transfer problem. The problem arises in three areas: how to raise the budget revenue for debt service in a noninflationary way, how to shift resources to the external sector so as to achieve the budget cut and trade surplus under conditions of high employment, and how to actually succeed in earning the foreign exchange with which to service the debt. At each step things can go wrong.

Among the factors influencing the ease or difficulty of servicing an external debt, four deserve special attention. The first is the burden of interest payments as measured by the ratio of interest payments to GDP. The second is the openness of the economy as measured by the ratio of exports to GDP. The remaining two are the position of the public sector budget and politics. These factors combine to determine the welfare losses arising from an external disturbance and the macroeconomic performance when exposed to a shock.

We now discuss each in turn, using the perspective of the transfer problem. Table 4 highlights two of the elements, the interest burden and the degree of openness (exports). The Brazil-Korea comparison is introduced to argue that superior Asian performance is in part a reflection of structural characteristics rather than policy choices.

The budget problem

The budget problem arises because much of the debt has been nationalized. Even where initially it was not debt by the public sector or public sector enterprises, the debt has in some cases been dumped in the budget in the course of financial collapse of the banking system. But this is a feature peculiar to Latin Ameria and, apparently, not common in Asia.

The budget problem of course arises because countries that already have difficulties financing their fiscal expenditures are suddenly forced to marshal resources worth several percent of GDP. The extra taxation is exceedingly difficult because it would fall primarily on wage earners, as capital effectively avoids taxation. Inflation, therefore, is the inevitable outcome (or sustained recession as in Chile), at least as long as the government has not found a way to cut spending. But financing an extra few percentage points

TABLE 4

Structural Characteristics of LDCs: 1984
(Percent of GDP)

	L. AMERICA	KOREA	BRAZIL
Interest Payments	4.7	5.1	5.5
Exports	16.4	37.3	10.3

Source: IMF and Morgan Guaranty

of GDP worth of debt service with an inflation tax means a dramatic increase in inflation. The problem is clearly not printing money, but having to service the debt.

In the foreign exchange market there is an easy offset. The public recognizes that the increased charge on the budget represents inflation and possibly asset taxation. If there is capital mobility, speculation against the currency will immediately lead to pressure on reserves and hence inevitably to a sharp depreciation of the exchange rate, further increasing inflation. The problem is aggravated when an already precarious budget situation is worsened by reduced foreign exchange revenues as, for example, is the case in Mexico.

If an exchange-rate collapse is to be avoided, asset holders have to be compensated by sufficiently high rates of interest. In Brazil, Mexico, and Argentina, real interest rates have been well into the double digit figures at various points during the past three years. Of course, the high real rates of interest ultimately breed their own instability since debts are being rolled over at these rates, and thus must eventually get entirely out of line with the tax base or the return from real capital. What looks like a holding action is therefore in the end yet another (domestic) debt crisis to be resolved either by repudiation or inflation.

The first problem, then, is the inflation cost, or real interest cost, of securing the budget revenue for debt service.

The foreign exchange problem

The second issue is to translate the increased budget revenue into earnings of foreign exchange. When the inflation tax is used to finance the government, the process is direct: the government issues money to buy foreign exchange, forcing the rate to whatever level necessary to buy the needed amounts. Private speculation goes the same direction, and hence real depreciation and high or even accelerating inflation are the rule. If taxation or expenditure cuts are used, the adjustment is more complicated. To maintain full employment, relative prices must now change. The real price of home goods must decline, releasing resources to the traded goods sector even as the public sector is cutting spending.

Real depreciation means in practice that the real wage must fall in terms of tradables. The only way a country can gain access

to extra foreign exchange is to reduce its dollar costs. The extent
of the required reduction depends on two factors. The first is the
domestic response of employment in the traded goods sector to the
real wage: the more responsive the employment, the smaller the real
wage cut. The second is the elasticity of demand for the country's
output. The size of the foreign trade sector certainly is a consideration here. The larger the trade sector, the easier it becomes, other
things being equal, to generate an extra percent of GDP worth of
foreign exchange.

With perfectly elastic demand the problem is entirely classical,
but if demand is less than perfectly elastic it becomes necessary to
put the country's resources on sale. Now it is possible that quite
substantial real wage cuts and cuts in the standard of living are required to achieve a given trade surplus.

The size of the foreign trade sector brings up the difference
in performance between Brazil and Korea. Faced with the need to
generate a given increase in the trade surplus, Korea has a much
easier task because the export sector accounts for a much larger
share of GNP. Other things being equal, only a small real depreciation is needed in Korea, whereas in Brazil it would need to be three
or even five times the size to have the same payoff in terms of net
foreign exchange revenues. That of course has an immediate impact on inflation as well as on the redistribution of income among
different sectors.

The point is reinforced in two ways. In Korea income distribution is exceedingly equal and social services are highly advanced.
Real depreciation is largely uncontroversial because it does not
significantly redistribute income among different groups. By contrast, income distribution in Brazil is highly unequal and real
depreciation is therefore an important real wage issue. An additional
effect is the following: in Korea real depreciation is practically a
growth machine since it applies to a very large share of GNP. In
Brazil, by contrast, it applies to a small share and hence is seen
primarily as a disruptive cost rather than an important policy for
growth. Moreover, because income distribution in Brazil is so unequal, indexation arrangements are essential to avoid political confrontation, and that in turn means real depreciation is largely
impossible.

The difference in structure explains why in Korea, real depreciation can be used to achieve external balance correction with little inflation and a large and favorable impact on growth. In Brazil, by contrast, adjustment takes much more the form of trade restriction and recession because real depreciation is so inflationary and disruptive.

System-wide problems

The transfer problem has a third dimension. Actual debt service, if there are no assets to be liquidated, can be effected only in kind. But that raises two separate difficulties. The first is that when many LDCs try, at the same time, to service their debts by trade surpluses, competition results. They are jointly pursuing a real depreciation policy that worsens their terms of trade. This situation represents a secondary burden of the transfer, which is unquestionably part of the LDC terms of trade deterioration.

The second difficulty is market access. Concerned about increased imports, the creditor countries respond to the increased cost competitiveness (due to devaluation) of the LDCs with the threat of trade restrictions. But if debt service is to continue, the restrictions mean that LDCs have to gain yet more in competitiveness to overcome the trade restrictions. Gaining competitiveness of course implies reduced real wages and a reduced standard of living.

Debt service fatigue

Given the intense difficulties involved in generating debt service, it is reasonable to ask why LDCs service their debts rather than default. One reason is clearly that the well-managed system simply excludes liquidity problems that make nonpayment inevitable. The other has been, for some time at least, the belief that failure to service debts would be extremely expensive in foreign policy terms: assets would be seized, trade would be disrupted, and the debtor countries might effectively become siege economies.

But at present a more fundamental argument has taken over in the major Latin debtor countries. The belief now is that action on the external debt will immediately translate into even larger *domestic* instability. Capital would try to leave through any channel and inflation control would disappear, accompanied by political stability. Moreover, once external debts are questioned it is a short step to asking questions about domestic debts and income distribution more generally. The politics are much too precarious to open that box. The most striking confirmation of this turn of thinking is President Alfonsín of Argentina. While he claimed a year ago that the debt could not be serviced with the blood and tears of the people, more recently he told the assembled national financial community that the international debt would be serviced with dignity. Even Mexico, entirely unable to meet her debt service, continued throughout much of 1986 to shy away from unilateral action and tried to maintain normal debt service against all odds. The means was to set interest rates high enough to attract a capital repatriation at the cost of a fierce decline in activity.

The working down of debt-export ratios that is under way is said to be in the interest of "the international system," as if the community at large had an interest. Clearly creditor banks do, but that is where things stop. Industrial countries as a group have little interest in paying for the premature interest receipt with increased unemployment. In the debtor countries the accelerated debt service is altogether perverse as it means not only a cut in per capita consumption, but also a deterioration of trend growth potential because saving finances debt service rather than investment. There is a growing gap between productive employment and the rapidly growing labor force. Lever and Huhne, in their authoritative analysis *Debt and Danger*, have drawn attention to the alarming results of debt collection as it is undertaken now:

> Debt needs our urgent attention for the threat it poses in itself—but also because it epitomizes a sickness in the West . . . The present dangers may be therapeutic. They concentrate the minds; but they must also elevate them. (p. 6)

Few are willing to argue that the present working-down of debt-export ratios is a strictly temporary policy, very soon to be reversed by renewed resource transfers from the industrial countries to LDCs. That of course raises the question whether the policy of forced debt service is not outright counterproductive. On a cash flow basis the debt problem is more or less under control, but debt service fatigue is building up even in the countries where the external balance is not the principal issue. Poor macroeconomic performance is rightly blamed on the difficulty of servicing debt at short notice. The banks cannot be expected to make the first gesture in adjusting debt service, but it is surely time for the IMF to recognize that its forceful assistance in debt collection is standing in the way of investment, year after year. It is not in the national interest of industrial countries, and more particularly of the U.S., that LDCs should service debts at a pace congenial to the international financial system as an open-ended commitment without targets, without growth, and without end.

The fiction of a return to voluntary lending is sharply contradicted by the steep discounts on LDC debts in the secondhand market and by the eagerness of the creditors to turn debt into equity before the debt goes even worse. The time is therefore ripe for limited debt write-downs as part of a constructive growth program for Latin America. No doubt there is room for a case-by-case approach. Argentina and Mexico, for example, seem in much more serious need than Brazil. But so far the case-by-case approach has been the primary vehicle for debt collection. It is appropriate now to use it as a means for controlled debt relief. A suitable action-forcing scheme is offered in the Bradley Plan.[6]

NOTES

This is the revised version of a paper prepared for the Inter-American Dialogue. It draws on material presented in Dornbusch (1986a, 1986b).

1. See Fishlow (1985), Simonsen (1985), and Dornbusch and Fischer (1985) for an analysis of the 1982 debt crisis.

2. See, for example, Simonsen (1985), Fishlow (1986) and Dornbusch (1986a).

3. See Cline (1984, 1985) and Simonsen (1985).

4. For a further discussion and derivation of these results, see Dornbush (1986a).

5. See Foreign Bond Holders Protective Council, *Annual Report for the Years 1946–49*, New York.

6. The plan proposed by Senator Bradley is reported in the *Herald Tribune*, June 30, 1986.

REFERENCES

Cline, W. 1984. *International Debt.* Washington, D.C.: MIT Press.

_____. 1985. International Debt From Recovery to Crisis. *American Economic Review*, May.

Dornbusch, R. 1986a. Policy and Performance Links Between Debtor LDCs and Industrialized Countries. *Brookings Papers on Economic Activity* 1.

_____. 1986b. *Dollars, Debts, and Deficits.* Washington, D.C.: MIT Press.

Dornbusch, R. and Fischer. 1985. The World Debt Problem: Origins and Prospects. *Journal of Development Planning* 10.

Fishlow, A. 1984. Revisiting the Great Debt Crisis of 1982. Unpublished manuscript. Berkeley, Calif.: University of California.

_____. 1985. The Debt Crisis: A Longer Perspective. Unpublished manuscript. Berkeley, Calif.: University of California.

_____. 1986. External Debt. In R. Dornbusch (ed.), *A Policy Manual for the Open Economy.* World Bank, forthcoming.

Kissinger, K.A. Building a Bridge of Hope to Our Latin Neighbors. *Los Angeles Times,* June 25, 1985.

Lever, H., and C. Huhne. 1986. *Debt and Danger.* Atlantic Monthly Press (U.S. edition).

Simonsen, M.H. 1985. The Developing Country Debt Problem. In G. Smith and J. Cuddington (eds.), *International Debt and the Developing Countries.* World Bank.

Wiesner, E. 1985. Latin American Debt. Lessons and Pending Issues. *American Economic Review*, May.

External Debt, Adjustment, and Development in Latin America

RICARDO FFRENCH-DAVIS*

In the 1980s, after three decades of marked economic growth, the Latin American countries suffered a serious recession that was associated with a rapid increase in their debt with the creditor banks in the 1970s and a deterioration in the international economy in the early 1980s. The crisis hit the Latin American nations when their economies had become accustomed to a high annual inflow of loans and had accumulated a very large debt stock in comparison with the preceding decades. Both factors have had an adverse impact during the subsequent adjustment undertaken by the debtor nations.

The per capita GDP has fallen to the level reached in 1977; the unemployment rate is twice as high as it was ten years ago; investment declined by close to 25 percent, and the net flow of funds from abroad has turned markedly negative since 1982.

Despite these adverse traits, well into 1985 there appeared to have been a general feeling of complacency among the leading actors (certain international institutions and creditors). This mood was based on the substantial improvement made in the trade and current account balances of the debtor nations since the outbreak of the crisis in 1982.

In fact, the adjustment achieved by the Latin American countries was quite spectacular. The current account deficit fell from $41 billion in 1982 to $14 billion in 1986. A large part of this change took place in the trade balance. After being almost at zero

---

*Vice President of CIEPLAN, Santiago.

in 1981 it rose to a surplus of $9 billion in 1982 and $39 billion in 1984. At the current exchange rates, this latter figure amounted to approximately 6 percent of the GDP of the region.

These results were obtained basically through expenditure-reducing policies and, to a lesser extent, through expenditure-switching policies (transfer of demand from foreign to national products).[1] After the 1984 recovery Latin American exports as a whole were reaching only their 1981 level, and in most of the countries their values were below those of 1981. As a result of the deterioration in oil prices, there was a large decline in oil exports in 1986, with non-oil exporting nations exhibiting export values close to those in 1981.

To sum up, a substantial trade surplus was achieved in 1983–86. This was due to a negative adjustment in which the quantum of exports rose by one fifth but prices fell, owing to the international recession, and *im*ports dropped by close to $40 billion — some 40 percent — mostly as a result of dramatic domestic recessions.

It is undeniable that there had been an excess of imports; at the end of the 1970s and early 1980s an increasing volume of luxury articles was financed by bank loans. But the decline in imports also drastically reduced purchases of intermediate and capital goods, and this, in turn, had adverse effects on the *rate of use of the resources* and on *the rate of formation of productive capacity*. For example, in the case of capital goods, the fall in the value of imports exceeded 50 percent.

The downturn in essential imports was closely associated with the restriction on domestic demand, which has produced higher unemployment and a decline in output. In other words, adjustment has meant a considerable fall in the rate of use of productive resources, labor and capital goods alike. With the exception of extreme cases of negative productivity, what misuse can be worse than making no use at all of a substantial volume of resources? Adjustment becomes inefficient when it leads to a widespread misuse of available resources.

Optimistic observers contend that the costs of the aforesaid adjustment were inevitable and that they represent in effect an investment for the future. Nonetheless, it should not be forgotten that these observers have been repeatedly mistaken in their appraisal of the external conditions that would confront the debtor nations. On average, in comparison with projections of institutions such as the IMF, access to export markets and prices paid have been worse, and net transfers (interest payments less net loans) to the creditor banks decidedly more unfavorable for the debtors (Ffrench-Davis and Molina, 1985; Dornbusch, Foxley, and Ossa, in this volume).

Adjustment was without doubt absolutely necessary. Nevertheless, its cost could have been much less and a positive structural adjustment achieved that would contribute to more favorable development prospects for the rest of the decade. In many ways the future is being undermined, and the productive capacity and political stability of the debtor countries are being jeopardized.

The complacency of the creditor institutions and more influential governments in handling the debt crisis has apparently dwindled in recent times with the recognition by officials of the United States, the IMF, and the World Bank that growth has been deficient in the debtor nations. With the launching of the Baker Plan this recognition acquired official status. Despite its delay, this recognition of a fact that had long been obvious to many developing countries is certainly welcome. However, the proposed prescription a) involves extremely limited additional funds and interest payments on commercial terms; b) lacks a realistic notion of how national and international markets function in present conditions; and c) seeks to impose on all debtor countries alike a single strategy of overall development, implying an extreme faith in the good behavior of private markets. Except in cases of arbitrary and haphazard interventionism, the *conditionality* with which the plan is likely to be associated may be very harmful to the economic and social development of debtor nations. In contrast, what is required is a constructive rather than destructive conditionality, and one with which debtors have agreed rather than one imposed on them.

AUTONOMOUS DEVELOPMENT AND EQUITY

One of the noteworthy features of the present situation is that decisions of the creditor banks and the IMF determine domestic policies on the basis of a shortsighted and unbalanced view. Their main objective has been to increase the immediate payment capacity of the debtor nations and not their development. This approach to the "transfer problem" is prejudicial for various reasons (ECLAC, 1984; Dornbusch and Fischer, 1985; Ffrench-Davis and Molina, 1985).

First, short-term considerations predominate overwhelmingly over long-term aspects. This is detrimental to economic growth, which requires a broad time horizon. Excessive emphasis is placed on short-run payment capacity, which was what gave rise to the complacent view that adjustment was proceeding satisfactorily, on the basis of the change observed in the debtor countries' balance-of-payments current account.

Second, uncertainty is rife. The availability of "fresh" funds has been determined in most cases on an annual basis, often when the period in question is well advanced. The amount of funds has been variable and has been decided by the IMF and the creditor banks, usually with limited participation by debtors. Once the amount of "fresh" funds has been established, variations in the terms of trade and finance alter the credit requirements, but hitherto it has been the debtor countries that have had to absorb the effects of adverse international markets. Hence, they have been compelled to reinforce the policies restricting aggregate demand.

Third, it is the weakest and poorest social groups in the debtor countries that have borne the weight of a considerable part of the adjustment. In the application of the standard adjustment programs there is a bias, conscious or not, against these groups. Drastic reductions in public food subsidies, severe wage controls, the relaxation of labor contracts, the rise in open unemployment, and the expansion of sectors of informal employment have helped to weaken the relative position of the poorest segments of the population (PREALC, 1985). In contrast, some high-income sectors have benefited from heavy subsidies to the exchange rates used to service their foreign debt, from the "watering down" of debts, and in other cases from the open acceptance of responsibility by the state for formerly nonguaranteed private debt. All sectors have tended to suffer from the crisis, but the people with fewest resources have generally been the hardest hit.[3]

Fourth, the positive effects of what the creditors regard as major improvements are barely noticed in the debtor economies. There is a general feeling that the creditors have not made a fair contribution to adjustment costs. The debtor nations have been exceedingly "responsible" in making their interest payments, despite having been subjected to a dramatic fall in the availability of foreign exchange. In 1983-86 they made net annual factor payments (disbursements of profits and interests minus receipts) amounting to $28 billion. But this was only part of the cost to the Latin American countries; in addition, the per capita product in the four-year period 1983–86 remained 7 percent below that of 1981, which represents a total annual GDP lower by over $40 billion. This is a conservative estimate of the underutilization of productive capacity (see Ramos, in this volume), owing to the severity of the external financial constraint and the weakness of international trade, and to the characteristics of the domestic adjustment programs put into force.

The actual cost to the banks has in fact been very limited. In general, the debtors have been paying their interest ($160 billion were remitted by Latin America in net interest payments during the five-year period 1982–86). In contrast, the banks' abrupt restriction of net loans has not only been prejudicial to the debtor nations; it has also meant that the countries of origin of the creditor banks have suffered a fall of around 40 percent in their exports to the debtor markets as a result of the adjustment. Nevertheless, the banks have managed to maintain in force the current recessionary and costly process of adjustment. Both in the industrialized and the developing nations there has been a tendency, since the 1970s, for financial aspects to take precedence over productive considerations. The expansion and increasing weight acquired by bank debt up to 1982, the subsequent approach adopted, and the preeminent position of the banks illustrate this trend, which has adverse effects on productive development and income distribution.

Fifth, the extreme vulnerability and limited maneuverability of the governments diminish their capacity to think of the future and invest in it. In fact, they capture a substantial part of management capacity, both public and private agents, in the debtor countries. The sense of national identity is weakened in the process, along with the ability to design effective development programs and to achieve national consensus. There is a growing feeling of disorientation in the quest for autonomous and equitable development. And this is not healthy for those who wish to see solidly based democracies and cooperative endeavors established on the continent.

The prospects for real improvements—even from an optimistic

view point — are at best modest and uncertain. It is more likely that the outcome will continue to be adverse unless systematic efforts are made to change the existing situation.

DEBT FINANCING AND MANAGEMENT

From 1982 the net annual flows of funds from the creditor banks have been negative for Latin America. Their evolution between 1978 and 1985 is shown in figure 1. The change of direction of the capital flows was unexpectedly brusque and considerable. A partial recovery in multilateral credits offset only a small pro-

FIGURE 1
Annual Net Flows of Bank Debt: Latin America, 1978-86
(US$ billions)

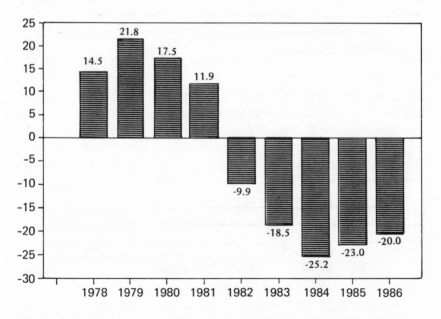

Source: Calculations made on the basis of the BIS, *The maturity distribution of international bank lending,* (Basle), and *World debt tables,* 1983-84 and 1984-85 editions. The figures for 1984 and 1985 are provisional, 1986 is an estimate.

portion of the deterioration in bank financing. Thus the total net outflow of funds from Latin America—including banks, official financing, and direct foreign investment—represented 5 percent of the GDP in the five-year period 1982–86. This is a particularly high negative figure compared with historical data.[4] It is even more dramatic when compared with the large positive net inflows of funds in the years before 1982. The substantial changes in their magnitude and direction imply that the current net outflows have been even more harmful to the debtor economies.

The flows from the banks are not the only source of financial constraint. Direct foreign investment (DFI) has also fallen drastically. The projections made by the IMF and the World Bank and the studies carried out by the Group of Thirty (1984) all indicate that DFI flows are expected to be modest and to represent at best only a fifth of the net capital movements that will occur in the years to come.[5] The same factors that discourage bank lending tend also to deter DFI.[6]

With respect to bank lending, after being compared with the actual outcome, the projections have been excessively optimistic since the outbreak of the crisis. Unless a meaningful change occurs in the most probable scenarios, the prospects are that the net flows of funds (net loans minus interest payments) will continue to be negative beyond the commencement of the 1990s. For example, on the basis of IMF (1986b) data, at the beginning of the next decade Latin America would be making net transfers in favor of the banks in the amount of $20 billion per year. The relationship with official creditors has shown a slightly favorable balance but threatens to deteriorate, as indicated in Feinberg in this volume. The continued transfer of funds abroad represents a considerable restriction on the investment capacity of debtor nations. For Latin America, total negative net transfers in 1985–86 were as large as the equivalent of between one-half and two-thirds of the annual increase of fixed capital stock.[7]

Thus the available data indicate that, instead of being a net receiver of foreign financing, the region would continue to be an exporter of funds even after the end of the decade. This situation is frankly incompatible with development. The region is becoming increasingly aware of the need to influence the course of events and not passively accept their results. Furthermore, it should be stated once again that the fact that the net flows are negative is a potential source of bargaining power for debtors.

The net outflow of funds is a matter that transcends the issue of debt rescheduling. Logically the latter is important and at present is a problem only a few countries have managed to solve. In fact, the creditors' determination to maintain strict control over debtors has led to the practice of the "short leash," that is, negotiations that include only amortization commitments maturing within one or a few years. Hence the debtor countries are being prevented from devoting their efforts of policy design and implementation to long-term economic development plans.

Under emergency conditions it was perhaps not possible to take fully into account the gravity of the problems or to create a framework appropriate for constructive adjustment; there may then have been a basis for operating with such a limited time horizon. Nevertheless, the restoration of development will call for new rules for refinancing amortization payments maturing in the coming years. Yet the extension of the time horizon does not imply giving carte blanche to the debtors. Rescheduling for several years can be based on and conditioned by the periodic fulfillment of the goals laid down in the negotiations. A major change in the current situation would be concerned not with actual control but with the length of time in which the debtor nations can program their economic development. Concerning the nature of conditionality, the aim should be to avoid the recessive bias implicit in the previously adopted adjustment policies, which rests unevenly on restrictions to aggregate demand and ignores or plays down questions of *national* development. The creditors, in their determination to maintain some control over debtors, should not hamper national efforts to develop nor place undue emphasis on the short run; nor should they try to impose on the debtors a specific economic strategy. What they can indeed demand is an effective program of structural adjustment, but one autonomously designed by the affected countries themselves.

There is another aspect of conditionality that has had a marked effect on the economic performance of debtor countries. The volume of funds provided by the banks and the IMF, and the goals laid down in the agreements with the latter, are based on their projections for international prices and interest rates. The projections for both variables have on average erred in a negative direction.[8] The continued worsening of the terms of trade, coupled with the instability of prices, has posed serious problems for the debtor countries in complying with the adjustment programs agreed to with the IMF, and has changed the financial needs of many developing countries.

As to real interest rates, the developing countries have been faced with inordinate levels. The floating rates in dollars, deflated by variation in the export prices of developing countries, appear in column 5 of table 1. This is a more appropriate indicator than that of inflation in industrialized nations for measuring the burden that interest payments impose on debtor countries.[9]

The implications of such large real interest rates are clear. The excess accumulated between 1981 and 1985 with respect to historical rates is spectacular. For instance, if a real rate of 3 percent is used, the cumulative excess is 106 percent of the initial debt stock. The gap between nominal interest rates and export prices is an extremely relevant explanation of the debt burden suffered by debtor nations during the 1980s.

The fundamental problem, therefore, lies in the magnitude of interest payments resulting from both a large stock of debt and real

TABLE 1

Real Interest Rates, with Alternative Deflators
(Annual Percentages)

	NOMINAL RATE (1)	INFLATION INDUSTRIALIZED COUNTRIES (2)	EXTERNAL INFLATION FACED BY LDCs (3)	REAL RATES Deflated by (2) (4)	Deflated by (3) (5)
1977–78	8.4	7.6	10.1	0.7	−1.5
1979–80	13.9	8.7	14.3	4.8	−0.4
1981	17.4	8.8	−2.2	7.9	20.0
1982	17.1	7.2	−5.6	9.2	24.0
1983	12.2	4.9	−4.3	7.0	17.2
1984	12.1	4.2	0.7	7.6	11.3
1985	10.5	3.8	−3.4	6.5	14.4
1986	8.6	3.3	3.1	5.1	5.3

Source: OECD (1986), Table V.17 for column (1) including spreads and fees; IMF (1986a; 1986b), Table A.9 and A.53 for column (2), which is the implicit deflator of the GNP of the industrialized countries, and Tables A.26 for column (3), which gives the unit price index for exports of net-oil-importing developing countries.

interest rates much higher than in the past. In general, the creditor banks have been receiving interest at the current market rates. At the same time, in 1982–84 they charged spreads and fees on new and rescheduled loans that were higher than those applied before the debt problem arose; only in 1985–86 did the spreads and fees return to levels comparable to those in force before the outbreak of the crisis. In fact, the creditor banks have not suffered appreciable direct losses as a result of the difficult situation they helped to create. Nonetheless, there is a risk for creditors that the debtor countries will not remain able to service their debt in the near future.

Various proposals have been put forward for the banks to share the costs of a situation for which they are partly responsible.[10] Without entering into detail on each type of proposal, the problem consists of reconciling three elements: a) the "reality" of the market; b) the need for the debtor countries to restore their development; and c) the contribution to a movement toward the "normal" operation of the international banking system. In our opinion, none of these three requisites is adequately taken care of in the current pattern of renegotiations and adjustment.

The excessively optimistic estimates have assumed—year after year since 1982—that the banks would shortly renew "voluntary lending." Yet experience has shown how doubtful it is that this will apply as a general practice in the near future. The suggestion that the debtors should "behave well" so as not to jeopardize their access to bank credit has no valid justification except for short-term trade financing; most likely there will not be any significant "voluntary lending," and net transfers would continue to be negative within the present framework. This is the "reality" of the market, which must be recognized.

For development to be restored, debtors must be allowed to choose their own development strategy, moderate the restrictions imposed by the scarcity of foreign credit, reduce instability, and lengthen the time horizon of lending. The movement toward a more normal functioning of the market requires a distinction to be made among the different components of bank debt; in particular, the prospects for the "normalization" of trade credit are better than those for other components of the developing countries' debt.[11]

Interest rates may be reduced via debt write-offs or by limits on interest rates. The following criteria for the payment of interest commitments might be applied to a scheme for sharing the costs between debtors and creditors.

(1) Trade credit and other new net loans might be made subject to market interest rates and commissions.

(2) The refinancing of amortization and the outstanding balance of the remainder of the debt might be tied to market interest rates; but the actual payments would be subject to a ceiling, similar to the historical average real rates in the neighborhood of 1 percent,[12] the surplus being "capitalized," and vice versa. A guarantee might be granted by multilateral agencies for the rescheduled amortization quotas with a long maturity term (for example, to installments maturing after 14 or 15 years).

The aforesaid surplus interest would be "capitalized," or added to the debt stock, with long-term maturities. However, there would be no subsequent capitalization of interest: the surplus would be non-interest earning. Aside from the debts that may be written off partially or totally,[13] this last characteristic involves a deferment and spreading over time of the creditors' losses, thus avoiding an immediate impact on recorded profits. In compensation, there would be less risk for the banks that the debtor countries would become unable to service their debt, thus reducing a dangerous source of instability for the international financial system.

The adoption of the system described above calls for a modification of regulations governing the banking systems of several creditor countries. Hence it is in the hands of the governments of these nations to adapt existing regulations and persuade the banks to accept an effective solution.

ADJUSTMENT WITH GROWTH

There is general agreement that the region needed adjustments; the countries had become accustomed to an excessive net capital inflow that could not be sustained for many more years. Consequently a critical attitude toward the ongoing processes does not imply an intention to avoid adjustment. The question at issue is how to improve it effectively. At the same time, however, it must be stressed that the creditors themselves should have realized that the annual average increase of 30 percent in the bank debt stock between 1973 and 1981 could not possibly have been sustained. Nevertheless, at the end of the 1970s the creditor banks were urging the debtor countries to increase their liabilities. Along with various international institutions and a number of experts, the banks were pressing for a great liberalization of capital movements and freer access to the foreign exchange markets in debtor countries.[14]

The governments that were unwilling to allow growing inflows of financial resources were pressed to change their policies and increase their external openness. This often meant that private borrowers without public guarantee accounted for a rising share of total debt in developing countries. The subsequent problems arose not only from poor judgment on the part of the governments of debtor nations, but also from errors shared by all parties concerned.

No one can deny that it was essential to reduce the aggregate demand and change its composition. The discussion centers on the nature and timing of the adjustment and on the sharing of the costs involved. There are serious and well-founded misgivings that adjustment, as designed and carried out, is prejudicial to growth and detrimental to the societies of the debtor countries. An adjustment process that contributes to economic growth (and social equity) should comply with a number of conditions.

First, it must be efficient. The intense output-reducing effects of the current adjustment are a sign of inefficiency. It is natural that in any process of adjustment some human and physical resources should become idle. But the average decline of 6 percent in the per capita GDP in the five-year period 1982–86, associated in most countries with the external shock, is a notorious sign of resource misuse. In other words, the availability of additional net external funds since 1982 would have signified a notably high rate of social return. In fact, in many countries the main obstacle to higher employment and greater use of installed capacity lies in the scarcity of foreign currency: the so-called external gap. It must be emphasized that it is not a question of maintaining a level of expenditure far above productive capacity—there is consensus on the need for adjustment, implying some reduction and reallocation of aggregate demand—rather the problem is that expenditure in general was so drastically and abruptly reduced that the *rate of use of productive capacity* has fallen dramatically.[15] This is damaging to growth, to social stability, and to future payment capacity.

Second, the improvement of the external balance will require, among other things, increased Latin American access to export markets. The importance of obtaining better access for exports to the developed economies has been repeatedly asserted in all the studies and reports on the debt problem.[16] In contrast, the trends observed are not encouraging: prices have been depressed for many years and access to these markets is menaced by protectionism and instability,[17] while the market outlook for Latin America's chief products is unpromising (Ibarra, 1986, in this volume). Intra-regional trade is also important for Latin America. Reciprocal trade has rapidly dwindled as a result of the decline in the region's markets. The revival of economic integration might help to improve export opportunities as well as play a positive role in industrial development. Economic integration programs with agreements on the liberalization of reciprocal trade, production agreements, promotion of regional enterprises, etc. may contribute to a better use of economies of scale and a more efficient reindustrialization.

Third, the scarcity of foreign exchange is producing a proliferation of import restrictions. The countries are making intense efforts to save foreign currency, as they did in the 1950s. On the whole the trend is in the right direction, since insofar as it reallocates expenditure and output, it helps diminish the output-reducing effect. There is a danger, however, that this will to some extent foster inefficiency in the corresponding drive toward import substitution industrialization (ISI). It is possible that most of the countries will be forced by the international economic framework to embark on a new stage of ISI, notwithstanding foreign political pressures in the opposite direction. Then efforts will be needed to improve its efficiency through a selective policy of import substitution that is made consistent with export promotion.[18] This is the constructive course, as opposed to simply advocating overall free-trade policies.

This topic brings us to the more general issue of trade policies. The United States government and the multilateral institutions have made great efforts to encourage free trade in developing countries. The Baker Plan undoubtedly has positive elements. It recognizes that the debt problem has not been adequately solved and indirectly acknowledges the shared responsibility for the crisis, and therefore the need for a contribution from the banks. Nevertheless, the plan threatens to become a notable example of the attempt to impose a specific strategy on the debtor nations. Serious and undogmatic consideration should be given to the implications of alternative trade policies for the developing countries.[19] Overall import liberalization has proved costly in the few cases in which it has been tried in Latin America, as Chile's failure shows;[20] but overall arbitrary protectionism has also proved inadequate. Hence better trade policies might be designed if energy and creativity were devoted to the setting up of moderate systems of protection, adjusted to the needs posed by the dominant external gap and geared to achieving a balanced combination of protection and competition, and of import substitution and export promotion. Analytical efforts in this direction have been very few, and the predominant thinking seems to be biased against them, despite the "heterodox policies" applied by successful exporters such as Japan, South Korea, and Brazil. A fruitful dialogue requires the acceptance of a legitimate diversity of needs and means. What is expedient for the more developed nations is not necessarily advantageous for semi-industrialized countries.

Fourth, an efficient adjustment needs longer-term horizons and economic stability, both in world markets and domestic policies. Prices and access to world markets are at present notoriously unstable. This is partly because of the different rates of recovery among the industrialized nations and the commercial and financial imbalances observed among them. But a major source of instability originates in the spectacular changes in price relations stemming from the variability of exchange rates. The appreciation-cum-instability of the U.S. dollar was a prime cause of uncertainty in the short run and produced distortions in the long-term allocation of the new resources. The same holds with the present depreciation-cum-instability, notwithstanding that it now moves around exchange rates closer to "normal ranges." Uncertainty gives rise to financial speculation, to the detriment of investment and improvements in productivity.

From a macroeconomic standpoint, the burden of instability has affected the debtor nations. The errors made by institutions such as the IMF in projecting the overall availability of foreign exchange—owing to a worsening of the terms of trade and of financing—have meant a tighter market for debtors. Contingency clauses are needed that will allow for more liberal and expeditious compensatory transfers from multilateral agencies and a similar compensatory adjustment of fund flows with creditor banks. The linkage of trade opportunities with debt servicing is a way to face this deficiency in the forms taken by debt negotiations, in other words, debt servicing tied to the actual performance of debtor exports. The IMF compensatory service scheme, though obviously positive, is clearly insufficient in view of the magnitude and persistence of the present crisis. It would therefore be necessary to increase resources for these objectives and broaden the coverage of the facility.[21] Additionally, because markedly unstable conditions are likely, efforts to improve the functioning of the world commodity markets should be revived. This would help producers in both developing and developed countries.

Fifth, long-term horizons are now limited by the terms of IMF agreements. The nature of such agreements has been directed toward solving balance-of-payments problems in "normal" world markets. These, however, are in a clearly recessive situation and need certain structural changes. Thus the countries must not confine themselves to a superficial correction of this imbalance, as they have done to this point. Of course, the change would not be achieved automatically with the recipe of across-the-board market liberalization and privatization that the Baker Plan appears to advocate. These programs reflect an excessive faith in spontaneous development in response to the standard package of policies contained in the IMF programs, or to their intensification in the same orthodox direction. The positive changes observed in 1979 in the IMF approach have been long forgotten or diluted in the present crisis. There is a need for systematic thinking on how to adapt (not avoid) conditionality, so as to contribute more effectively to adjustment-cum-growth and respect for national autonomy.[22] The proposal would add to the present conditionality prescriptions for reducing the size and functions of the public sector, liberalizing imports, and relaxing the regulations on direct foreign investment which are neither effective nor sensible recommendations in the present circumstances. What is needed is an "alternative conditionality" consistent with selective economic policies. Various possible components of a new constructive conditionality are outlined in this volume.

Some serious rethinking is required as to the nature of the IMF recipe, and more recently of the World Bank, with due attention to the viewpoint of developing nations and to unorthodox approaches. A high-level task force should be commissioned to propose changes in the programs that are being applied to minimize the recessive and regressive biases and introduce more pragmatism into these formulas.

Sixth, an important link between the short and long term is the behavior of investment. Investment rates rose appreciably during the period of increasing indebtedness, which suggests that foreign resources contributed to regional development as a whole. There were differences, however, among countries. For example, nations that markedly liberalized capital inflows, domestic financial markets, and imports tend to show both lower investment and lower national savings (Bacha, 1983). Again, performance was better in those countries which reformed their trade and financial policies moderately and selectively.[23] This points to the need to accept a diversity of policy approaches, abandoning the mechanical transfer of recipes that are dysfunctional for the development of semi-industrialized countries.

In the present adjustment process, investment and imports of capital goods are considerably below precrisis levels (table 2). It is important to understand the reasons behind that outcome. The recessive domestic situation, the persistent uncertainty, and the constraints on public investment have reduced the rate of capital formation. Increased investment is required to create new employment opportunities, revive growth of output and the coverage of basic needs, and ensure a sustained long-term payment capacity. To achieve these targets, the present service of the debt and the size of negative transfers must be reduced substantially. In this

TABLE 2

Rate of Gross Capital Formation in Latin America

1977–79	24.4
1980–81	23.1
1982–83	19.1
1984–86	17.5

Source: IMF (1985), Table 16 and (1986b), Table A.7. Above table refers to the Western Hemisphere as defined by the IMF and to the gross capital formation as a percentage of GDP.

connection the excessive pressure exerted by creditors in the prevailing adjustment process is more likely contributing to reduce the future payment. Thus by thinking only of their short-term interest the creditors may be jeopardizing their prospects of collecting in the longer term and of having a healthy trading partner in the south.[24]

The fall in the rate of use of productive resources — labor and capital — leads to a decline in savings. Both households and private and public enterprises tend to reduce total savings, while lower wages, unemployment, and idle installed capacity have gradually undermined national savings. This has been aggravated by the negative net flow of funds between the creditor banks and the debtor nations, which has reduced notably the volume of funds available for investment.

An increase in both investment and savings is needed to obtain reasonable growth rates. Yet this is not easy to achieve. Within each country a better macroeconomic framework with a more normal level of domestic demand, a national development stategy broadly accepted by the social forces, and a relaxation of the external gap is required. All this calls for a mix of public and private investment. At least until the macroeconomic framework becomes settled, public investment may be the decisive factor in fostering private investment. Instead of a "crowding out," there might be a "crowding in." Seeking to force the privatization of public enterprises during the present crisis most probably tends to deepen it. Recovery in semi-industrialized countries calls for increasing public investment over its present depressed levels and using private funds to create new productive capacity (and not to purchase public enterprises).[25]

Redistributive efforts can also be directed to supporting instead of discouraging investment and savings. For instance, assistance to small enterprises, peasants, and cooperatives may contribute to increased employment and productivity, and help to mobilize dormant energy and idle resources.

We have indicated that efforts should be made to improve the working of the public sector; in addition, the design of public policies and regulations and controls on public enterprises are important factors. How to make the performance of the government and public enterprises more efficient is undoubtedly a crucial issue. A systematic bias against the public sector usually discourages efforts to improve its efficiency; the outcome also tends to be a destructive adjustment.

What can be demanded from the industrialized nations? By way of example, on the basis of the foregoing analysis, *five* strategies can be mentioned: a) modification of some banking regulations; b) pressure on the banks to accept more pragmatic solutions including a longer time horizon and substantially reduced interest charges; c) greater bilateral and multilateral official financing;[26] d) coordination of macroeconomic policies to permit a sustained recovery of their markets and slackening of protectionism; and e) a move away from the present increasing ideologization of the issue of conditionality on the part of some industrialized countries, led by the United States and multilateral creditors; and, instead, a sincere search, conducted jointly with the developing nations, for more efficient and equitable approaches in North–South and in debtor–creditor relations.

In the present conditions of the world economy and those foreseen for the near future, it seems imperative to seek procedures that will result in stable long-term solutions for the problems caused by the indebtedness of developing countries. It should be recognized that any solutions should imply losses which are shared by the parties involved. Postponement of a solution may be worse for all concerned. If the debtor countries are forced to continue assuming this heavy burden on their own and to submit to more orthodox conditionality than in recent years, the effect may be to create untenable domestic situations that will result in further disturbances in the goods and financial markets. We maintain that this might be avoided by a cooperative approach.

NOTES

A previous version of this article was presented at the Seminar on "External Debt, Negotiating Strategies, and Economic Policies in Latin America," Campinas, December 7–8, 1985; at the CIEPLAN Workshop on International Economics; and at the working meeting of the Inter-American Dialogue. I am grateful for the comments made on these three occasions and also for the suggestions offered by R. Devlin, J. De Gregorio, J. Estévez, R. Feinberg, A. Foxley, C. Ossa, and J. Ramos.

1. This is somewhat different from the classification "tradable/non-tradable." It becomes important because of the underutilized capacity in the production of national importable goods.

2. Figures for 1986 as compared to 1981 (ECLAC, 1986b). Between 1981 and 1986 the volume (quantum) of exports of goods rose 15 percent, while unit values dropped 29 percent. Thus, the region made a substantial effort, with a negative outcome, in response to world recessed markets and to policies pursued by industrialized nations. See Ibarra in this volume.

3. A rough estimate indicates that the real value of the available per capita product would have declined by close to 15 percent between 1981 and 1985; the per capita GDP by 7 percent and the terms of trade by 10 percent (related to exports of goods and services equivalent to 18 percent of GDP), while the net transfer of funds fell by $40 billion (from plus $10 billion to minus $30 billion) equivalent to 7 percent of the GDP. The figures are based on ECLAC (1986a), except for GDP, which we have assumed to be $600 billion (approximately its value at current exchange rates).

4. In some years of the 1950s negative net flows were recorded, mainly influenced by foreign investment. The amount, however, was very small compared with 1982–86. See Feinberg, in this volume, with respect to fund flows with official sources.

5. Debt-equity conversion has acquired some importance since 1985. It should be noted that in the short run it does not represent an additional financial contribution. In turn, it tends to weaken the debtors' bargaining position in the medium term insofar as the debt is reconverted at a high percentage of its face value or is exchanged for equity valued at recessed prices.

6. In this context, the indiscriminate liberalization of existing regulations on foreign investment in the debtor countries serves mainly to increase the "economic rent" of the existing stock. A recent analysis of the performance of DFI appears in White, in this volume.

7. The rate of fixed capital formation was close to 17 percent of GDP and net transfers reached 5 percent. If capital depreciation is estimated at 7 percent, 10 percent of the GDP would be used to augment capital stock and transfers would equal one-half of that figure. The coefficient of two-thirds corresponds to a depreciation rate of 9.5 percent of GDP.

8. Even in 1984, the relative improvement recorded in that year did not compensate for the overestimates of 1982–83 (Ffrench-Davis and Molina, 1985). In 1985 the estimates were once again overly optimistic; the fall in interest rates did not offset the dwindling of net lending and the worsening of the terms of trade.

9. The relation between the two categories of price indices will tend to be reversed with the devaluation of the dollar from September 1985. The IMF (1986a) predicts an increase of 7.6 percent in export prices in 1986. It should be noted that price levels relate to a different aspect than that of the terms of trade ratio.

10. Comparative analyses can be found in Bergsten, Cline, and Williamson (1985) and ECLAC (1984).

11. Paradoxically, in spite of representing only a small proportion of the debt (around one-tenth), this is the chief instrument of bank pressure on the debtor countries.

12. Table 1, however, illustrates the difficulties of defining the "real" levels. See also Ossa, in this volume. The term "real" ought to have an equivalent expression in nominal rates. In case of sufficiently negative price changes, the nominal rate would need to be negative, too. In order to avoid the effect of changes in the rate of inflation on effective amortization, only the real component of interest rates might be paid, with the disguised amortization component of nominal rates being capitalized.

13. The bank claims to be written off include, for instance, debt of bankrupt firms and debt of private firms unable to finance its service without public subsidies. It is common that governments of debtor nations have been subsidizing or "nationalizing" private debts, thus freeing creditor banks from write-offs of non-performing private debt. Other criteria could be a percentage of write-off associated to secondary market discounts, or to "excess" interest payments in the 1980s, or to output losses derived from the external restriction.

14. See, for example, Robichek (1981). On the basis of the neo-classical argument of the resulting gap between marginal and average costs, various authors concerned with the increasing exposure to risk frequently argue in favor of a tax on capital inflows. Given the functioning of the capital market, this proposal is not effective in regulating short-run speculative movements or medium-run cyclical movements. See Arellano (1982), Devlin (1985), and Ffrench-Davis (1979, chaps. 5 and 6).

15. The drop has tended to be larger in the countries that have applied across-the-board demand restriction and that have made limited use of selective or discriminatory policy tools. See papers by Carneiro, Foxley, and Webb, and panels by Ffrench-Davis and Ramos in this volume.

16. See, for example, the analysis in Cline (1984) on the requirements of economic growth in industrialized countries and the access of debtor countries' exports to these markets.

17. Export prices expressed in U.S. dollars are affected by the exchange rate with other currencies; as already indicated, the recent devalua-

tion of the dollar would tend to increase the level of international prices. This would help reduce the real burden of the debt.

18. This argument acquires more weight if a) the GDP of the industrialized countries, as is predicted, grows more slowly than in 1950–80; and b) the international markets function with a world trade income elasticity substantially lower than in the past three decades.

19. A proposal for selective active policies which include a differentiated tarriff system is developed in Ffrench-Davis (1979, chaps. 7 and 8; 1983b).

20. See references in Ffrench-Davis (1983b).

21. Its financing could be linked, for example, to the resumption of the issues of SDRs.

22. Analyses in this respect are given in Dell (1981); Griffith-Jones (1985); Group of 24 (1985); Killick (1984); and SELA (1986).

23. See the various articles contained in the collections of essays complied by Ffrench-Davis (1983a) and Wionczek (1985).

24. However, as discussed above, the strategy has been very profitable for banks in the short-run. They have benefitted at the expense of LDC debtors and of productive sectors in industrialized nations.

25. In Chile, which has gone furthest in privatizing public sector enterprises, the government is in numerous cases handing over more funds (as preferential dividends to the new owners) than it is receiving (as capital payments by the purchasers).

26. This financing, preferably multilateral when possible, should be linked with projects in investment and imports of intermediate goods and equipment and machinery. It should be destined to raise the volume of net funds available for debtor nations, not to increase interest payments to commercial banks, which, as has been observed in some countries, only helps to postpone the solution of the current crisis.

REFERENCES

Arellano, J. P. 1982. Macroeconomic Stability and the Optimal Degree of Capital Mobility. *Journal of Development Economics*, June.

Bacha, E. 1983. Apertura financiera y sus efectos en el dessarrollo nacional. In R. Ffrench-Davis (ed.), *Las relaciones financieras externas: su efecto en la economía latinoamericana*. Lectura, no. 47. Mexico: Fondo de Cultura Económica.

Bergsten, F., W. Cline, and J. Williamson. 1985. Bank Lending to Developing Countries: The Policy Alternatives. *Policy Analyses in Inter-*

national Economies 10. Washington, D.C.: Institute for International Economics, April.

CIEPLAN. 1985. Deuda externa, industrialización y ahorro en América Latina. *Colección Estudios CIEPLAN* 17, special issue edited by R. Ffrench-Davis.

Cline, W. 1984. *International Debt: Systemic Risk and Policy Response.* Washington, D.C.: MIT Press.

Dell, S. 1981. On Being Grandmotherly: The Evolution of IMF Conditionality. *Essays in International Finance*, no 144. Princeton, N.J.: Princeton University Press.

Devlin, R. 1985. La deuda externa vs. el desarrollo económico: América Latina en la encrucijada. *Colección Estudios CIEPLAN* 17. Santiago, September.

Dornbusch, R., and S. Fischer. 1985. The World Debt Problem: Origins and Prospects. *Journal of Development Planning*, no. 16. New York: United Nations.

ECLAC. 1984. Política de ajuste y renegociación de la deuda externa en América Latina. *Cuadernos de la CEPAL*, no 48. Santiago, December.

_____. 1986a. Estudio Económico de América Latina y El Caribe, 1985: Síntesis preliminar. Santiago: United Nations, April.

_____. 1986b. Balance preliminar de la economía latinoamericana, 1986. Santiago: United Nations, December.

Ffrench-Davis, R. 1979. *Economía Internacional: teoría y políticas para el desarrollo.* 2nd ed. (1985). Mexico: Fondo de Cultura Económica.

_____. 1982. International Private Lending and Borrowing Strategies of Developing Countries. *Journal of Development Planning*, no. 14. New York: United Nations.

_____. (ed.) 1983a. *Las relaciones financieras externas: su efecto en la economía latinoamericana.* Lectura, no. 47. Mexico: Fondo de Cultura Económica.

_____. 1983b. Una estrategia de apertura externa selectiva. In *Reconstrucción económica para la democracia.* Santiago: CIEPLAN-Ed. Aconcagua.

_____. 1984. Deuda externa y alternativas de desarrollo en América Latina. *Colección Estudios CIEPLAN* 15. Santiago, December.

Ffrench-Davis, R., and S. Molina. 1985. Prospects for Bank Lending to Developing Countries in the Remainder of the 1980s. *Journal of Development Planning*, no. 16. New York: United Nations.

Griffith-Jones, S. 1985. Proposals to Manage Debt Problems: Review and Suggestions for Further Research. Mimeo. Institute of Development Studies, University of Sussex.

Group of Twenty-Four. 1985. Informe preparado por el grupo interguber-
namental sobre asuntos monetarios internacionales. Seoul, October.
Group of Thirty. 1984. Foreign Direct Investment, 1973–87. New York.
IBRD. 1986. *World Debt Tables 1985–86*. Washington, D.C.: The World
Bank.
IMF. 1985. *World Economic Outlook*. Washington D.C., April.
———. 1986a. *World Economic Outlook*. Washington D.C., April.
———. 1986b. *World Economic Outlook*. Washington D.C., October.
Killick, T. 1984. The IMF Case for a Change in Emphases. In R. Feinberg
and V. Kallab (eds.), *Adjustment Crisis in the Third World*. Wash-
ington, D.C.: Overseas Development Council.
OECD. 1986. *Financing and External Debt for Developing Countries,
1985 Survey*, Paris.
PREALC. 1985. *Beyond the Crisis*. Santiago.
Robichek, W. 1981. Some Reflections about External Public Debt Man-
agement. *Alternativas de políticas financieras en economías pequeñas
y abiertas al exterior*. Estudios Monetarios. 7, Banco Central de
Chile.
SELA. 1986. *El FMI, el Banco Mundial y la crisis latinoamericana*. Mex-
ico: Siglo XXI.
Wionczek, M. (ed.) 1985. *Politics and Economics of Latin American Debt
Crisis*. Boulder, Col.: Westview Press.

Latin American Debt:
Renegotiating the Adjustment Burden

RICHARD E. FEINBERG*

Five years after the debt crisis struck Latin America, it continues to dominate hemispheric economic relations. Creditors and debtors alike have been swinging from panic to euphoria, from the hope that sustainable progress is being made to the fear that default is at hand. These gyrations in mood reflect a widespread awareness of the unstable underlying reality: the debt burden is big in relation to the debtors' economies and to the creditors' capital base. Debtors and creditors are also aware that purely economic criteria may not, in the final analysis, determine the outcome: the debt crisis may be influenced by foreign policy considerations and by popular opinion as interpreted or molded by national leaders.

For Latin America, debt servicing affects all aspects of economic policy. It absorbs substantial proportions of domestic savings and therefore reduces investment rates. It limits imports and so determines consumption levels, which in turn place ceilings on government spending and on wages. It consumes substantial portions of government outlays, thereby reducing resources for other expenditures while generating pressures for new taxes. It factors importantly in trade policy, initially fostering government intervention to ration available hard currency, more recently stimulating trade liberalization to enhance export competitiveness. Through these and other mechanisms, the debt overhang strongly influences not only short-term stabilization policies but also future growth potential and development options.

*Vice President, Overseas Development Council, Washington, D.C.

Today, Latin American governments define themselves by the postures they strike on debt. Some governments have sought to demonstrate their adherence to Western norms by adopting "responsible" positions even at great internal cost. Other governments have attempted to play upon nationalist and populist sentiments by criticizing international banks and multinational financial institutions. Most governments have claimed that their debt strategies have gained concessions from foreign banks and governments.

Furthermore, debt is a major factor in Latin America's bilateral relations with the United States. Even though U.S. banks account for only about one-third of Latin America's debt to the private banks, Washington has become the focal point for policy discussions. Moreover, both parties attempt to use the debt issue as a bargaining chip to win concessions on other matters.

For the economy of the United States, Latin American debt looms less large. Nevertheless, it constrains monetary policy because the Federal Reserve Board fears that higher interest rates would jeopardize Latin America's debt service capacity. It has harmed U.S. exports and fostered protectionist pressures by stimulating Latin American nations to cheapen their exports. The resulting belt-tightening has impaired the profits of U.S. subsidiaries and darkened the climate for future U.S. business and investment opportunities in Latin America. Most importantly, of course, the debt crisis has weakened confidence in the U.S. banking system, lowered the value of some banks' equities, and forced banks to increase their capital and reserves. It has also compelled U.S. government agencies to counter the trend toward deregulation of domestic banking by intervening more forcefully to stabilize international credit markets.

Broader U.S. foreign policy interests are also at stake. The United States has sought to use Latin America's debt predicament to gain short-term diplomatic leverage, particularly with regard to softening opposition to U.S. policies in Central America. Working with the IMF and the World Bank, the U.S. has pressured for long-desired economic reforms. At the same time, the United States risks a sharp deterioration in hemispheric relations if Latin Americans perceive that Washington is either ignoring or unduly benefiting from the debt crisis. For the United States, the debt crisis presents both a major danger as well as an historic opportunity to advance both its influence and its interests in Latin America.

This essay discusses the strategy that the creditors have so successfully employed to manage the debt crisis since 1982, and the resulting international distribution of the costs of adjustment. The question is posed: Why have the debtors acquiesced to a chronic transfer of financial resources from South to North? The likely future supply of public and private funds for Latin America is then explored. The essay concludes that the probable pattern of future financial flows is neither in the interests of Latin America nor arguably in the long-term interests of the United States, and suggests ways to produce a different financial future.

THE ADJUSTMENT PROCESS, 1982–85

The props were pulled out from under the Latin American economies in the early 1980s. The global recession narrowed export markets and squeezed commodity prices, while tight monetary policies in industrial countries forced up global interest rates and increased the real burden of Latin America's bloated debt. Alarmed at the deteriorating creditworthiness of the region, bankers closed their lending windows. The region's loan and export revenues dropped, without a corresponding decline in the region's demand for foreign exchange to purchase imports and service the debt. The cumulative result was the famous telephone call from Jesus Silva Herzog, the Mexican Minister of Finance, to the U.S. Treasury Department on August 12, 1982, announcing that the Mexican treasury was dry and without means to meet debt obligations.

In the short run, it seemed easier to alter the region's demand for foreign exchange than to affect the supply. The willingness of financial markets to extend new credits depends on subjective assessments of future economic conditions abroad that governments cannot easily alter. The supply of funds is also determined by global commodity prices and interest rates that are determined by complex and often stubborn variables. But methods for contracting a nation's demand for foreign exchange are well known: reducing domestic purchasing power and raising the cost of foreign goods will predictably cut the demand for imports. So governments throughout the region slashed budget deficits, lowered real wages, and sharply devalued their currencies. The resulting austerity had the desired result: Latin American imports fell from $98 billion in 1981 to $59 billion in 1984.[1] Governments were thereby able to husband scarce foreign exchange to meet at least a portion of their debt obligations.

Even draconian austerity measures were insufficient, however, to generate enough foreign exchange to allow countries to pay back old debts. Previously, the custom had been to repay old loans with the proceeds from new ones. The sudden refusal of the banks to continue to extend new loans destroyed the assumptions underlying this process. There was, however, a ready alternative that had the same net effect on debtors' balance of payments: rescheduling. Banks traditionally dislike reschedulings because they imply that the rescheduled debt may be bad debt and because they restrict management prerogatives. But the global recession and the banks' own shutdown had placed Latin America in a liquidity squeeze that made debt rescheduling unavoidable. Both creditors and debtors quickly adjusted to this new reality, and the rescheduling of principal payments became a regular if often rushed occurrence. Importantly, however, banks required debtors to demonstrate the soundness of the debt by exempting interest payments from reschedulings.

The compression of imports and the rescheduling of principal payments substantially eased the region's liquidity position. Still, some countries needed some extra funding to cover pressing cash-flow problems or to place a floor under imports. Industrial-country governments worked closely with multilateral agencies—notably the IMF and the Basel-based Bank for International Settlements (BIS)— to arrange the extra financing. A portion was provided by bilateral sources, and governments agreed to increase resources available to the IMF by about 100 percent. In addition, the IMF coerced the commercial banks to extend some additional loans. Backed by the U.S. Federal Reserve Board, the IMF threatened to withhold stabilization loans if the banks were unwilling to help with at least small amounts of financial support. Bankers at first objected, but quickly realized that an uncontrolled creditor stampede against the debtors would trample all parties.

The IMF and industrial-country governments summarized their strategy in three points: the debtors should adjust their economies to levels consistent with available financing; the creditors should be willing to reschedule existing debts; and official and private lenders should provide some new financing to debtors undergoing approved stabilization programs. Public and private creditors quickly rallied behind the strategy and imposed it universally upon the debtors. Only the numbers were worked out "case by case."

This three-pronged plan was designed to cope with an immediate emergency. The total strategy contained a fourth dimension: an expanding global economy, led by a resurgent United States, would provide markets for an export-led growth that would enable developing countries to work their way out of debt. So long as the debtors restrained new borrowing and interest rates moderated, expanding exports would generate gradual improvement in debt profiles. The key ratios of debt service to export earnings and of total debt to GNP would fall to sustainable levels, and countries would eventually regain their creditworthiness. The debt crisis would thus be permanently resolved.

During 1983–84 the creditors' four-point strategy seemed to be working. Moreover, some countries—notably the more industrialized nations, led by Brazil—succeeded in expanding exports primarily to the buoyant U.S. market. In 1985, however, new storm clouds appeared on the horizon. Several assumptions behind the export-led recovery strategy proved to be shaky. The prices of many commodities remained weak and even declined during 1985. Interest rates reacted slowly to lower inflation rates, and the real cost of money hovered at historically high levels. Nor did commercial banks respond to the improved trade and current-account positions of the debtors; as pressure from the IMF to make new loans abated, the banks quietly ceased to make them. Thus, the Latin American recovery began to falter, and the region's growth rate fell from approximately 2.6 percent in 1984 to 2 percent in 1985 and therefore below the rate of population increase. Even more ominous, the disequilibria in the U.S fiscal and trade accounts and rising protectionist pressures in the U.S. and Western Europe raised doubts about future growth prospects in industrial countries and therefore the entire debt strategy.

WINNERS AND LOSERS

No one has emerged unscarred from this wrenching adjustment process. All parties—industrial countries, the Third World, and the commercial banks—have paid for past mistakes. But the debtors have paid disproportionately.

U.S. manufacturing, financial, and foreign policy interests have suffered some losses. As a result of the contraction in Latin American markets, U.S. exports fell from $42 billion in 1981 to $30 billion in 1984. Some 400,000 workers, or 0.4 percent of the U.S. labor force, lost jobs as a result.[2] The private banks have also had to take some losses. The regulatory authorities have required the banks to set aside reserves against "value impaired" loans to Nicaragua and Bolivia, and some losses have been taken on claims against private firms not secured by government guarantees. As noted earlier, confidence in the equities of the major money-center banks with large international portfolios has suffered, and banks' reported profits have been hit by stiffer requirements regarding loan loss reserves and capital-asset ratios. Nevertheless, the overwhelming reality is that bank profits on Latin American loans have remained large during this entire period, and the banks continue to carry on their books the large majority of loans at face value. The equity markets and the regulators seem to believe that the banks will be subject to harder "hits" in the future, but so far they have weathered the storm surprisingly well.

In addition, the U.S. government has made a small financial contribution to the management of the debt crisis. The U.S. Congress appropriated $8.4 billion for the IMF; in recent years Latin America accounted for 48 percent of all borrowings from the Fund.[3] Furthermore, U.S. bilateral aid—impelled primarily by concern for the security of the Caribbean Basin—totalled nearly $2 billion above previous levels during 1982–85.[4] The Latin American portion of the U.S. contribution to the IMF ($4 billion) plus the increase in U.S. bilateral loans since 1982 equal $6 billion. This figure can be considered part of the direct cost of the Latin American debt crisis to the United States.

Both the United States government and the banks have had to make some political adjustments. The banks have suffered government intervention in their decision making and are being more closely monitored. The Reagan administration has had to set aside its ideological distaste for government interference in markets and for multilateral financial institutions.

The losses sustained so far by the U.S. economy and the private banks, however, pale in comparison to the costs paid by Latin

America. If the U.S. had to provide $6 billion to help finance the IMF and the Caribbean Basin, an amount equal to less than 0.2 percent of one year's GNP, Latin America has been paying $30–40 billion in net resource transfers to service its debt, equivalent to about 6 percent of GNP.[5] Interest payments are consuming 35 percent of Latin America's export earnings and draining about 25 percent of domestic savings, depriving the region of badly needed investment capital and thereby reducing its growth potential.[6]

Latin American negotiators might argue that they have succeeded in extracting some concessions. In the first phase, they cajoled creditors into providing some additional funding and to restructure old debts. In the second phase, when credit markets seemed to have steadied, the commercial banks were persuaded—with help from the IMF and the Federal Reserve Board—to reduce fees and commissions and to lower interest-rate spreads to pre-crisis levels. Some debtors also gained multiyear reschedulings, thereby introducing more order and predictability into their balance of payments. More recently, the United States government has offered to increase future financing through the World Bank and the Inter-American Development Bank, and to pressure the commercial banks to resume modest levels of new lending.

Certainly Latin American governments have had numerous reasons for pursuing cautious debt policies. Initially, the crisis caught them by surprise. They also considered their own bargaining positions to be weak and judged that cooperative solutions with the creditors were more likely to enhance their financial stability, and yield some marginal concessions, than policies of confrontation. They hoped that good behavior would lower their credit costs and reopen their access to private credit markets (the first expectation has been realized, the second largely not). They feared that aggressive tactics might provoke retaliation—the curtailing of trade credits and possibly the seizure of overseas assets—that could severely disrupt imports and stimulate a domestic financial panic.[7]

DEBTOR INDIVIDUALISM

If each debtor nation felt weak and vulnerable, why haven't the debtors forged a coordinated strategy? Reasons of timing, tactics, personalities, national interests, and domestic politics have all played a part. The crisis peaked in different countries at different times. In its rush to avoid default, Mexico lacked time to coordinate actions with other debtors. When the Alfonsín government sought international backing to confront the IMF and the banks, rather than line up behind Buenos Aires, the other major Latin American debtors sided with the creditors in urging Argentina to come to terms. Fearing that an Argentine default would harm their own creditworthiness, they even extended short-term credits to enable Argentina to cancel interest arrears. Ironically, this coordinated action among central banks—wherein the major Latin American debtors applied friendly but firm persuasion to discipline Argentina—was the foremost example of Latin American "solidarity" during this entire period. Such was the degree to which the Latin American governments had bought into the creditors' strategy.

Individual nations also decided that their unique financial or geopolitical position warranted a go-it-alone approach. Because of its strong reserve position, Venezuela judged that it did not need new credits, or an IMF standby, and could therefore negotiate a specially tailored deal. Mexico reasoned that it, too, could extract somewhat more favorable terms by cultivating its special relationship with the United States. And none of the major debtors wanted to tarnish its image through association with such "basket cases" as Bolivia, Nicaragua, or Peru.

During this period, Latin America lacked the strong national leader who might have spearheaded a working alliance. Many governments were confronted with severe economic and political problems, and were too preoccupied or fragile to devote their energies toward participating in a risky debtors' cartel.

Exceptional episodes aside, Latin America does not have a history of close hemispheric cooperation. The two major debtors in particular—Mexico and Brazil—have generally stood apart from the rest; Mexico has concentrated on its bilateral ties with the United States while Brazil has always felt a bit removed from its Spanish-speaking neighbors. Most foreign ministries lack the personnel, technology, and experience to organize a hemisphere-wide campaign. In any case, central banks and finance ministries tended to control international economic policy, and they leaned toward working cooperatively with creditors rather than seeking solidarity with other sufferers.

No clear strategy emerged to guide a multilateral approach. Governments did sign several declarations—at Cartagena, Colombia, in June 1984 and again in Lima, Peru in July, 1985—but they were more a list of ideas than a coherent and workable plan. The Latin Americans lacked the power to impose the recommendations aimed at improving the global economy; they had no leverage over U.S. fiscal policies, and only very weak bargaining power to forestall growing protectionism in Western Europe.

Finally, it might be argued that many Latin Americans identified with the creditors. While capital flight had once been an elite privilege, during the 1970s and early 1980s the middle classes in many countries opened bank accounts abroad. Their diversified portfolios gave them a stake in the strength of the dollar and in the stability of the international financial system. Indeed, some actually benefited from the sharp devaluations and recessions that devastated their nations, since their dollars appreciated in relative terms, enabling them to purchase domestic assets at bargain rates. At the same time that the middle classes were being integrated into international capital markets, the Latin American labor movement and leftist political parties had declined markedly in many countries, weakened by repression, recession, and botched attempts at governing. Thus, some governments felt under greater pressure from external forces and from cautious middle classes than from the citizenry at large.

The Latin American nations—individually or collectively— never really had their own debt strategy. The creditors' four-point strategy has directed the adjustment process. Whereas the creditors—public and private—overtly organized to coordinate strategies for managing old debts as well as for providing new loans under certain conditions, the debtors remained independent from each other. Individual debtors, too, failed to devise or articulate very clear strategies beyond seeking to remain current on interest payments, regain creditworthiness, and minimize the costs of refinancing. Some governments also sought to ameliorate their adjustment process by squeezing "softer" terms from the IMF. But these were modest efforts to alter at the margins a broader strategy imposed by others.

THE CHANGING PATTERN OF CAPITAL FLOWS

Within the declining capital flows to Latin America, the relative weight of the different sources has shifted significantly. Most notably, official credit—provided by bilateral and multilateral sources—has doubled in value since 1980–81 (see table 1). And whereas official credit accounted for only about 10 percent of total flows in 1980–81, since 1983 official agencies have been providing the lion's share of credit. Indeed, in 1985 the contribution of governmental institutions may have surpassed 100 percent, as net private flows may have turned negative.

The increase in official flows was partially the result of increased disbursements by the World Bank and the Inter-American Development Bank, both of which adopted special programs to speed credit to recipient nations, while also seeking to expand new loan commitments. Gross disbursements by the World Bank to Latin America rose from $1.6 billion in 1980 to $3.2 billion in 1984, while the IDB increased its contribution from $1.4 billion to $2.4 billion (see table 2).

The boost in official flows—augmented by IMF lending—was insufficient to offset movements in private markets. While official lending rose by some $5 billion, private lending to Latin America fell by $40 billion or more. Most significantly for the future, increases in official lending were quickly engulfed in the flood of interest payments being paid the commercial banks, which hovered at levels in excess of $30 billion.

THE FUTURE FLOW OF FUNDS

A survey of the probable availability of funding for Latin America over the next several years suggests a continuing scarcity of new credits. Interest payments seem likely to continue to exceed net inflows by a substantial margin. Contrary to expectations that the commercial banks would quickly resume lending once countries reduced their current-account deficits, bank opposition to substantial new lending seems to be hardening. The IMF is looking forward to repayments from its short-term stabilization loans, while the IBRD and the IBD are in need of major capital increases if they are not also to become drains on the region's resources. U.S. bilateral flows are constrained by Congress and by the shaky financial position of the Export-Import Bank.

Commercial banks

The more optimistic scenarios that predicted a smooth and relatively rapid resolution of the debt crisis foresaw bank exposure increasing at a nominal rate of 5–7 percent per year to the major debtor nations.[8] This was a rate of increase well below the rapid expansion of the 1970s and early 1980s, and only slightly above

TABLE 1

Sources of Capital for Latin America and the Caribbean 1980–86
(U.S. $ billions)

SOURCE	1980	1981	1982	1983	1984	1985	1986P
a) Private creditors[a]	35.9	54.1	28.8	2.0	7.0	–0.6	2.3
b) Long-term borrowing from official creditors	4.2	5.3	5.6	9.5	7.3	3.3	9.1
c) Reserve-related liabilities[b]	1.9	1.2	9.0	8.2	3.4	1.8	–1.8
Net External Borrowing	42.0	60.6	43.3	19.7	17.7	4.5	9.7

p equals projection
Source: IMF, *World Economic Outlook*, April 1986, Table A41.
a. Calculated by the IMF as residual.
b. Includes IMF credit, arrears, and short-term government-to-government borrowing.

TABLE 2

Sources of Official Multilateral Capital for Latin America and the Caribbean,
1980–85 Gross Disbursements (U.S. $ billions)

	1980	1981	1982	1983	1984	1985
IBRD	1.59	1.71	1.97	2.45	3.18	3.14
IDB	1.43	1.54	1.66	1.73	2.38	2.34
IMF[a]	0.29	0.56	1.86	6.61	3.99	1.86
Total	3.31	3.81	5.49	10.79	8.97	7.34

Sources: IBRD, *World Debt Tables* (1986), p. 250; IDB, *Annual Report* (1985[a]), p. vii; IMF, *International Financial Statistics Yearbook* (1985), p. 21; IMF, *International Financial Statistics* (May 1986), p. 29.
a. Gross Purchases, including drawdown of reserves

inflation. However, the banks have proved unwilling to undertake even such a marginal addition of risk. From the end of 1983 through March 1985, international banks increased their net lending to non-OPEC developing countries by only 1 percent; since March 1984, outstanding loans to Latin America have actually fallen slightly, from $212.2 billion down to $211.8 billion.[9] U.S. banks have followed this global trend. Their exposure in Latin America and the Caribbean increased by less than $3 billion from June 1983 through June 1985, to $72.6 billion, a rate of increase well below the rate of inflation.[10]

Alarmed at the deteriorated quality of their assets in Latin America, the commercial banks have adopted a strategy of reducing their exposure in relation to their overall assets as well as their capital. When the debt crisis first hit, the banks found their exposure to be a multiple of their capital; nine major banks had loans outstanding to Mexico and Brazil alone that nearly equalled their total capital.[11] Banks are working hard to reduce their vulnerability by holding down new loans while building up their primary capital (which includes loan loss reserves). U.S. banks have succeeded in lowering their exposure in developing countries as a percentage of their capital, from a peak of 186 percent in 1982 to 141 percent by the end of 1984; the ratio for Latin American countries dropped from about 120 percent to 93 percent. For the nine largest U.S. banks, the ratio of loans to developing countries in relation to their capital has fallen from 288 percent to 224 percent, and for Latin America from 177 percent to 146 percent. Morgan Guaranty has calculated that if the banks continue to expand their primary capital at current rates (by issuing equity and setting aside reserves out of profits), they could lower their LDC loan-to-capital ratio to 93 percent for all banks and to 155 percent for the nine major banks by the end of the decade, providing that they limit the growth of new loans to 4 percent annually.[12]

Bank lending decisions are influenced by the pressures that management feels from owners and borrowers. Bank managers currently emphasize that their directors and stockholders are nervous about Latin America's economic future. While not saying so publicly, bank managers have also been impressed by the willingness of most Latin American nations to live with little to no new credit. Rather than being persuaded to reward "good behavior" with new loans, banks seem to have concluded that the debtors require few concessions to adjust their economies and to stay current on interest payments.

Current bank objectives are the reason behind the slump in new lending, despite the heroic adjustment undertaken by the Latin Americans. So long as the banks' primary objective is to reduce their vulnerability, and their directors and stockholders perceive them to be badly overexposed in developing countries generally, no degree of economic reforms is likely to call forth substantial amounts of new loans.

Assuming that the banks' objective of reducing their vulnerability to Latin American debt is legitimate, the key issues are how fast and how far they should adjust their portfolios and balance sheets. A larger volume of new lending would be possible if the banks accepted a more gradual improvement in their risk position, and if they were willing to settle on a somewhat higher final level of risk. Alternatively, a faster accumulation of primary capital would also make more lending possible.

The banks might also be cajoled into making new loans if public-sector institutions were willing to absorb a portion of the risk. The banks would like to see official export credit agencies and the World Bank expand their loan guarantee programs. They may also be persuaded to do more in the presence of implicit assurances by the U.S. government. More favorable regulatory treatment of Third World loans could be one manifestation of such an official commitment.

Direct investment

The near-term contribution of direct investment to the region's capital needs is likely to be disappointing. Discouraged by contracting markets and excess industrial capacity, net foreign investment inflows fell from a yearly average of $7.2 billion in 1981–82 to an estimated $3.8 billion in 1983–84.[13] The Overseas Private Investment Corporation (OPIC) and the World Bank's International Finance Corporation (IFC)—and two new agencies, the IDB's International Investment Corporation and the World Bank's Multilateral Investment Guarantee Authority—can use their lending and insurance authorities to promote foreign investment. However, the region's unsettled business climate is likely to preclude a rapid recovery.

Official lending

Both the World Bank and the Inter-American Development Bank have attempted to pump more funds into cash-starved Latin America. Jointly, their disbursements have jumped from $3.0 billion in 1980 to $5.6 billion in 1984 (see table 2). Given the need, however, their performance is less impressive. Both agencies were hampered by the deep recessions in the region which not only made it hard to find new investments to fund but even halted construction on existing projects for lack of local ("counterpart") finance. The IDB was further constrained by internal budgetary ceilings, which included limitations on lending to the major debtors. These country limits of $250 million per year were established in earlier years to assure funding for the smaller, poorer nations in the region. The World Bank was less immediately constrained by budgetary ceilings, but found itself unable to fully utilize its program lending because countries were unwilling to accept the accompanying conditions. Sectoral and structural adjustment loans required policy reforms that were more strenuous, detailed, comprehensive, and intrusive than some governments were willing to accommodate. Resenting IMF conditionality, governments shied away from placing themselves under the long-term tutelage of the other Bretton Woods organizations. Jamaica and Costa Rica were willing to sign structural adjustment loans with the World Bank, but negotiations with the larger nations proved more difficult. As a fallback position, the Bank moved to negotiate more narrowly focused sectoral loans that involved fewer conditions, and reached agreements with Colombia and Chile in 1985.

New capital injections for the IBRD and IDB will be negotiated during 1986–87. Because reflows from past loans are mounting rapidly and interest charges are at near-market rates, the banks' net financial contribution will be negligible unless lending levels increase very substantially (see table 3). Even allowing for a modest increase in commitments, the IBRD's net transfers to Latin America could well turn negative by 1990, although some countries would continue to receive a net inflow. Similarly, whereas the IMF responded

boldly and rapidly to the debt crisis, providing net flows of over
$10 billion to Latin America between December 1982 and mid-
1985, it is scheduled shortly to become a net recipient of capital
from the region as its medium-term loans fall due. Thus, the
multilateral institutions could become part of the problem.

U.S. bilateral loan programs include the Agency for International Development and the Export-Import Bank. Driven by security
rationale, AID has increased its lending to about $1 billion a year
for the small economies of Central America and the Caribbean
islands. Being the largest single donor, AID has in some cases taken
the lead in providing macroeconomic policy advice, pushing the IMF
aside. AID's balance-of-payments loans have somewhat cushioned
the adjustment process in several countries, particularly El Salvador,
Honduras, and Costa Rica, although poor terms of trade, high debt
burdens, and political strife have kept their economies stagnant.[14]

Guided by more traditional risk-aversion criteria, the U.S.
Export-Import Bank (Eximbank) has reduced its lending to troubled
Third World areas. As a self-financing institution, the Eximbank
is concerned by its mounting losses, delinquencies, and forced reschedulings, as well as record claims being filed against its guarantees
of private credits. Moreover, the demand in recession-ridden countries for its big, capital-intensive projects has declined. Total Eximbank loan authorizations fell from an annual average of $5 billion
in fiscal years 1980–81 to only $650 million in 1983–84; for Latin
America, new loans dropped from $830 million to $450 million

TABLE 3

*Projected IBRD and IDB Net Transfers^a to Latin America
and the Caribbean, 1985–90 (Fiscal years, U.S. $ billions)*

	1985	1986	1987	1988	1989	1990
IBRD	0.6	0.5	0.5	0.3	0.1	−0.3
IDB^b	1.0	0.8	0.7	0.3	0.1	0.7
Total	1.6	1.3	1.2	0.6	0.2	0.4

Source: Author's calculations and IDB estimates
a. Net transfers equal disbursements minus repayments and interest charges.
b. Figures are projected on the basis of anticipated funding through 1986, while
1987–90 figures are estimated with no projected replenishment of IDB funds.

(see table 4). This pattern was repeated by other industrial country export credit agencies, whose net provision of loans and guarantees to developing countries declined from an annual average of $12.5 billion in 1979–81 to $8.8 billion in 1982–84.[15] For seven major Latin American nations, net flows declined from $2.6 billion to $1.1 billion.

Because the Eximbank is sensitive to presidential directives, it followed White House appeals for special loan guarantee lines to Mexico ($500 million) and Brazil ($1.5 billion) that were part of larger financial packages, as well as to Central America ($300 million).[16] However, overall activity levels are likely to remain constrained by the perceived riskiness of business in developing countries, unless either the White House or Congress provides new guidelines and, perhaps, additional funding.

THE BAKER PLAN

In his address to the joint World Bank–IMF meetings in Seoul, Korea, on October 8, 1985, U.S. Secretary of the Treasury James Baker recognized the insufficiency of funds flowing into the major debtor nations. He urged both the multilateral development institutions and the commercial banks to increase their disbursements to the major debtors, in support of adjustment policies that moved beyond austerity to a renewed emphasis on development. He argued that "there must be a commitment by the banking community—a

TABLE 4

*Export-Import Bank Authorizations for Latin America
and the Caribbean, FY 1979–85 (U.S. $ billions)*

	1979	1980	1981	1982	1983	1984	1985
Loans	.60	.59	1.07	1.64	.11	.14	.20
Guarantees	.36	.55	.57	.43	.51	.42	.67
Medium-term insurance	.36	.44	.36	.29	.17*	.21	.15
Total	1.32	1.58	2.00	2.36	.79	.77	1.02

* Excludes special facilities for Mexico and Brazil
Source: U.S. Export-Import Bank, annual reports, 1979–1984

commitment to help the global community make the necessary transition to stronger growth."[17] Specifically, he called on the banks to commit publicly to net lending in the range of $20 billion over three years, and urged the World Bank and IDB to increase their disbursements to principal debtors by roughly 50 percent from the current annual level of nearly $6 billion. In return for these increases, the recipient nations should agree to "comprehensive macroeconomic and structural reforms," including fiscal stringency, competitive exchange rates, higher domestic savings, more liberal policies toward trade and foreign investment, and increased reliance on the private sector.

Baker's address marked a fundamental shift for the Reagan administration in several conceptual areas. First, it was a clear public admission that, contrary to numerous previous statements, the existing strategy was inadequate, and that not only did serious problems remain but that some "setbacks" had also been experienced. Second, Baker abandoned the lukewarm posture he had adopted toward the World Bank at the 1984 annual meetings and awarded the Bank a central role in the future global adjustment process. Third, he implicitly recognized the fallacy of the previous assumption that the commercial banks would rapidly begin to lend voluntarily to debtors who improved their external accounts. In short, the United States government would have to provide firmer support to official financial institutions and would also have to renew efforts to coerce the banks to increase their exposure. While to some degree Baker's proposal was a replay of the about-face made by the U.S. Treasury at the time of the first debt crisis in 1982, he was saying in effect that a strong public-sector role was not just a short-term emergency departure from market principles, but must be a central feature of international financial relations for the foreseeable future.

Baker's assessment properly focused attention on the key issue of inadequate capital flows and the need for a greater public role, but three problems remain. First, Baker's numbers simply do not approach the size of the financing gap that his address seems to recognize. In addition, the plan was announced unilaterally, without consulting the debtors being asked to undertake revolutionary changes in their political economies, or even other industrial countries whose banks and taxpayers will be expected to contribute.

Finally, Baker's rhetoric is replete with "supply side" phrases, emphasizing tax cuts and the free market, which if taken seriously could imply an effort by a fortified creditor cartel—this time led by the World Bank—to impose a particular, ideologically charged development model; the outcome could be a new phase of confrontation between North and South.

REALLOCATING THE BURDEN

The industrial countries and commercial banks have been highly successful in passing the lion's share of the adjustment burden onto the debtor nations. This success was embedded in the banks' foresight during the 1970s to switch from fixed to floating interest rates, and was solidified by the superior unity, strength, bargaining skill, and ideas that the creditors demonstrated in the 1980s. The Latin Americans' corresponding weaknesses have prevented them from striking a more balanced bargain, and the trend may be unfavorable: as banks improve their loan-to-capital ratios, they will feel less vulnerable to any pressure that the debtors might mount.

But the creditors' success is unstable and is arguably not in the long-term interests of either the banks or the U.S. government. The net outflow of capital from Latin America is so great that it seriously impedes new investment and growth. While exports can grow briefly through diverting production away from the domestic market, sustained growth requires new investment; thus, the ability to service debt is ultimately impaired when a country is deprived of a sizable portion of domestic savings. Left to their own devices, the banks have been reverting to a defensive posture of not increasing exposure, which makes sense from the viewpoint of each individual bank, but which decapitalizes clients and thereby reduces the value of everybody's assets. The size of the net capital outflow also raises questions in the minds of the debtors about the costs and benefits of seeking to please a financial community whose reaction to good behavior seems to be simply to demand yet more and more reforms.

Several other U.S. interests are also at risk. Most concretely, U.S. exporters and subsidiaries of U.S. firms producing for domestic markets find their sales are inversely related to interest payments. More broadly, important U.S. foreign policy interests are at stake in whether Latin America can resume growth, and whether Latin Americans perceive that the United States played a constructive role in rekindling that growth. In the short run, it is true that austerity has not automatically produced political upheavals, and those changes that have occurred have generally been in the direction of centrist, civilian regimes. Nor have most governments adopted strong anti-U.S. rhetoric. But the danger exists that prolonged austerity combined with a large net capital outflow could erode the legitimacy of governments and create fertile ground for fervent nationalism. One need not wave the red flag of pro-Soviet revolutions to imagine a very rocky period of political instability and nasty hemispheric relations.

Finally, prolonged austerity is likely to weaken the finance ministers and central bankers who are generally more favorably inclined toward open markets and good relations with the United States. If their strategies cannot deliver, they will likely lose ground in debates within governments, and their attitudes have never been popular with the masses. While severe financial crises do sometimes strengthen the hands of fiscal conservatives and free-market reformers, a policy of squeeze is a high-risk one, especially if applied on a hemisphere-wide scale over an extended period.

REDEFINING THE PROBLEM AND THE PROCESS

Building on Baker's conceptual breakthroughs, it should be possible to devise a new bargaining objective and procedure. The central concept would be to seek a more equitable distribution of the adjustment burden by reducing the net capital transfers from debtors to creditors. The diplomatic benefits from this redistribution could be maximized by including the debtors in a negotiating process whereby the new bargain is struck. In return for an agreement to reduce the net capital outflow, the Latin Americans would make commitments to long-term structural reforms in their economic management.

Focusing on net resource transfers is not a new concept.[18] The international community is accustomed to talking about the percentage of donors' GNP that they devote to foreign assistance, and private flows are sometimes included in these statistical series.[19] Just as the donor community has had the target of 1 percent of GNP for aid flows, the international community might agree to gradually reduce the net capital outflow from Latin America to a certain percentage of hemispheric GNP. Bilateral accords might be reached with individual Latin American nations that set country-specific targets.

A broad range of mechanisms is available for reducing the net outflow. Some focus on increasing inflows while others seek to reduce outflows.[20] The IMF, World Bank, IDB, Eximbank, and AID could each raise its projected contribution. Using their various formal and informal cofinancing and guarantee schemes, they could also seek to catalyze more private credit. Through their persuasive powers and the carefully crafted treatment of international loans, the Federal Reserve Board and the other regulatory agencies could also stimulate private creditors to do more.

Once contentious but now routine, the rescheduling of principal payments is one element in a package to reduce the capital outflow. Other proposals that attack interest payments are more controversial. The president of the IDB, Antonio Ortiz Mena, among others, has suggested that the commercial banks agree that a certain percentage of interest payment be automatically reinvested in-country.[21] Alternatively, if market interest rates rose above a predetermined rate, a portion of the payments falling due could be postponed and rolled into principal ("capitalized"). More drastically, payments above the interest rate "cap" could simply be canceled. An interest-rate ceiling that reduced rates on existing loans by two percentage points for the four largest Latin American debtors (Argentina, Brazil, Mexico, and Venezuela) would eliminate only an estimated 13 percent of earnings for the major U.S. banks, while a cut of five percentage points would reduce earnings by 33 percent.[22] While far from negligible, neither sacrifice would force banks to dip into their essential equity base. Whether the banks might suffer a catastrophic loss of confidence would depend on the magnitude and likely duration of the concessions and the measures taken by the regulatory agencies. Still more drastic measures, including loan write-downs, might be appropriate for some lesser debtors such as Bolivia, Nicaragua, and Costa Rica, whose export potential seems too weak to carry existing debt.

Numerous combinations or permutations of such proposals

could produce the desired result. The ultimate package should seek to reduce the net outflow in ways consistent with eventually restoring the creditworthiness of Latin American nations and maintaining the stability of the international financial system. Judgments regarding the likely direction of interest rates will be crucial: lower rates would suggest a package more heavily weighted toward new lending, while higher rates would increase the need for restructuring existing debts.

The exact formula should not be decided by the United States alone. On the contrary, involvement of the debtors in designing the program could bring several benefits. The diplomatic gains will be much greater if the debtors play a meaningful role in determining their own futures. Moreover, the U.S. administration would be in a stronger position to sell the plan to the commerical banks and the Congress if it takes the form of an international agreement backed by friendly democratic states. Indeed, the package could be sold on strategic grounds — as essential for the economic viability and therefore endurance of Latin American democracies, and vital for maintaining warm hemispheric relations in an increasingly fragmented world. While the direct budgetary costs of the package are likely to be small, Congress will have to accept the potential or indirect costs of guaranteeing lending by multilateral agencies and allowing banks to write off any losses against their taxes. But Congress could be persuaded to accept these costs if the banks are shown to be making their contribution, and if the security arguments are convincing.

Multilateralism is not without risks. The debtors might press for exorbitant demands, or indulge in polemics. However, if the United States convened the meeting, and carefully selected the time, place, and participants, and proposed the agenda, it should be able to avoid losing control. The U.S. Treasury Department — as the lead governmental agency in international finance — could organize the meeting and limit attendance to its counterparts in the governments of the major Latin American debtors. By circumscribing attendance to financial agencies, the danger of the meeting degenerating into a rhetorical confrontation is reduced; instead, the finance ministers — who have behaved so responsibly to date — have every incentive to demonstrate that their closer working relations with Washington can bring real rewards. The larger debtors are also likely to behave reasonably because they hope to regain access to private capital markets.

The governments and banks of other industrial countries will of course have to be consulted early in this process, and eventually included in the negotiations. Non-U.S. banks account for over half of Latin America's debt to the international banking system. Because the United States is by far the region's largest single creditor, and has been working closely with several Latin American nations to manage their debts, it is logical for the U.S. government to play a leading role.

From an analytical perspective, inviting just the leading four to eight debtors makes sense because they account for two-thirds or more of the total debt. Indeed, it might be wise to devise a wholly separate strategy for dealing with the second and third tiers of debtors—those whose debts are relatively small from a systematic point of view and manageable with some special alterations, and those whose economic situation is so desperate that only highly concessional solutions seem valid. Such debtors might be invited to later meetings where their particular problems head the agenda. Finally, the applicability of the agreements to extra-hemispheric debtors will have to be considered.

The IMF and World Bank should participate in the meetings to provide the analysis necessary for a most important part of the agreement—the Latin American commitment to structural reforms. By pledging to improve their economic management, the Latin Americans would lay the foundation for meeting future debt service, as well as guaranteeing that the debt relief package not be merely a short-term palliative.

The "multilogue" would face some knotty problems. It would want to calculate the level of capital outflow consistent with an agreed-upon growth rate for the hemisphere—a task that the multilateral agencies are well staffed to perform. Perhaps its greatest challenge would be to design a program of economic reforms whose policy substance and monitoring provisions are both acceptable to the Latin Americans and credible to the commercial banks. But Secretary Baker, in his Seoul address, has already asked the World Bank to shoulder this task.

In seeking to negotiate such an accord, the United States government would, in effect, be mediating between the commercial banks and Latin America. It would be aiming to right a balance that the Latin Americans, by themselves, have lacked the organization and power to accomplish on their own. The U.S. would be asserting a leadership role that recognizes that the long-term interests of the nation do not necessarily accord with the deals that private powers produce. Such leadership has been demonstrated at crisis moments, and is now required to produce a lasting settlement.

A hemispheric agreement that sets targets to reduce the capital drain which is exhausting Latin America and that establishes a reform agenda which the Latin Americans themselves agree would yield a more productive future, could transform a crisis into a covenant, and open a healthier era in U.S.–Latin American relations.

NOTES

The author would like to thank Robert Cassen, Peter Hakim, Robert H. Johnson, Joan Nelson, and Mary L. Williamson for their insightful comments on an earlier draft of this article, and Chika Kuno for able research assistance.

1. United Nations Economic Commission for Latin America and the Caribbean (1985).

2. See Sewell and Contee (1984).

3. See International Monetary Fund (1985).

4. United States Agency for International Development, Congressional Presentation, mimeo, various issues.

5. Inter-American Development Bank (1985).

6. Discussions of the adverse impact of the debt crisis on growth prospects can be found in Krueger (1985); IDB (1985b); and in Appendix A, "The Impact of Import Availability on Domestic Output," in Bergsten et al. (1985), pp. 203–210.

7. For persuasive arguments that some of the fears were probably exaggerated, see Kaletsky (1985).

8. Feinberg (1984), p. 8

9. BIS (1985).

10. Federal Financial Institutions Examination Council, Washington, D.C., Statistical release E. 16.

11. Lissakers (1984), p. 53.

12. Morgan Guaranty (1985a), p. 8.

13. Goldsbrough (1986), Table 1.

14. Feinberg and Bagley (1985).

15. Morgan Guaranty (1985b), p. 11.

16. These open lines of credit were largely underutilized because of procedural complications, the relatively high cost of Eximbank funds, and low demand for investment goods.

17. James A. Baker, III, Statement before joint Annual Meetings of the IMF and Wold Bank, October 8, 1985, Seoul, Korea, Treasury News, mimeo, p. 9.

18. For a classic discussion, see Domar (1950).

19. For example, see Development Assistance Committee (1984), pp. 244–260.

20. For discussions of the many proposals to manage the debt crisis, see Bergsten et al. (1985); Kaletsky (1985); and Feinberg (1984).

21. For example, see Bogdanowicz-Bindert (1985), p. 6.

22. Feinberg (1984), pp. 12–13. Estimates are for after tax based on banks' 1983 performance.

REFERENCES

Bank for International Settlements (BIS). 1985. *International Banking Developments, First Quarter, 1985*. Basel: BIS, July.

Bergsten, C.F., et al. 1985. *Bank Lending to Developing Countries: The Policy Alternatives*. Washington, D.C.: Institute for International Economics.

Bogdanowicz-Bindert, C.A. 1985. Small Debtors, Big Problems: The Quiet Crisis. ODC *Policy Focus*, no. 2.

Development Assistance Committee. 1984. *Development Co-operation: 1984 Review*. Paris OECD.

Domar, E.D. 1950. The Effect of Foreign Investment on the Balance of Payments. *American Economic Review* 40 (December): pp. 805–826.

Feinberg, R.E. 1984. Restoring Confidence in International Credit Markets. In R. Feinberg and V. Kallab (eds.), *Uncertain Future: Commercial Banks in the Third World*. Washington, D.C.: Overseas Development Council.

———. 1985. International Finance and Development: A Surging Public Sector. In R. Feinberg and V. Kallab (eds.), *U.S. Foreign Policy and the Third World: Agenda 1985–86*. Washington, D.C.: Overseas Development Council.

Feinberg, R., and B.M. Bagley. 1986. *Postponing Development: Recent Economic Policies in Central America and Alternative Development Strategies*. SAIS Papers in International Affairs. Boulder, Col.: Westview Press, June.

Goldsbrough, D. 1986. Past Trends and Prospects for Foreign Direct Investment in Developing Countries: The Link with Bank Lending. In T. Morán (ed.), *Investing in Development: New Roles for Foreign Capital?* Washington, D.C.: Overseas Development Council.

Inter-American Development Bank. 1985a. *Annual Report.* Washington, D.C.: IDB.

_____. 1985b. *Economic and Social Progress in Latin America: 1985 Report.* Washington, D.C.: IDB.

International Bank for Reconstruction and Development. 1986. *World Debt Tables.* Washington, D.C.: IBRD.

International Monetary Fund. 1985. *International Financial Statistics Yearbook 1985.* Washington, D.C.: IMF.

_____. 1986. *International Financial Statistics* 29 (no. 5, May).

Kaletsky, A. 1985. *The Cost of Default.* A Twentieth Century Fund Paper. New York: Priority Press Publications.

Krueger, A.O. 1985. Developing Countries' Debt Problem and Growth Prospects. Lecture delivered at the Atlantic Economic Society Conference, Washington, D.C., August.

Lissakers, K. 1984. Bank Regulation and International Debt. In R. Feinberg and V. Kallab (eds.), *Uncertain Future: Commercial Banks in the Third World.* Washington, D.C.: Overseas Development Council.

Morgan Guaranty. 1985a. *World Financial Markets*, July.

_____. 1985b. *World Financial Markets.* Sept./Oct.

Sewell, J. and C. Contee. 1984. U.S. "Costs" of Third World Recession: They Lose, We Lose. ODC *Policy Focus*, no. 2.

United Nations Economic Commission for Latin America and the Caribbean. 1985. *Preliminary Overview of the Latin American Economy 1985.* Santiago: CEPAL, December.

The Foreign Debt Problem from a Latin American Viewpoint

ALEJANDRO FOXLEY*

Latin America has reached an impasse. After more than four years of harsh adjustment programs, the prospects for economic growth in the major debtor countries are far from promising. Current projections, based on an oil price of $18 per barrel and interest rates of around 8 percent, show a likely rate of growth of GDP for the rest of the decade of not higher than 3.7 percent per year. [1] At this growth rate, Latin America will be barely recuperating its pre-crisis levels of GDP. A full decade of growth would be lost (Cepal, 1986). On the other hand given a labor force that grows at more than 2 percent a year, the employment perspectives do not look favorable for the rest of the decade. The debt-export ratio would still be, on average for the region, higher than 300 percent, and by some estimates Latin America would still be needing on the order of $30 billion in net capital inflow per year.[2]

These figures are important because they confirm widespread doubts about the viability of the strategy implemented so far. By the end of the 1982–83 debt crisis, expectations for a more permanent solution to the problem were bolstered by the rapid growth in world trade, which would have enabled significant expansion in the economies of the debtor countries and increased their ability to pay back their debts. This optimistic perspective was influenced by the views of the creditor banks on resolving the crisis, and prevailed until early 1985.

The strategy of the banks consisted of trying to achieve two

---

*President, CIEPLAN, Santiago

The strategy of the banks consisted of trying to achieve two simultaneous objectives. First, they wanted their financial position to improve rapidly. They would achieve this by reducing their credit volume in Latin America and capitalizing a high proportion of their profits in order to cover themselves against the risk of nonpayment by some of the debtors. Their success in fulfilling this objective meant that by mid-1985, their financial position was already equal (in terms of the ratio between banks' claims in debtor countries and the banks' capital) to the level in the years preceding the debt crisis (Morgan Guaranty, 1986).

Second, the banks wanted to improve the ability of three major debtors in particular — Mexico, Brazil, and Argentina — to make their payments. The banks closely followed the performance of these economies, and in-depth studies were undertaken to evaluate their prospects at the end of the decade.

Banks measure a country's creditworthiness on a variety of aggregate ratios. The one that is most often used is probably the debt-export ratio. A country is considered to be solvent and creditworthy when this ratio is under 200 percent.

It should not be surprising, then, that the banks felt confident when some financial institutions made projections for Brazil and Mexico and found, under plausible assumptions, that these countries could reach the year 1990 with a debt-export ratio under 200 percent. There was still concern about Argentina, whose situation was particularly difficult to forecast because of both the government's unclear position on the debt payment and the uncertainty surrounding the application of an internal economic adjustment policy which Argentina did not appear ready to accept.

When, in June 1985, Argentina implemented a shock policy that was even harsher than IMF's, showing a willingness to catch up on foreign debt interest payments, it seemed that the main obstacles to solving the debt problem in Latin America had dissipated. Of course, the banks were aware that the situation of the other countries in Latin America was not necessarily the same as for the largest debtors. In fact, projections for the small and medium-sized countries, such as Chile, Peru, Bolivia, Nicaragua, Jamaica, and others showed that their debt-export ratios did not reach the minimum necessary to be regarded as creditworthy. The position the banks took on these other countries was that governments and multinational agencies should aid their economies with easy credit terms.

However, the current situation of the principal debtors has modified the banks' optimistic outlook. The September 1985 issue of *World Financial Markets* reviews its previous projections of the economies of Argentina, Brazil, and Mexico. By the end of the decade none of the three countries even approaches the threshold of a 200 percent debt-export ratio. The levels projected for 1990 are about 300 percent for Brazil and Mexico; and 350 percent for Argentina (Morgan Guaranty, 1985). These estimates do not consider the impact of oil price reduction in the Mexican economy, which is already having a devastating effect on that country's ability to meet its debt obligations.

The deterioration of the economies in these countries is not an isolated occurrence. It is clearly a regional problem. According to bank sources, around October 1985, ten Latin American nations were behind in their interest payments; six others had not been successful in meeting the goals of the adjustment programs established by the IMF; and two others refused even to negotiate with the IMF.

In 1985, Bolivia and Nicaragua fell behind in their payments, and Peru unilaterally announced a ceiling on the interest that it would pay and refused to negotiate with the IMF. The Dominican Republic and Jamaica struggled to maintain a precarious level of stability in their domestic policies in the face of extremely severe austerity policies. Chile entered into a new period of economic stagnation. Mexico held back payment of nearly $1 billion and requested more than $6 million to keep up with its payments in 1986. The IMF declared Mexico to be out of compliance with the established goals. Brazil kept up its interest payments but was not able to settle differences with the IMF regarding an adjustment program.

This economic backdrop was accompanied by political pressure from Latin America's main debtor countries for a new approach to solving the debt problem — one that would be compatible both with the banks' goal of avoiding a solvency crisis and with the resumption of the economic growth in Latin American economies, which was seen as indispensable to payment of the foreign debt. Some analysts interpreted these political reactions of the governments as a symptom of "adjustment fatigue."

GOING BEYOND "ADJUSTMENT FATIGUE"

Growth perspectives for Latin America do not offer expectations of improvement in the living conditions in Latin America. The current adjustment effort is at times seen by some countries as pointless. It is important to note that, in spite of that perception, most of the countries have not considered the option of a moratorium, as occurred in the 1930s. This is because, until now, they have believed that the costs would be too high. On the one hand, considerable emphasis has been placed on the possibility of a liquidity crisis, which could arise if the flow of credit of a country were suddenly interrupted. On the other hand, there has been hope that "good behavior" in the form of timely payment of the debt would create conditions which would quickly reestablish voluntary credit channels through the international banking system.

Another important consideration in the past was the internal political situation. On the one hand, authoritarian governments who saw their internal base of support weakening attempted to strengthen their principal sources of outside political and economic support from the U.S. government, multinational institutions, and creditor banks. Thus, for example, Chile became the most faithful observer of conditions favored by the IMF, the banks, and the U.S. government. This observance was maintained despite the catastrophic social consequences of the imposed adjustment.

Paradoxically, Latin America's new democracies arrived at similar political conclusions, but for different reasons: the fragile nature of these new democratic systems and the absolute importance of avoiding any economic disaster set off by a sudden break in the flow of credits from banks led governments, such as those in Argentina, Uruguay, and Brazil, to be overly cautious in their approach to the debt questions and, despite their reluctance, to follow the policies suggested by the IMF and the banks.

The perception of these costs, however, has been changing since the end of 1984. Despite their "good performance," some of these economies are currently going through severe liquidity problems. Recent events in Mexico suggest as much. On the other hand, one has only to look at the figures to see where the problem lies. The net credit from private international banks to the seven major debtor countries in Latin America grew by only 2.5 percent in 1983 and by 1.6 percent in 1984. During first-quarter 1985, the net flow was negative (Morgan Guaranty, 1985).

The cost associated with losing access to voluntary bank loans in the future is also diminishing in view of the general impression in financial and political circles that the banks will not, before the end of this decade, voluntarily renew a normal flow of credit, except perhaps to larger countries such as Brazil, which have been able to sustain solid recovery with significant levels of economic growth. The cost of less concerted actions with banks and more concerted actions between countries is considered lower now, not only for these reasons, but also because in several cases these governments have been able to considerably strengthen their internal basis of political support. The examples set by Alfonsín, Sanguinetti, García, and Sarney illustrate this point very well.

It could in fact be argued that precisely this perception of the economic crisis combined with the impossibility of improving the economical situation by depending, as in the past, on high levels of external credit would make it possible for Latin America's new leaders to launch an appeal for large-scale nationwide mobilization to solve the debt crisis through domestic savings and internal efforts.

The recent experience of Argentina could serve as a lesson. So long as the country's economic situation did not deteriorate drastically, it was impossible to attain the political support necessary for economic adjustment. Alfronsín's political talent enabled him to recognize the critical point of crisis and convert it into an opportunity. When the gravity of the crisis became well known and there was no other alternative to Alfonsín's, the government took harsh economic measures—the so-called Plan Austral—which the population supported despite the immediate costs to each particular group. Alfonsín came out of the crisis in a stronger position and was able to gain time before tackling the underlying structural problems behind the current economic crisis in Argentina. The same happened in Brazil in early 1986, when the "Plan Cruzado" was put into practice, with widespread popular support.

The point is that it *is* possible for a country subject to severe external constraints to achieve dynamic levels of growth. But it needs leadership capable of mobilizing the population through a national development plan which spurs the country's imagination and encourages it to make a special effort to save and work in order to free itself from crisis. What countries need are their own national strategies for overcoming constraints, as historical experience indicates.

What blocks this path for Latin American countries in the 1980s is their governments' limited autonomy in defining national development plans in response to their own institutional structures, experience, and knowledge on the basis of past successes and failures.

A NEW CONDITIONALITY?

Current efforts by the U.S. government point to a shift in the focus of its approach to the debt problem, to acknowledging the need for economic growth to pay off debt. Greater emphasis is now being placed on the importance of structural change to renewed growth.

Structural readjustment would be a necessary condition for the proper use of capital that agencies such as the World Bank might make available to debtor countries at higher levels. This increase in resources would be subject to compliance with long-term development policies consistent with the "correct policies" view held by these agencies and/or the governments that have the greatest influence on them. This would represent a new form of conditionality that would be superimposed over that defined so far by the IMF. The extension of this principle of conditionality to the sectoral or structural change programs undertaken by the developing countries may imply limiting the ability of each country to find the development scheme most effective in mobilizing its creative energies.

Public statements by Secretary Baker seem to be saying to the multinational development organizations that their new mandate is to loan to those indebted countries that are willing to try moving towards "reagonomics" in a serious way: privatization of public enterprises, free-market policies, free trade practice, liberalization of financial markets, and supply-side incentives through lower taxes. It would seem that this new form of conditionality takes little account of the past experiences of some countries that have used such policies, particularly in the Southern Cone in Latin America. The new conditionality has already been applied in Jamaica.

Jamaica has been subjected to the simultaneous and super-imposed conditionality by the IMF and the World Bank over its economic policy and development program. Its structural adjustment program includes more than twenty simultaneous conditions that cover domestic concerns (such as privatization of state-run bus companies and publically held land, reorganization of the stock exchange, and a program for reforming public administration, government-run hotel rates, public radio commerical rates, and staff-reduction quotas in specific state-run companies) in addition to the more standard conditions in the foreign trade, taxation, and finance areas.

If this form of conditionality becomes more widespread, countries will be severely constrained in defining their own development programs and will have no leeway in their application; in some cases, they will be led into repeating the same errors committed by those Latin American countries who hurriedly liberalized their economies in the 1970s. The alternative for these countries would be to seek a deliberate delinking from the international economy. This may become an appealing alternative for some countries in the area, but the historical lesson is well known: isolated, autarchic countries with "war-time economies" inevitably end up restricting civil liberties and developing very authoritarian-looking "war-time policies."

EXTERNAL AND INTERNAL ADJUSTMENTS

Two aspects contribute to the fragility of the current strategy for solving the debt problem. The first is related to the notion that industrial countries' growth will be the basic mechanism by which debtor countries will be able to grow out of the debt problem. The second has to do with the difficulty of sustaining the massive transfers of funds from debtor countries to developed countries, which has been occurring since the inception of the debt crisis.

The locomotive theory

According to the "Locomotive Theory," the debt problem could be solved without the need for government intervention if stable, strong growth rates were achieved in the industrial economies.

Strong growth rates—above 3 percent for the OECD economies—
would make it possible to expand the exports of developing countries to annual rates of at least 6 percent.[3] With real interest rates
in the international markets projected between 4 percent and 5 percent, the higher growth of exports would make it possible for the
countries to allocate even fewer exports to debt service maintenance.
Thus, the solution for the problem would not be short-term, but
a favorable result would be guaranteed in the medium term, with
no other intervention than that necessary for maintaining sound
macroeconomic policies.

The developed economies in 1984 grew at a respectable 5 percent, this high rate stemmed from the 6.8 percent economic growth
in the U.S. economy that year. In 1985, however, the situation took
a sudden turn. Industrialized nations as a whole grew at a rate of
only 2.8 percent. This modest growth was accompanied by continued deterioration in the purchasing power of Latin American exports, which in 1985 alone, decreased by 4.6 percent (CEPAL,
1986). Most analysts agree that the deteriorated terms of trade for
Latin America are not likely to recuperate in the short to medium
term (Project LINK, 1986). These figures show the fragility of the
mechanism on which the debt-payment capacity of debtor countries is based.

The "locomotive" mechanism, which presumes that rapid,
stable growth in the industrialized economies would create a sweep-
ing demand for Latin American exports as well as an automatic improvement in the region's terms of trade, does not seem reliable
enough to bring about an "automatic" market solution to the debt
problem in Latin America. Governments and international lending
institutions must intervene to "guide" the process, neutralizing the
negative impact of external "shocks," until the economies are able
to recover their ability to grow in a sustained manner and pay off
the debt.

*Can internal efforts for paying the debt in Latin America
be sustained?*

Since 1983 Latin America has annually transferred about $30
billion to the industrialized countries. This represents approximately
5 percent of the region's GNP.

To effect this transfer, Latin American economies had to free resources that would otherwise have been added to internal savings for investment. Transfers were paid with the foreign exchange produced from surplus trade balances. If the economy is at full employment, these surpluses are achieved by reducing internal spending to generate the savings that need to be transferred abroad.

To ensure their ability to transfer resources for paying the debt, countries apply adjustment programs negotiated with the IMF. Although the nature of these programs is well known, two aspects should be emphasized: the dual conditionality to which the countries are subjected, and the fact that the IMF programs tend to ignore particular circumstances and new economic constraints arising from the debt crisis itself.

Dual conditionality occurs because different entities—the banks on the one hand and the IMF on the other—each pose their own conditions. After the debt crisis, the international banks decided to limit the total amount of loans a given country may receive. This total is determined by three criteria: the banks' need to reduce their exposure in a given country, to increase reserves to cover from the risk of nonperforming loans, and to give out new loans only to the extent required by a given country to allow it to continue interest payments without affecting its creditworthiness.

As a consequence, the internal effort that the country has to make is determined by the size of its debt and the level of the interest rate, as well as by the banks' upper limit in their desired lending to the country in question (Dornbusch, in this volume). The resource constraint for the country is thus determined by the amount of new external credit the banks and official agencies are willing to provide. The magnitude of the internal adjustment effort that the country must make is in turn conditioned by the ceiling imposed by the banks on the new lending that is available. This is the first conditionality constraint.

The second conditionality constraint is present when the country asks the IMF to help finance a balance-of-payments deficit. The IMF usually sets two types of conditions. First, the country should reduce imports by tightening spending, and second, the country has to take measures that would allow it to divert resources to the production of either exportable goods or goods that can be used to replace imports.

The adjustment that began in 1982 in Latin America showed just these features, and the results were as expected. Imports dropped very rapidly, followed by significant reductions in production.

The drops in production resulted from Latin America's traditional dependence on imported raw materials and imported capital goods for full capacity use and internal production expansion. When imports fall 40 percent in two years, as was the case in 1982–83, the resulting shortages in raw materials and intermediate goods inevitably bring down output levels in the economy.

Internal adjustment policies have also created huge complications in the fiscal sector. The IMF has always placed emphasis on reducing the fiscal deficit, with a very simple recommendation. The rule of thumb seems to be "cut the deficit in half each year, regardless of its relative level."

After the period of financial liberalization in Latin America, the following events occurred. The governments, state-run companies, and the private sector borrowed excessively abroad. When external funds dried up, it became inevitable that loans had to be renegotiated. At this point the international banks pressured governments to take over external liabilities contracted by the private sector. This was achieved either by government guarantees on the private debt or by having the public sector assume the obligation to make payments in dollars.

To make the interest payments on the foreign debt, governments had to purchase dollars with surplus internal resources obtained either by reducing spending, by printing more money, or by issuing bonds that were placed on local financial markets. If the choice was to reduce spending, this accentuated the contractionary trend set in by the IMF adjustment policies regarding the nonfinancial deficit. Contractions in government expenditures usually had the largest impact in the areas of investment and spending for social services.

The other options for governments consisted of either borrowing in the domestic capital market or, alternatively, in printing more money. When the first alternative was chosen, the interest rate rose, which accentuated recession; when the second alternative was chosen, inflationary pressures immediately increased, as in the cases of Argentina and Brazil, where inflation shot up to the three-digit level.

Furthermore, the requirement to convert government savings into foreign exchange to pay the debt in dollars meant that the governments had to purchase this foreign exchange, thereby creating upward pressure on the exchange market. The anticipation of a devaluation that this generated could be countered only by providing a strong inducement to hold domestic currency. This in turn implied increasing domestic interest rates. This was the mechanism chosen by Alfonsín's economic team, and variants of this mechanism have also been used in Mexico and Brazil, which explains the extremely high real interest rates that prevailed in these countries during the adjustment period.

All of these aspects have obvious repercussions on the economic climate of the countries during the post-crisis adjustment phase. The undesired consequences of austerity policies against a background of excessive borrowing can be summarized as follows: slow growth or outright stagnation in production levels, aggravation of the financial position of firms, high rates of real interest, pressure on the dollar, and a permanent climate of economic uncertainty.

Uncertainty is perhaps the most significant unintended consequence of the drastic adjustment effort. IMF targets for the main macroeconomic variables have to be continually revised, because of the inability of most countries to meet them. While this occurs, the IMf interrupts the flow of external funds until conversations with each country's policymakers are reinitiated. These conversations take months, during which time the economic agents can do nothing but wait.

In this environment it is impossible to maintain a stable economic policy. Frequent changes make the public lose trust in the policy. What suffers most are investment levels. Economic agents do not feel they can make rational decisions in such an uncertain environment, and often choose to hedge against uncertainty by buying dollars. Capital flight turns out to be the last escape valve in a climate of economic deterioration and uncertainty. In fact, the figures for capital flight from Latin America are impressive. During the 1983–85 period alone, it reached $31 billion for the ten largest Latin American debtors (Morgan Guaranty, 1986).

The picture depicted here would not be balanced unless one recognizes the valuable role that the IMF played during the crisis in preventing a collapse in the international monetary system. The

IMF's key function was to put pressure on countries and banks to maintain payment flows and minimum levels of new credit that were essential to prevent the "debt bomb" from exploding.

On the other hand, it cannot be denied that the debt-burdened countries had to adjust their economies to the new conditions of scarce credit. To achieve this, greater fiscal discipline was necessary, along with internal savings efforts and a redirection of national production toward external markets. It is also clear that the achievement of greater international competitiveness continues to be the best basis for a solid solution to the debt problem.[4]

But what is not often recognized by international lending agencies is that economic policy approaches in Latin America in the 1980s are more sophisticated and pragmatic than old stereotypes would admit. Most governments and policymakers in Latin America today would stress the importance of the market and its proper functioning as a necessary, although insufficient, condition for the efficient allocation of resources in these economies. This approach recognizes the reality of mixed economies in Latin America as a valid historical formation that has existed and will continue to exist in the future, beyond the ideological intents of the extreme left or right.

Latin America today has a greater understanding than ever of the need to promote more incentives for the development of entrepreneurial capacity. What is needed is a dynamic private enterprise that is productive and competitive at the international level.

Furthermore, critical evaluations of past free-market experiments are currently under way in Latin America. It is generally accepted now that naive and radical hands-off attitudes on the part of the governments lead to serious distortions in resource allocation: low investment, high capital flight, etc. This was like a domestic capital market that in some countries produced real interest rates in the range of 20–50 percent for several years; to persistent goods and labor markets' disequilibrium, to unchecked speculative behavior by economic agents, to imperfect world markets for key export products, etc. Thus, it seems that an active regulatory role for the governments is needed, as well as more protection for the poorer sectors through vigorous development of social programs.

The difference between this active government presence and old-fashioned statism lies in the fact that what is stressed now is a decentralized, smaller government that opens channels for the private sector and organized labor to participate in the decision-making process. Discussions in Latin America today focus more on decentralized development with social pacts and concerted action and less so on an omnipresent State or on the advocacy of unrestricted free markets.

Lessons to be learned from dual conditionality

The IMF's mandate is to promote the international financial order by conditioning its financial support of countries in difficult situations on their compliance with measures to normalize the balance of payments. In addition to the necessary emergency measures, the success of external adjustment depends most importantly on strengthening the ability of the economy to export and to substitute imports efficiently. An aspect that is usually ignored in the redirection of production toward export goods is that success hinges on the impact that the macroeconomic adjustment policies will have at the microeconomic level, that is, on the firms themselves.

Adjustment policies during and after the debt crisis were characterized by reductions in investments of up to 30 percent and by the persistence of a recessive trend in the economy. For firms this meant low sales levels and chronically idle capacity. Stagnation in sales weakens the ability of the companies to pay off debt. Recessive adjustment with restricted credit pushes interest rates up and sales down. This in turn sets off an *internal* debt crisis: firms cannot pay back their credit and the proportion of banks' nonperforming loans goes up sharply, resulting in bankruptcy in some banks and financial institutions, and government intervention to stave off bankruptcy in others. Efforts to save productive firms from bankruptcy lead either to liquification of the debt through inflation, as in the case of Brazil and Argentina, or to repeated renegotiation of the debt with the banks, as in Chile. In the latter case the governments, through their central banks, end up subsidizing the renegotiated interest rates and assuming the exchange risk, if for any reason the private debt is "dedollarized."

Private enterprise, saddled with debt, is unable to recover because of prevailing recessive conditions. Investment in projects to modernize production and expand capacity cannot be undertaken because the cumulative effect of the prevailing recession and its accompanying uncertainty forces business to turn to purely defensive, survival-oriented strategies. The government is pressed to cancel private firms' debts and reduce the size of the work force, as well as wages and benefits for employees. When the situation becomes critical, the private sector lays off even its most highly skilled workers.

The private sector enters a period of stagnation and sluggishness; the morale of both managers and employees drops. Uncertainty over work and wage conditions decreases interest in work, and this affects productivity levels. Under such conditions, no incentives remain for the internal creativity that is essential to achieving international competitiveness.

Can the successful export experience of East Asia be repeated in a microeconomic climate that stifles innovation, creativity, and modernization of the production process? The real cause of the recent decline of private enterprise in Latin America does not lie so much in crowding-out by the government or in an excess of government control. On the contrary, the economic climate was on the whole quite permissive for private enterprise during the 1970s. Its current problems can better be explained by errors committed during the period of liberalization, such as excessive borrowing and the prevalence of interest rates far above the rate of return on assets. Without a doubt the greatest source of problems was the adjustment policy, conceived as a purely macroeconomic process, whose effect on industry at a microlevel did not receive adequate consideration.

The lesson is that if the IMF's conditionality is to strengthen export capabilities, attention must be focused on the microeconomic conditions necessary for production firms to recover from their current debilitated state.

The first requisite is internal financial housecleaning of the firms. The IMF, however, normally limits itself to imposing conditions at the macroeconomic level for the central bank to tighten credit, a large part of which is used precisely for salvaging companies, private or state-run, which would otherwise go bankrupt. Reducing this credit has a negative effect on the position of these firms.

Naturally, the ability of these firms to pay back their debts depends on their profits, which, in the short run, depend on anticipated sales levels. An adjustment policy without prospects for a reactivation of demand makes it impossible for the firms to move from a purely survival-oriented strategy to another, more active strategy that would normalize their financial position, while preparing the ground—through relatively high exchange rates and low tariffs—to direct firms more toward the external market.

How can private enterprise be strengthened when it simultaneously faces debt problems and a decline in markets? Who will take on investment projects to put the paralyzed economy back on its feet? Government and public sector enterprises have important roles in this situation, as was shown by the successful strategy used by industrial and Latin American economies to recover from the Great Depression in the 1930s. At that time private enterprise suffered from problems that, like those faced in Latin America today, kept it from becoming an active factor in ending the recession and reinitiating growth.

Even with private enterprise on the way to recovery, there is still the problem of stengthening export capabilities. This depends on more than just financial rehabilitation and favorable exchange rates. It requires research on new products, improvements in product quality, and access to new markets. According to most estimates, future conditions in external markets will be difficult: world trade is expanding at a slower rate than in the 1970s; there is more protectionism; and more countries are attempting to increase exports simultaneously to the same markets. It is unlikely that this type of strategy will be successful unless it is based on a close relationship between current or potential exporters and the government. This was the method used in post-war Europe and, more recently, in East Asia.

World economic conditions in the 1980s are characterized by instability, volatile interest rates, and potential external shocks from adjustments in industrialized economies. The presence of these factors would seem to indicate the advisability of carefully thought-out government action to reduce uncertainty and stabilize expectations of domestic economic agents, which will allow them to consider new investment decisions and modernization plans to increase productivity and international competitiveness. Mechanisms to coordinate and exchange information with private enterprise and to involve labor organizations could aid in reducing uncertainty and stabilizing expectations about the future.

Other lessons related to the IMF's conditionality acknowl-
edge various structural complications that may interfere with the
economy's recovery. One is the high incidence of the financial
component — payment of the foreign debt — in current government
budgets in Latin America. If this is not adequately recognized and
the condition is imposed mechanically that, regardless of the level
of spending, the deficit of the public sector must be cut in half, the
government will find itself facing a dead-end. For it would then be
forced to suspend the very same investment projects necessary for
reactivation and to reduce spending for social services, which are
aimed precisely at compensating the worst effects of the recession
on lower-income groups. Last, the policy will ultimately produce
a rise in interest rates, which is needed to attract resources toward
the government, so that it can finance the payment of interest on
the public debt. Overkill in the reduction of public spending has
gone so far in some cases that countries have been prevented from
using World Bank credits because the required counterpart of domestic public resources is just not available.

Another valid lesson to be learned from recent adjustment
policies is that the combination of tight domestic credit policies and
the liberalization of the foreign exchange market are likely to induce capital flight which is very difficult to reverse once it has started.
The lesson is that the government should control the foreign exchange market and actively regulate the flow of external funds to
avoid the worst consequences of procyclical behavior on the part
of external creditors and domestic borrowers alike. This is in turn
what will allow the country to recover some degree of autonomy
in monetary and financial policy.

A final lesson can be drawn from the dual conditionality imposed by the IMF and the banks: the banks' strategy of rapidly reducing exposure forces governments to adjust too drastically. Because
adjustment occurs through import reduction in the short run, this
has a negative impact on the exports of industrial countries. Jobs
are lost in industrialized economies.[5] The magnitude and speed of
the productive employment loss generated by this process in industrialized countries is ultimately determined by the velocity at
which the major private international banks decide to withdraw from
the credit market in debtor countries, because this is what regulates
the intensity of the adjustment effort needed by their domestic
economies and, thus, their required import reduction.

This tight lending policy on the part of the banks will probably accent, rather than moderate, the contractionary characteristics of the adjustment programs that, as argued before, tend to weaken production units the most and therefore end up jeopardizing the ability of Latin American economies to pay off debt, recover, and grow in the medium and long term.

WHAT TO DO?

The concern of the banks and the United States government over the apparently unsuccessful debt strategy has resulted in a policy shift. A proposal has been made to increase the role of the multinational organizations by expanding credits granted by the World Bank and the IDB. This would entail a $9 billion increase in net new loans over a period of three years, plus the creation of mechanisms that would allow cofinancing by the World Bank and private banks, as well as World Bank guarantees on some of the loans made by private banks (as has already occurred in Chile). It is hoped that this will help the debtor countries attract $6–7 billion per year in private credit.[6]

Some of the proponents of these measures want the World Bank, possibly in cooperation with the IMF, to condition new loans on obligatory structural reforms and economic policy reforms on the part of debtor countries. Proposed changes include the privatization of state-run companies, the liberalization of trade and financial flows, and, in general, the active promotion of a free market and pro-private enterprise policy. This new form of conditionality would be a third dimension added to the conditions already imposed by the banks (ceiling for the total of new external credits available) and to IMF conditions pertaining to the specific type of economic policy the country should adopt to adjust the economy in the short run. The new conditionality would be based on the process now being applied by the World Bank in its structural adjustment loan (SAL) programs, which in turn reflect current U.S. government policies of promoting liberalization and privatization.

No doubt the proposed increase in the availability of government and private funds constitutes a move in the right direction. However, the new forms of conditionality do not necessarily constitute a step forward. The basic challenge, which is now all but unanimously accepted, is to create conditions that will enable Latin American economies to resume their normal economic growth. Otherwise, their ability to pay the debt will become increasingly weaker with time.

Growth in Latin America has come to a standstill as a result of the insufficient level of imports that the region is currently able to finance. Around 1981, imports to Latin America were on the order of $100 billion. In 1985 they totaled $57 billion. A "normal" level, based on that which existed in the second half of the 1970s, would be around $80 billion in 1985.

To recover this level, an additional $20–25 billion will be required each year. This would make it possible to increase imports by one-third. Using the import elasticities estimated by Lessard and Williamson (1985), this could lead to an 8–15 percent increase in the region's GNP, with a probable 5 percent reduction in the unemployment rate.

Latin America's new inflow of capital in 1984 and 1985 was on the order of $8 billion annual average. Adding between $20–25 billion in new resources would produce a net capital inflow similar to the one that existed immediately prior to the boom period of 1978–81. So long as reserves remain constant, this would represent a deficit in the current account of the balance of payments similar to 1976 and 1977 levels, a period when growth rates could be characterized as "normal" with annual GNP growth at about 5 percent. The availability of $30 billion in net new external funds would be equivalent to 8 percent of Latin America's combined debt. Assuming annual rates of growth in the 5 percent range and 3 percent inflation, net credit expansion would be consistent with maintaining the ratio between the region's debt and its GNP, constant in the future.

How can this capital expansion be financed? Fishlow (1984) and others have suggested a formula based on two principal components. The first puts a ceiling on the interest rate paid on credits. Any excess over this limit would be capitalized; as a result, the real value of the debt would remain constant. The second component of the formula would require an expansion in official credits— governmental and from multinational lending agencies.

If a reduction of 4 points in nominal interest rates could constitute an acceptable target for the maximum rate to be paid in any one year by indebted Latin American economies and the difference with respect to market rates were capitalized, Latin America would reduce by this means its current net transfer of capital outside the region from $30 billion to $18 billion. How can the difference be financed so that $20 billion can be generated per year?

In a climate of resumption of economic growth and rational, more stable economic policies, one could expect current low levels of direct foreign investment of around $2 billion per year to return to their previous levels. Foreign investment in Latin America as a whole exceeded $4 billion annually in the 1981–82 period. Hence, it would be possible to obtain an additional $2 billion per year.

The remaining $6 billion would still have to be financed with new official credits to the region. Two points of reference should be noted. First, this amount is equivalent, in 1985 dollars, to the annual average level of external government financing available to Latin America in the 1961–70 period (the Alliance for Progress years). Second, under the Marshall Plan, U.S. government transfers were equal to 14 billion in 1985 dollars per year between 1948 and 1951. Over 85 percent of these funds were grants. That financing effort represented 1.2 percent of the United States' GNP each year. A similar percentage of the United States' GNP today would represent an average annual level of aid of $46 billion.[7]

Our proposal is that a Latin American Development Fund could be established to grant long-term credit at interest rates not in excess of 2 percent in real terms. These credits would be used to aid countries by cofinancing with the countries themselves their development programs and investment plans. Decisions of the Fund would be made jointly by representatives of the government agencies providing resources to the Fund and by representatives from Latin America chosen on the basis of their technical capabilities and their political significance in the region.

The conditionality criteria to be applied to these credits should avoid the exaggerated forms of "policy conditionality" often required by multinational agencies, and should be tailored to specific circumstances. It would be advisable for the IMF to continue supervising the adjustment of imbalances in the external sector of the economies. The forms for internal adjustment should vary, however, depending on the nature of the imbalance and the structural characteristics of the particular economy. As Bacha (1985) points out, the IMF should not, as it frequently does, apply a rigid conditionality for the internal adjustment of the economy. Rather, it should leave the country free to design its own domestic adjustment program as long as the goals set for the balance of trade and the balance of payments are met.

It has been noted that Brazil improved its balance of payments at the end of the 1970s through highly unorthodox domestic economic policies (Cortázar, 1985; Carneiro, in this volume.) It increased rather than decreased government investment, directing it toward sectors of tradable goods and thereby creating conditions for the subsequent expansion of exports and substitution of imports. Thus, Brazil in recent years has been able to generate strong trade surpluses (about $12 billion a year), which have enabled it to continue paying the interest on its gigantic foreign debt.

Countries should be able to proceed more selectively in their internal adjustment. IMF-mandated adjustment policies have the strongest impact on wage earners (because they increase unemployment), and on the poorer strata of society (because these groups are affected by the general drop in income and by cuts in public spending that reduce social services). A strong argument based on equity considerations can be made that a selective fiscal and spending policy should be applied.

Conditionality in a development fund should concentrate on increasing investments, particularly in the areas of exports and substitution of imports, and on the absorption of unemployment. The instruments for achieving these goals should be tailored to the specific characteristics of each country.

These criteria contrast with the current concept of policy conditionality, which assumes that a particular instrument of economic policy, if used in a certain way, will necessarily produce the same results in any context. Albert Hirschman has called this view "mono-economics," arguing that it tends to ignore the validity of development economics as a whole. The discipline of development economics arose in the post-war era, along with the awareness of the specific nature of economic problems of developing countries and the need to identify those factors that distinguish these countries among themselves as well as from industrialized countries. Within the discipline, attempts were made to design strategies and use policy instruments to remove obstacles to development in a particular historical and structural situation.[8]

The key issue in the theory and practice of development economics is the mobilization of existing resources to revitalize the national economy. Also important is the way local production factors should be combined so that innovations in technology and production methods are forthcoming to allow for sustained growth in production and productivity levels. When a country finds its own formula for development—a scheme capable of mobilizing and promoting creativity and innovation—it reaches a level of development that has the potential to sustain itself in the future because conditions for achieving permanent increases in productivity are met.

If this view of the development process is accepted, it follows that conditionality should neither stifle the search for this development formula nor impose economic conditions that will leave the government with nothing to offer in the future to motivate economic agents. The combination that should most be avoided as the result of excessively restrictive conditionality is that of tough, uniform policies applied by weak governments. From greater rigidity in conditionality will come greater weakness in government.

Conditionality should be consistent with the idea of energizing a society, that is, putting it in tension for development. It should increase the society's degree of freedom and enhance its indigenous problem-solving capacity, not reduce them.

What follows from this is that conditionality should be flexible enough as to allow for nonuniformity in the policies applied in different institutional, structural, and even historical contexts. Why recommend further financial and trade liberalization in the countries of Latin America's Southern Cone when their current economic crisis was due at least in part to an unrestricted application of the very same policies being recommended now by some lending agencies? What would be the purpose of pushing for the privatization of banks and state-run firms in those countries where these public firms often had a more efficient performance in relation to external shocks than private firms did?

Take the case of Chile. During the boom, the State Bank was careful to lend only to firms whose projects—after careful evaluation—proved profitable. Additionally, it did not engage in the extended practice of private banks to lend (in fact, overlend) without guarantees.

It might also be useful to point out that many public enterprises were able to perform better than their private-sector equivalents during the recession. To be sure, this was the consequence of their quasi-monopoly situtation that allowed them to stay in the black by upward adjustments in utility rates.

The recognition of different situations and of flexibility in conditionality criteria are part of the necessary ingredients in a suitable economic policy which should be more pragmatic and draw from past successes and failures rather than from ideological preferences. In economic policy, good sense cannot be substituted with simplistic, ideological criteria. The conditionality that is applied to adjustment in the short term must be consistent with long-term development. If the outcome of adjustment policies is a drop in investment of 25 to 30 percent, for four or five years in a row, as recently observed in Latin America, then something is inconsistent between the short- and long-run elements of the desired policy package.

The problem is no mere technical matter. If what is required is a government with broad support and with the ability to lead the country in mobilizing human and physical resources to overcome the external constraint, then an excessively rigid and premature conditionality may nullify the process through which the government is gaining credibility and legitimacy so that it can actually implement the required economic program. Otherwise, as suggested by the case of President Alfonsín, it is the expansion in political legitimacy—which can occur only under a full democracy—that will enable a government to achieve the levels of freedom that are needed to later apply economic measures that may involve harsh sacrifices for the population.

The sequence of these actions is essential for any adjustment-with-growth program to be successful.

NOTES

This paper was written at the Kellogg Institute for International Studies, University of Notre Dame, October 1985. The author would like to thank J.P. Arellano, C. Bradford, R. Cortázar, J.M. Dagnino-Pastore, R. Devlin, R. Feinberg, R. Ffrench-Davis, P. Hakim, C. Ossa, and K. Stenzel for their comments and suggestions. The author alone, however, is responsible for the contents of this paper.

1. Projections by Project LINK at the University of Pennsylvania, March 1986, and by IDB, March 1986.

2. Estimates by IDB, March 1986.

3. There has been much discussion on the relation between the economic growth of OECD countries and the expansion in exports of developing countries. The most complete discussion of the topic is found in Dornbusch and Fischer (1985). See also Fishlow (1984).

4. Krueger (1985) develops this point. She maintains that most countries have already adjusted their economies. The main problem now would be how to reduce the debt overhang that constrains the export capacity of many countries.

5. The Chemical Bank has estimated 800,000 jobs were lost in the U.S. economy because of this effect alone. See the *Washington Post*, September 29, 1985.

6. The official figure is $20 billion in three years.

7. This information was supplied by Konrad Stenzel in a personal memo.

8. A given policy instrument used in the same manner in structurally different developing countries can produce very different results. Dornbusch, in this volume, shows this by comparing the effect of a devaluation of the exchange rate in Korea and Brazil.

REFERENCES

Bacha, E. 1985. The Future Role of the International Monetary Fund in Latin America. Mimeo. Depto. Economia P.U.C., June.

Bergsten, E. 1985. The Second Debt Crisis is Coming. *Challenge*, May.

CEPAL. 1986. The Economic Crisis Policies of Adjustment, Stabilization, and Growth. April.

Cortázar, R. 1985. Employment, Real Wages, and External Constraint: The Cases of Brazil and Chile. Mimeo. PREALC, September.

Dornbusch, R., and S. Fischer. 1985. The World Debt Problem. *Journal of Development Planning*, no. 16. New York: United Nations.

Ffrench-Davis, R., et al. 1985. Deuda externa, industrialización y ahorro en América Latina. *Collección Estudios CIEPLAN* 17, Santiago, September.

Fishlow, A. 1984. Coping with the Creeping Crisis of Debt. *Working Paper* no. 181. Dept. of Economics, University of California, Berkeley, Calif., February.

IDB. 1986. *Economic and Social Progress in Latin America*.

Krueger, A. 1985. Developing Countries' Debt Problems and Growth Prospects. Mimeo. World Bank, August.

Lessard, D., and J. Williamson. 1985. Financial Intermediation Beyond the Crisis. *Policy Analysis*, no. 12. Institute for International Economics, September.

Morgan Guaranty. 1984. Morgan International Tables and Charts, November.

———. 1985. *World Financial Markets*. September.

———. 1986. *World Financial Markets*. February.

OCDE. 1985 Economic Outlook. June.

PREALC. 1985. *Informe no. 6*. March.

Project LINK. 1986. Projections. March.

Comments

CRISTIÁN OSSA*

I would like to focus my comments on three major topics: diagnosis, proposed solutions, and the recent change in the world economic outlook. Concerning diagnosis, there is a relatively high degree of consensus in the three papers on the origins of the debt problem and its consequences. Richard Feinberg emphasizes the interaction of the economic situations of the Latin American countries and aspects of the balance of power between the banks and U.S. policy toward Latin America, Alejandro Foxley stresses the internal costs of a predominantly recessive adjustment in our region, and Ricardo Ffrench-Davis concentrates on the financial and productive aspects. However, the three authors agree on how the problem arose and why attempts to solve it have failed. Relative agreement is also evidenced by the fact that all three feel that if other policy lines had been taken, a significant portion of the adjustment costs could have been avoided. Personally, I concur, for the most part, with the historical analysis contained in the articles. Therefore, I will only briefly refer to a few points that I believe are important yet were not sufficiently developed.

The first point is the assignment of responsibility. There are three factors: the countries themselves, the banks, and the policies of the major participants in the world economy. In 1983 the analysis of the IMF attributed most of the balance of payments erosion in the debtor countries to factors outside their control.[1] Nevertheless, all the steps taken to solve the problem are based virtually on the assumption that the blame rests entirely with the debtors. Moreover,

*Chief, International Economic Relations Branch, DIESA, United Nations, New York.

some important institutions have begun arguing that all of the difficulties were caused by excessive fiscal spending in these countries.
In fact, for a number of debtor countries, the truth is quite different.
The fiscal deficit was a direct result of the abrupt change in the international economic environment in the late 1970s and early 1980s.

On the one hand, fiscal revenues eroded because they depended
largely on import and export flows, which were affected by the
stagnation of international trade and the drop in the flow of external credit (Tanzi, 1986). On the other hand, there was a sudden
change in the interest rate structure, causing a rapid increase in fiscal
expenditures for the public external debt. Obviously, the debtor
countries are not primarily responsible for a monetary policy in the
developed world that was excessively expansionist in the 1970s,
leading to negative interest rates, and then excessively restrictive
at the beginning of the 1980s.

Another point not sufficiently analyzed is the respective roles
of the public and private sectors. The neoconservative movement
of the late 1970s and early 1980s in the developed countries, especially the United States, portended and prompted an increasingly
minor role for the public sector, even in the developed countries.
However, because of the debt problem, in the debtor countries the
state seems to be indispensable and its role of greater importance.
In some economies even the banking system is nationalized, not as
a result of the government's socializing strategy but rather as a means
of strengthening the national financial system, which was seriously
threatened by the repercussions of the external debt problem. But
there is still another paradox related to the debt problem. The spontaneous solution prescribed by the market for credit-based investments that ultimately result in losses, unless there is backing, is the
partial or full write-off of the debt. In current circumstances the
market solution has not worked: creditors have united to exert concerted pressure for the full payment of all credits granted, including
those that were for private activities of a speculative or highly risky
nature.

The last point I would like to make regarding diagnosis concerns the excessive optimism exhibited, as recently as 1982, by
creditors and debtors alike with respect to the future course of individual economies and the world economy in general. As Ricardo
Ffrench-Davis affirms, in this case everyone is to blame. Creditors

and debtors alike were largely uncritical in their acceptance of projections and prognoses on the growth of the world economy and
exports, which were consistently overestimated. Debtors, in turn,
did not concern themselves sufficiently with negotiating contingency
clauses, so that each time external variables performed worse than
expected, the adjustment became much more difficult.

Concerning the proposed solutions, the three authors agree
that simultaneous action is required in a number of areas. The solution basically includes six elements: 1) a new type of adjustment,
with a conditionality that is jointly agreed to rather than imposed
by the creditors or the IMF; 2) a significant increase in official
credits, especially from the World Bank and the IDB; 3) formulas
to reduce or partially defer interest payments; 4) an increase in bilateral credits; 5) soft aid to the most vulnerable countries; and 6)
a possible increase in foreign direct investment. I agree with the
position that action is necessary in all these areas and that all efforts
should be coordinated to solve the debt problem in the least con-
flictive manner. The initiative of the U.S. Treasury Secretary—the
Baker Plan—is also oriented along some of these same lines. However, as the analysis of the three articles reveals, this plan seems
overly optimistic about the possible contribution of private banking and the restoration of its confidence in the debtor countries in
the near future.

In regard to the solutions proposed in this volume, I would
like to make three comments: one on interest payments, another
on the political viability of some of the proposals and, finally, one
on the overall situation of the world economy.

Among the solutions proposed for reducing interest payments,
the effects of cutting the rate to be paid on already contracted debt
to only 4 or 5 percent, that is, half the current rate is analyzed by
one of the authors. This formula offers various advantages over
proposals for deferring interest payments or establishing maximum
real interest rates. It is very difficult to determine real interest rates
when prices vary in a fundamentally different way for creditors and
debtors. A fixed rate would permit improved financial programming
ming for both creditors and debtors. The implicit loss for the banks
would be absorbed over a long period of time, if banking regulations would permit it. In this regard, it should be noted that projections on the earnings of U.S., European, and Japanese banks were

recently revised upward and the price of bank stocks, as well as stocks in general, has risen dramatically.[2] The problem would still have to be resolved of whether a measure of this type can be negotiated or implemented only as a unilateral action on the part of the debtors. There is a potentially significant risk of creditor reprisals, but, as Feinberg points out, this risk has often been exaggerated. It is not a coincidence that in the December 23, 1985 issue of *Fortune* magazine Carol Loomis proposes this formula as a means of conciliation between banks and debtor countries, with obvious advantages for both, provided that the debtors honor their agreement to pay the five percent rate.

It is not easy to give an opinion on the political viability of many of the proposals presented. However, an essential component of all of them is a significant contribution of resources from the U.S. government, either in bilateral form or through multilateral institutions. The current political situation in the United States does not, however, seem conducive to this end. Implementation of the Gramm-Rudman-Hollings Act of 1985, the objective of which is to balance the budget by 1990, is likely to involve significant cuts in bilateral aid programs and reductions in the growth of multilateral aid. There would have to be a drastic change in the attitude of Congress to obtain significant resources through this channel. Nevertheless, there are two areas in which U.S. policy could have a decisive impact on improving the situation, without requiring the disbursement of additional resources.

First of all, it could change its position with respect to the issuing of special drawing rights by the IMF. The technical study of the secretariat of the IMF recently concluded that an issue was justified. But this still met with the opposition of key members, including the United States. Second, the United States, within the context of the group of five or seven participants in the summit meeting, could pressure its allies, particularly those with current account surpluses and greater fiscal equilibrium, to increase the flow of resources to Latin America.

Finally, concerning the solutions, I want only to emphasize the global dimension of the debt problem. The debt did not spring up as an isolated phenomenon. In fact, it was one of the most virulent expressions of the world economic crisis at the beginning of the decade. It is critical that the analysis not overlook the global aspect of the source of the debt, despite the fact that many believe that the solution should only be approached on a case-by-case basis.

Any solution, including those calling for even greater curbs on demand in the debtor countries, will require significant changes in the international economic environment. Without more dynamic international trade, all efforts to ease the current situation and to restore long-term growth will be insufficient.

This brings me to the last of the three topics I mentioned, the short-term outlook for the world economy. After 1985, which was a fairly deceptive year for the world economy and especially for Latin America, the world economic situation has tended to improve markedly. Various factors were responsible for this turnaround. Inflation in the developed countries fell off considerably, affecting nominal interest rates and restoring confidence in the financial markets. The recent depreciation of the dollar lessened the possibility of increasing exchange instability. The Group of Five decided to coordinate monetary policies, and the U.S. government adopted a more determined attitude toward reducing the budget deficit. This combination of factors strengthened the confidence of consumers and investors. Since December 1985 the drop in oil prices has significantly improved the position of energy importing countries and has afforded them greater room for maneuver. It is estimated that a drop in the price of a barrel of oil on the order of $8 leads to growth in the OECD countries of more than one-half percent, and a fall in the rate of inflation of about 1 percent after twelve months. In fact, and in anticipation of lower inflation, the key developed countries implemented a coordinated reduction in the discount rate of their respective central banks, which rapidly led to a drop in interest rates.

Although we probably cannot call it euphoria, there is unusual optimism in many institutions and, especially, in the developed countries. Production and price indicators are not the only things beginning to improve. Commodity exchanges have recorded all-time highs in New York, London, and Tokyo, as well as in other European financial centers. The OECD and the IMF have revised their projections, and it is expected that the growth of the developed countries will be above 3 percent at least until the close of the decade. Perhaps as important as the indicators themselves is the fact that two basic imbalances of the system seem to be on the way to being resolved. The current account deficit and the federal deficit of the United States should begin to decrease significantly in 1987.

Compared with an undoubtedly more promising outlook for the developed world, the probable economic growth of the Third World seems in no way satisfactory. It is interesting to note that the multilateral institutions are gradually approaching consensus in their recent analyses of the growth prospects of the developing countries; for the majority of these countries growth will continue being slow—considerably less than 4 percent—up to the close of this decade. This growth is clearly unsatisfactory, especially if we consider that the population in these countries is growing between 2 and 3 percent and that per capita income fell significantly in the first half of this decade. The performance of Latin America is expected to be similar to that of the Third World in general.

There are four elements that, at the global level, explain this wholly unsatisfactory situation.

First, the great majority of the oil-exporting developing countries will suffer losses, in terms of trade, in excess of 30 percent in 1986. Second, everything points to there being no significant recovery in the real prices of other primary products. In other words, it is expected that in the world markets the prices of primary products, excluding oil and its byproducts, will rise at a rate equal to or less than the price of manufactured goods. Third, the accelerated growth of the developed countries will lead to comparatively moderate growth in international trade. It is expected that the volume of world trade will grow approximately 4 or 5 percent in the remainder of the decade. This rate, although higher than at the beginning of the decade, does not seem sufficient to produce the required dynamism in the world economy. Fourth, the debt or countries, and Latin America in particular, will continue facing a limited supply of capital. The drop in the interest rate will undoubtedly provide significant relief in debt service. However, because of the moderate growth of world trade and, consequently, of debtor country exports, there will be no significant change in certain key financial indicators. Only for a few countries will exports grow at a rate higher than the level of interest rates (that is, 7 to 8 percent per year) and the debt/export ratio will decrease only slowly throughout the rest of this decade. Up to 1990, only a very few countries will have regained the confidence of the banks.

In conclusion, for Latin America as a whole, enormous efforts will be needed to bring about any improvement in the standard of living in 1986 and 1987, and this will be true up to the end of the decade. The legacy of the debt will continue being a severe restraint on its economic growth.

NOTES

1. In the Annual Report of the International Monetary Fund (IMF, 1983, p. 34), it is claimed that for all non-oil-producing developing countries the erosion of their current accounts is due almost entirely to the worldwide recession, terms of trade deterioration, and high interest rates.

2. Stock market values reached record levels in London, New York, and Tokyo in the first quarter of 1986. Bank stocks generally kept pace with the movement of the market, and some bank stocks even exceeded it.

REFERENCES

IMF. 1983. *World Economic Outlook*. Washington, D.C. April.

Tanzi, V. 1986. LDC Fiscal Policy Responses to Exogenous Shocks. *American Economic Review*, May.

Comments

JOSÉ MARÍA DAGNINO-PASTORE*

I am going to concentrate on a comparison of the recommendations for the future set forth in the papers by Richard Feinberg, Ricardo Ffrench-Davis, and Alejandro Foxley, as topics for further discussion on the future agenda of the Inter-American Dialogue.[1] I am well aware of the complexity of the task of updating the diagnosis, for, as Foxley has said, it changes rapidly from month to month. Table 1 provides a summary comparison of the recommendations of the three authors grouped according to the entities addressed: creditor banks, international organizations, and creditor countries.

CREDITOR BANKS

The first recommendation is broad rescheduling of the debt—regardless of how much the financed amount increases—so that each time loan maturities are discussed a sufficient grace period is accorded, which would obviate the frequently recurring need to restructure the payments. The temporal structure of a country's debt is generally decreasing, as the graph on page 110 illustrates.

When already matured debt is rescheduled in period 1, an insufficient grace period is granted and the outstanding debt is carried over into the following periods [for example: four years with no grace period]. Such a carryover almost unavoidably leads to new

---

*Former Economic Minister and Former Secretary of the National Development Council of the Republic of Argentina.

defaults [for example: second to fifth year] and renegotiations, as shown in the graph on page 111.

This is what is known as giving "short rein," and it brings up a key topic: the handling of economic policy under conditions of continuing uncertainty. The cost is high and the money lost is not recovered by the countries since everyone knows that an exchange crisis is scheduled at least every twelve months. Thus, in addition to increased financing, the topic of rescheduling maturities is im-

TABLE 1

Comparison of Recommendations

RICHARD FEINBERG	RICARDO FFRENCH-DAVIS	ALEJANDRO FOXLEY
Creditor Banks		
1. Reschedule maturities	Reschedule maturities	
2. Interest rate ceiling with or without subsidy	Interest rate ceiling with or without subsidy	Interest rate ceiling with or without subsidy (Savings of $12 billion)
3. Automatic reinvestment		
4. Write off the debts of small, insolvent debtor countries		
International Organizations		
1. More credit	More credit	More credit Create L.A.D.F.[a] ($6 billion)
2.	Adapt design; increase the amounts and time frames of IMF financing	
3.	Nonideological conditionality	Objective conditionality, adapted to the country More investment ($2 billion)
Creditor Countries		
1.	Amend world economic policy	
2. Multilaterality		
3.	Amend creditor bank policy	

a. Latin American Development Fund

portant. This is still not resolved because of the fear of losing control over the economic behavior of the countries if all the joint negotiations are not updated every twelve months. My suggestion is to recommend broad rescheduling but with measures that satisfy the creditors' need for control, so that their fears of giving "loose rein" can be alleviated.

The second recommendation is the interest rate ceiling, which, in Foxley's proposal, could mean a savings of $12 billion per year. There are different mechanisms for implementing it, although — as shown in the example given by Cristián Ossa in this volume — regulating it would be complicated because wide price swings make it very difficult to define. For example, what is meant by keeping a thing constant in real terms? In short, two extreme types of clauses are possible: either fixing the amount to be paid and capitalizing the rest, or fixing the capitalized amount and paying the rest. A problem not often mentioned — but not unnoticed either — is that if large amounts are capitalized, the debt increases exponentially.[2] I believe that even with the difficulties of concretely defining the objective, exponential growth of the debt must be avoided. My suggestion is to recommend setting an interest rate ceiling, but to define a reasonable criterion to keep the debt from running out of bounds.

The third recommendation is establishing a mechanism for reinvesting interest, which is a variation of the above and a pro-

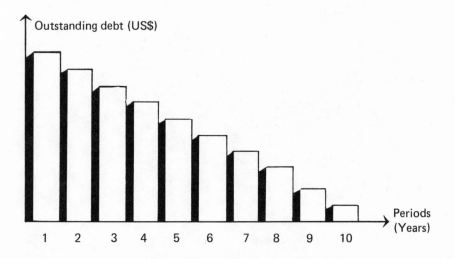

posal made by Ortiz Mena. Once it is determined that a portion of the unpaid interest will be capitalized at the end, that portion is added to the balance of capital loaned to the debtor country; optimally, it should be added automatically in an agreed form. This must be determined in a manner acceptable to both parties; if no more favorable way can be found than increasing the aggregate total of the debt, it is better not to do it. But I think there are better ways. Less tied loans with less conditionality is one possibility, but the question of how to define the method of reinvestment should be explored.

The last recommendation is writing off credits to small, heavily indebted countries. Here I believe that the resistance of the creditors is "How do we make a selection? To which countries do we limit ourselves? What effect will publicity have?" and so on. These concerns stand in the way of a solution, and so long as this situation remains unresolved these debtor countries are totally excluded from the financial world, without any possibilities whatsoever. What is needed is a solution that is tenable for the creditors and fast-acting for the debtors. It occurs to me that converting to soft credits is the most direct way, in the sense that it normalizes the situation

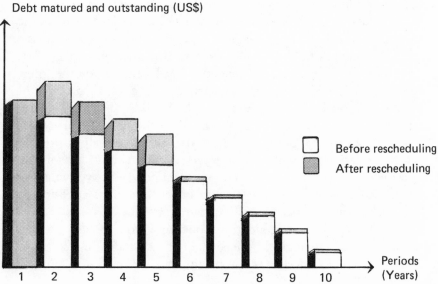

Debt matured and outstanding (US$)

Before rescheduling

After rescheduling

Periods (Years)

1 2 3 4 5 6 7 8 9 10

of the countries and creates no problems or intolerable precedents for the creditors.

INTERNATIONAL ORGANIZATIONS

Moving to the topic of organizations and taking the same approach, the first recommendation of the three authors is again: more credit. Foxley mentions $6 billion per year. There is no disagreement on this point. The roads are familiar; the only thing lacking is to expedite the political decision to take them.

The second recommendation refers to the need for the International Monetary Fund to work with longer time periods, with different designs and also with larger amounts, at least with respect to compensatory loans.

Concerning the International Monetary Fund, we have overlooked a long history of flaws in its administration in the interest of getting along well with the Fund. But, in fact, it seems to me that this is a rather important subject—well worth another look—because the IMF is, after all, the foremost short-term organization in the world. What concerns me, in institutional terms, is what might be termed its irresponsibility, not in the pejorative sense of acting irrationally, but in the sense of not having to answer for its actions to an independent authority. I fail to see clearly what the auditing or technical management supervision of the Fund consists of, since in specific cases I have observed gross errors. This does not mean that there have been no overall benefits for the international financial system, particularly in the very difficult circumstances of the 1980s, where, under the leadership of La Rosiere, it has responded very well to the crisis. But in specific programs there is evidence of poor adaptation of policies to the priorities of each country, even in technical aspects. It seems more reasonable for the countries to request some type of supervision over what the Fund does, so that it is obligated to pay a little more attention to the technical aspects of specific programs.

The third recommendation concerns conditionality, which should not be ideological but specific for each individual country. I consider this subject very important, but we must not "put the carriage before the horse." There is no conditionality worse than that of refusing to increase the financing; in that case we are truly constrained because we have no funds in our domestic policy. In any case, because of the objectives imposed by conditionality, there are always some subjects left out, which the international organizations and the creditor countries are not very interested in discussing. It is these I wish to discuss. One is import substitution, another is regional integration, and the third is tying the organizations' credits more to the generation of foreign exchange in the projects they finance, and less to the source of supply of the equipment used in the projects.

The subjects of import substitution and regional integration are fairly well covered. Literature abounds in articles on suboptimal tariff policy suggesting how to design better protection systems. The international organizations initially operated as export banks in the industrialized countries. But now that the developing countries must generate foreign exchange to service their debts, it is time for these organizations to round out their operations and to finance projects based on their foreign exchange content and not their imported component. There has been some progress, but there is still much to be done.

The fourth recommendation is more foreign investment in the debtor countries. This recommendation would not apply to the international organizations, but according to Foxley's presentation, they are involved because their credit policies should promote greater investment of this type. One possibility is the willingness of the industrialized countries to support these multilateral organizations so that they can invest funds; the other possibility — since most of the resources must come from commercial bank financing — would be the creation of special funds: Latin American Development Funds, for example. I believe that the idea of exploring the creation of new funds, to be managed by existing institutions and not by new bureaucracies, is a valid one. One role that the countries can play is to reduce the risk of the refinancing provided by the banks. The risk is lessened by lending — not to the debtor countries directly — but through a fund, where there could be some guarantee from the creditor countries. There could be two types of funds, one for long-term credit and one for venture capital.

CREDITOR COUNTRIES

The authors' recommendations are to support multilateralism, to amend international economic policy, and to take action to change the policy of the creditor banks, or, in general, to provide political support for the implementation of technical solutions.

The points I have outlined for the Dialogue's Agenda in the peceding sections can serve as technical suggestions for negotiators, but they do not solve the central issue, "How to negotiate?" Actually, the debtor countries have so far been very cautious: they have followed the policy of negotiating individually within the existing framework and attempting to push collectively for a change in this context. Everything that has been said shows that without a change in this framework, there is no clear answer to the question. The recommendation does not go much further than what the Inter-American Dialogue has already said: it is necessary to petition collectively at the highest level (that is, Presidents) for a change of context. I believe that this should be done in an increasingly insistent manner and with increasing frequency.

NOTES

1. The search is for points upon which reasonable agreement is possible, rather than solutions involving confrontation, which are more costly and traumatic for all concerned.

2. Except that recapitalized amounts do not accrue interest. However, this is not refinancing, but rather subsidization, which may be unavoidable in certain cases.

PART II

External Trade
and Foreign Investment

Crisis and the External Sector in Latin America

DAVID IBARRA*

It is commonplace to state that the economic crisis in Latin America is the most profound, prolonged, and generalized of the entire postwar period. Less common is the assertion that after five years of declining per capita income and heavy sacrifices by the people, the objectives of the "adjustment policy," implemented by the great majority of governments at varying intervals and with the normal variations, are still a long way from being achieved.

Per capita income fell 9 percent between 1980 and 1985. National income appears to have shrunk even further, judging from the erosion in the terms of trade (23 percent) and the increases in external debt service (ECLAC, 1985). Certain countries — particularly certain social sectors within these countries — may well have lost between one-fourth and one-third of their former income.

An encouraging sign was that during these same years the deficits in the balance of payments current account fell markedly, from over $40 billion to $4 billion. However, rather than indicating an improved position, this perhaps shows that the course of the adjustment was essentially recessive (ECLAC, 1984; BIRF, 1985).[1] The trade balance went from a negative $1.6 billion to a positive $34.3 billion. This remarkable phenomenon cannot be attributed to an increase in foreign sales — which were virtually stagnant in nominal terms, despite the fact that movements in relative domestic prices generally favored "tradable" goods. The adjustment of this

---

*Former Finance Minister of Mexico

balance, then, is associated with an abrupt, recessive decrease in imports, in the neighborhood of 40 percent.

During these years, the external debt rose from $222 to $368 billion, not so much because freely available new resources were received but because of the capitalization of interest agreed to *de facto* in the renegotiating process. With a slight improvement over 1982, service of the interest on the debt equaled 36 percent of the total goods and services in 1985 and is also the single most important item explaining government budget deficits. Debt has become a dead weight; it even wipes out the traditional contribution of external savings to capital formation in the developing nations, forcing countries in crisis to become net exporters of capital or to limit drastically the investment and development capacity of their governments beyond the present decade.

Despite the reduction in world inflationary pressures and the rather widespread application of severely restrictive measures to limit increases in domestic demand (cutbacks in public expenditure and credit, higher taxes and interest rates, only partial restoration of purchasing power of wages, foreign exchange rationing), inflation, far from abating, appears to have acquired renewed vigor over time. From 1979 to 1981 the weighted consumer price index maintained annual growth rates of just over 50 percent. From then on, however, it rose abruptly, soaring to 185 percent in 1984 and 328 percent in 1985. In effect, the dramatic efforts at domestic stabilization have been frustrated in many countries. What is more, the all too common presence of strong distortions in relative prices is grounds for anticipating new upward adjustments in the future. The most recent attempts of applying unorthodox adjustment strategies — in Argentina, Brazil, Peru, and Costa Rica — are the most encouraging sign that solutions will be found to problems that appear resistent to conventional treatment or at least that the sacrifices demanded of the people of the region will be reduced.

Crises and adjustment policy have debilitated the public and private capital formation process — the investment ratio fell from 22 percent to 16 percent between 1980 and 1985 — consequently limiting the flexibility of the economies either to promote essential structural changes or to absorb their inevitable costs — and this factor determines the countries' capacity to strengthen their internal economic autonomy or achieve greater integration into the international economy.

Clearly, Latin America's crisis is closely associated with changes in the international economic environment and with the new role that productive links with the exterior have played throughout the postwar era. With this in mind, this paper examines the export trade structure and the restrictions imposed by external indebtedness, in order to evaluate what is needed and how much time is required to enhance Latin America's share in the international division of labor. Next, it discusses changes and adjustments in the economic relations between the industrialized countries insofar as they affect these countries' economic capacity or political willingness to participate in finding a lasting solution to the development of Latin America. Finally, in light of recent developments in the foreign trade policy of the leading Western nations, it makes some final comments on the impact of trade on the future growth of the economies of the region.

THE REGIONAL PANORAMA

In Latin America trade problems tend to be viewed as an unjust exchange between the centers and the periphery. The international division has assigned to the region the production of raw materials or primary goods where there is no concentration of technological progress nor high demand elasticities that guarantee foreign exchange inflows compatible with the goal of bridging the development gap.

There is an element of truth in this position, particularly if the evolution of exports and trade prices in the 1980s is examined. Faced with the lack of foreign exchange associated with reversal of the sign of the external savings flow, all the countries of Latin America have made desperate attempts at increasing their marketing of goods abroad. Thus, despite a shrinking world economy, export volumes have been systematically increasing, while unit prices have been decreasing. Between 1980 and 1985, export volumes rose 24 percent whereas unit prices fell by almost one-fifth. Consequently, despite the enormous efforts expended, the growth rate for foreign exchange earnings was less than 3 percent. In contrast, the unit prices of imports remained unchanged during this period. The terms of trade registered a cumulative decline of over 16 percent between 1980 and 1985, which affected oil- and non-oil-producing countries alike, although in different cycles (see table 1).[2]

From a structural standpoint, the composition of Latin American exports adheres to a somewhat obsolete pattern of specialization in primary products, the demand for which in international

TABLE 1

Latin America[a] Volume and Unit Value of Exports
(1980 = 100)

	VALUE		UNIT VALUE		VOLUME		TERMS OF TRADE
	Exports	Imports	Exports	Imports	Exports	Imports	
1980	100	100	100	100	100	100	100
1982	97	80	88	105	110	81	84
1983	98	62	83	100	118	65	83
1984	109	65	86	100	126	68	86
1985	103	64	83	99	124	64	84

Source: ECLAC, based on official figures
a. The estimates are for 19 countries: those of the Latin American Integration Association (LAIA), the Central American Common Market (CACM), and Haiti, Panama, and the Dominican Republic.

TABLE 2

Latin America: Intra-Regional Exports
(Millions of dollars FOB)

	LATIN AMERICA[a]	LAIA	CACM
1970	1,920.6	1,599.6	314.0
1975	5,834.5	5,160.1	646.6
1980	13,828.8	12,349.9	1,304.8
1981	15,729.6	14,311.3	1,263.9
1982	13,026.8	11,926.4	998.8
1983	10,422.1	9,337.0	1,006.5
1984	10,914.5	9,832.3	999.7

Source: ECLAC, based on official figures
a. Includes the countries of the LAIA, the CACM, Haiti, Panama and the Dominican Republic.

trade has already peaked or is on the wane. In some cases (coffee, cocoa, sugar, bananas), per capita consumption in many industrialized countries is either reaching the saturation level or the markets for these products are affected by changes in consumer preferences, for example, away from foods rich in calories or carbohydrates. In other cases, raw materials used as inputs for activities that no longer constitute key sectors in the industrial world or are being replaced by substitutes that are lower in cost or have fewer energy requirements (bauxite, copper, iron, cotton, sugar, hard fibers, textiles) are technologically obsolete. Another group of products is affected by the protectionism of the industrialized countries or by their efforts to subsidize exports that are no longer competitive (sugar, textiles, wheat, corn, meat, footwear, steel). On the other hand, there are practically no goods that now generate the maximum trade in international transactions. Finally, the payment crisis of all the countries has led to the imposition of intraregional trade restrictions, affecting the manufactured goods of Latin America's leading industries in particular. Intraregional exports and those of the LAIA countries fell approximately 45 percent between 1981 and 1984, and those of the Central American Common Market 20 percent (table 2).

A quick review of the growth of the eighteen principal products in Latin American foreign trade (table 3) shows a lack of manufactured goods as well as the fact that, with the exception of zinc and bananas which remained stable, prices for 1985 were below those of 1980, and, in some cases, this decline approached or exceeded 30 percent (sugar, lead, copper, wool, fishmeal).

Although exports of manufactured goods increased almost tenfold between 1970 and 1981 (table 4), they represented scarcely more than 8 percent of the total goods sold, and in 1985 their share of the world industrial goods trade was still less than 2 percent (table 5). Moreover, the capacity to export manufactured goods is highly concentrated in a few countries (Brazil, Argentina, Mexico); more than 30 percent of these goods are marketed within the region or to other developing economies. The principal developed markets in which these goods are sold are almost evenly divided between Europe and the United States, while contacts with the more dynamic Japanese market are still minimal. In a few countries industrial exports exceed the total sales of commodities by 20 percent (Brazil,

TABLE 3

Latin America: Prices of the Principle Export Products
(Dollars at current prices)

	ANNUAL AVERAGES							GROWTH RATES			
	1970–1980	1980	1981	1982	1983	1984	1985	1982	1983	1984	1985
Raw sugar	12.8	28.7	16.9	8.4	8.5	5.2	3.8	-50.3	1.2	-38.8	-26.9
Coffee (mild)	121.8	178.8	145.3	148.6	141.6	147.3	147.8	2.3	-4.7	4.0	0.3
Cocoa	86.3	118.1	94.2	79.0	96.1	108.7	101.5	-16.1	21.6	13.1	-6.6
Bananas	11.8	18.9	19.2	18.4	20.4	19.0	19.1	-4.2	10.9	-6.9	0.5
Wheat	125.1	176.0	178.5	162.0	158.0	153.0	138.0	-9.0	-2.5	-3.2	-9.8
Corn	127.5	210.0	181.0	137.4	162.2	167.3	135.1	-24.1	18.0	3.1	-19.2
Beef	82.2	125.9	112.2	108.4	110.7	102.6	97.4	-3.4	2.1	-7.3	-5.1
Fishmeal	354.7	504.0	468.0	353.0	453.0	373.0	275.0	-24.6	28.3	-17.7	-26.3
Soybeans	232.4	296.0	288.0	245.0	282.0	282.0	228.0	-14.9	15.1	—	-19.1
Cotton	61.2	94.2	85.8	72.8	84.8	80.3	63.8	-14.7	16.5	-5.3	-20.5
Wool	131.5	194.5	178.2	154.6	144.0	141.6	133.9	-13.2	-6.9	-1.7	-5.4
Copper	69.6	98.6	79.0	67.2	72.2	62.5	64.6	-14.9	7.4	-13.4	3.4
Tin	3.9	7.6	6.4	5.8	5.9	5.6	5.4	-9.4	1.7	-5.1	-3.6
Iron ore	18.3	28.9	25.9	27.1	25.2	23.8	22.9	4.6	-7.0	-5.6	-3.8
Lead	25.3	41.1	33.0	24.8	19.3	20.1	17.7	-24.8	-22.2	4.1	-11.9
Zinc	29.7	34.6	38.4	33.8	34.7	40.6	35.6	-12.0	2.7	17.0	-12.3
Bauxite	103.5	212.5	216.3	208.3	179.5	165.0	164.3	-3.7	-13.8	-8.1	-0.4
Crude oil											
Saudi Arabia	10.0	28.7	32.5	33.5	29.3	28.5	27.9	3.1	-12.5	-2.7	-2.1
Venezuela	10.1	27.6	32.0	32.0	28.1	27.0	26.9	—	-12.2	-3.9	-0.4

Source: UNCTAD, *Monthly Bulletin of Commodities Prices, 1960–1980* and November 1985 Supplements; International Monetary Fund, *International Financial Statistics*, 1981 and December 1985 Yearly Reports, and ECLAC (1985).

Argentina, Mexico, Colombia, Jamaica, Guatemala, El Salvador, Costa Rica). In the majority of these cases, the phenomenon is due more to the influence of regional or subregional integration agreements than to the success of strategies properly aimed at opening the country to foreign trade.

TABLE 4

Latin America: Total and Intraregional Exports of Manufactured Goods (Millions of dollars FOB and percentages)

	TOTAL EXPORTS OF COMMODITIES	EXPORTS OF MANUFACTURED GOODS			
		Total		Intraregional	
		Value	% of total	Value	% of total manuf. goods
1970	15,052	2,284	15.1	773	33.8
1975	36,262	6,959	19.1	2,757	39.6
1980	90,411	20,238	22.3	7,184	35.5
1981	96,560	21,820	22.6	8,043	36.9
1982	85,906	18,070	21.0	6,020	33.3

Source: UNCTAD, *Manual of International Trade and Development Statistics*, Supplement, 1979, 1980, 1981, and 1984.

TABLE 5

Latin America: Share of Manufactured Goods in the World Trade in Said Goods (Percentages)

1970	1.0
1975	1.2
1980	1.5
1981	1.8
1982	1.8
1983	1.8
1984	1.8

Source: ECLAC

Notes: 1970 and 1975, includes the LAIA and the CACM countries, Barbados, Guiana, Jamaica, Trinidad and Tabago, Surinam, the Bahamas, Haiti, Panama, the Dominican Republic, the Netherlands Antilles, Bermuda, French Guiana, Guadeloupe, the Virgin Islands, Martinique; 1980 and 1981, same countries as 1970 and 1975, plus Antigua and Bermuda, Dominica, Grenada, Montserrat, St. Kitts and Nevis, St. Lucia, St. Vincent and the Grenadines, Cuba and the Falkland Islands (Malvinas); and 1982 to 1984, includes the LAIA and CACM countries, Barbados, Belize, Guiana, Jamaica, Surinam, and Trinidad and Tabago.

Brazil alone has a little more than 15 percent of its foreign sales in machinery and equipment; in the rest of the countries these sales are less (between 4 percent and 6 percent in Argentina and Mexico) or insignificant. The same thing occurs with exports of chemical products, which in the best of cases do not usually account for more than 5 percent, despite the existence of large oil-producing countries (table 6).

A few conclusions may be drawn from the above. It is almost certain that even a sustained recovery of the international economy will, in the immediate future, have less of an impact on the Latin American economies than the conditions of the last three decades of the postwar period. With the possible exception of Brazil, these nations are ill-equipped to forge ahead at a time when competition for international markets has intensified to a point hitherto unknown. At the very least, these countries will have to transfer investment and technical resources to activities whose consolidation will require considerable time. There is a sharp time lag between

TABLE 6

Latin America:[a] *Export Structure*
(Percentages)

	1982	1983
Minerals	49.1	45.6
Agriculture and foodstuffs	26.8	28.8
Textiles	3.3	3.2
Leather	1.7	1.9
Paper and wood	1.9	1.9
Processed nonmetallic minerals	0.4	0.4
Chemical products	3.4	3.7
Metals	6.2	7.7
Machinery	3.2	3.1
Transport equipment	2.7	2.3
Tools and weapons	0.3	0.3
Precious materials	0.7	1.0
Others	0.2	0.2
Total	100.0	100.0

Source: IDB, INTAL, *Commercial Trade Statistics of the Latin American Countries, 1980–1984*, Buenos Aires, 1985.

a. Includes 19 countries: those of the LAIA, the CACM, Haiti, Panama, and the Dominican Republic.

making adjustments on the demand side— which can and have been implemented fairly quickly—and reallocating resources to effect changes in the supply structure, where the length of time needed to achieve results is much longer.

The institutions and experience needed to advance industrialization according to the well-worn precepts of internal growth strategies are already in place, but not those corresponding to a model of sustained development in international trade. After the Second World War, protection cemented the most intense and sustained phase of development in the history of the region since the culmination of the independence movements. Moreover, import substitution has been carried out both nationally and at the regional or subregional level, where integration programs have permitted the use of large economies of scale.

The problem with many of the substitution strategies is that they were not coupled soon enough with systematic efforts to raise domestic or regional competitiveness, improve productive efficiency, progressively select likely activities for penetrating foreign markets, or pursue active policies to foment technological change. Furthermore, since the 1970s, a variety of obstacles, including those of a political nature, have hindered the further development of multinational integration programs.

All of these factors have contributed to the loss of dynamism in Latin America's characteristic development model. In addition to the tensions in the foreign exchange markets, which usually accompany primary import substitution programs, the maintenance of which requires a constantly positive flow of external savings, beginning in 1979 the situation was further complicated by the combined action of the worst foreign demand crisis—structural and cyclical in origin—of the last fifty years and the generalized problem of the region's indebtedness.

Allowing for the differences and specific characteristics of each economy, the gradual demise of the Latin American development model can be verified in a number of ways. Viewed in the most direct terms, the average growth rate fell from 6.4 percent in the 1970–75 period to 5.5 percent in the following five-year period, and has continued at predominantly negative rates so far in the 1980s. The decline in Latin America's external sector and its diminished contribution to development caused the share of regional exports in the world economy to stagnate between 1970 and 1984, hovering below 50 percent of the level of the early 1950s. At the same time, the crisis has not only erased the possibility of improving the standard of living, it has also upset the equity of these countries' economic systems by imposing the greatest costs on workers. The obsolescence of the development model is demonstrated by the growing inability to achieve the main goals of economic modernization, equitable distribution, and national autonomy, which have lent legitimacy to Latin America's governments since the crisis of the 1930s.

From another standpoint, the break in the pattern of dominant growth is also manifested in the inability of the industrial sectors to continue to promote the development of the debtor nations. While the growth rate for the added value of manufactured goods exceeded that of the economies as a whole by 25 percent and 21 percent in the 1950s and 1960s, this differential fell to only 9 percent in the following decade and turned negative between 1980 and 1983 (ECLAC/UNIDO, 1985). A process of involution, though perhaps temporary, is at work in Latin America's manufacturing sector, as indicated by the fact that the degree of industrialization in 1984 was the same as it was fifteen years earlier in 1969.

The loss in dynamic potential of Latin American industrialization is related in part to the success of the import-substitution process, where the greatest advances are usually made in manufacturing activities not known for having the most elastic demand or the most dynamic emerging markets. Mention has already been made of the relative sluggishness of the capital goods and chemical products manufacturing industries. The same thing is occurring with even greater intensity in what has become the world's most dynamic group of activities (electronics, computers, robots, pharmaceutical products, electrical equipment, etc.).

Problems have arisen from the lack of organic integration of research, development, and new technologies, on the one hand, and production processes on the other. Expenditures for research and technological development are below the absolute standards of other countries. However, this is hardly the main problem. Qualitatively most important is the fact that the vast majority of academic and reasearch centers have divorced themselves from the problems of production and the real economic processes.

Structural flaws and the insufficient development of the mechanisms necessary to facilitate flexible adaptation to change recur in many other areas essential to the adoption of successful strategies for opening the economies to foreign trade. Although there are sometimes remarkable differences from case to case, international transportation and research and development services are deficient, while support services (marketing, quality control, transportation and research and development services are deficient, while support services (marketing, quality control, transportation, insurance, packaging, information, financing) are poor. In addition, Latin American multinational corporations, which are essential to the development of effective strategies for competing in world markets, are practically nonexistent.

In other words, however justified and accepted the need to make the external sector and technological change the cornerstones of the future regional development, any turnaround in economic strategies is hampered by the obstacle common to any radical change in the growth pattern: the inadequacy of existing institutions, mechanisms, and processes, coupled with the inexperience and inability of administrative personnel to successfully undertake new tasks.

Some forces of structural and institutional inertia linked to a wide range of vested interests cannot be simply cast aside but must rather be recognized as a legitimate expression of defense on the part of potentially affected groups. The elimination of industrial protectionism may be a key element in eradicating domestic sources of inflation and inefficiency. Even so, the removal of existing barriers cannot be abrupt, and it must be accompanied by integral industrial reconversion programs, wherein the bases for new agreements among business, labor, and government are carefully established. If improperly handled, the opening of markets leads to unemployment and, almost certainly, to the failure of structural adjustment policies.

It may be inferred, then, that altering the development model is not a question that admits a simple solution, nor is it a matter that can be settled in the short term. Adjusting the relative price structure in favor of exportable goods—the objective of decreased protectionism—is a precondition for transforming the external sector. It is not enough, however. Time, effort, and resources must be invested in adapting the institutional organization and making acceptable changes in content and performance standards of social contracts or agreements. The risks involved in attempting sudden, far-reaching changes in economic policies are underlined by the experiences of the nations of the Southern Cone, where reversals in industrial development and enormous social costs were sustained without effecting any real change in the traditional methods of penetrating world markets.

No doubt the majority of Latin American countries need to update their development policies as soon as possible. However, they also need to minimize the industrial and institutional conversion costs that the change of strategies entails. Here a serious, unknown quantity is added to the uncertainty over the profile that the new international division of labor will assume. For the first time in decades there is a danger that the widespread protectionist trends in the First World will supplant the pattern of liberal multilateralism, or that prolonged commercial conflicts will erupt. Similarly, by destroying the stability of the former comparative advantages, the ubiquity of modern production and the impact of technological change make the outcome of the search for new Latin American foreign trade specializations uncertain.[3]

From a domestic standpoint, the unknown quantity introduced by altering the development model refers to the possibility of causing stagnation in the renewal of productive activities, and even in the social groups that have been exercising economic leadership. As noted, the capital-formation process is at an all-time low and the ability of the governments to act is severely limited. The available resources for structural change are few, and fewer still are those that can be utilized to ease the social tensions that accompany such change. Moreover, it becomes increasingly difficult to demand new sacrifices of people already overwhelmed by the social costs of the economic crisis.

Despite the enormous complexity of these tasks, the importance of stabilizing fluctuations and imparting dynamism to the export sectors of Latin America cannot be overemphasized. Only with great difficulty can the payment crisis be overcome without a substantial increase in the access of the region's products to world markets.

The interdependence of trade and external ties is too familiar a subject to be discussed here. Suffice it to note that, given the reversal of the sign of net capital flows, when an economy's growth rate is less than the interest rate, the debt can be serviced only by curbing domestic consumption. Under the same conditions, when the growth rate for export earnings is consistently below the interest rate, the ability to service the debt can be strengthened only by reducing foreign purchases. Consequently, when imports and consumption have been drastically cut in the space of five years, it becomes increasingly less viable to repeat such an effort without weakening fragile economic structures and/or encountering mounting social resistance. Therefore, the idea that growth is the only available means of creating the conditions necessary for satisfactorily servicing the external debt begins to gain credence.

The need to find answers to the decline in Latin American export trade becomes a basic imperative in light of the reversal of the sign of external savings flows. From 1982 to 1984, the external net financing (credit and investment inflows deducted from factor payments, dividends, and credit amortizations) available to Latin America was already showing cumulative negative figures of more than $100 billion. Paradoxically, if the present situation persists, the renewal of international loans will simply constitute a temporary solution which later on will only serve to exacerbate the initial disequilibria. This situation is not likely to change in the immediate future, as evidenced by the successive rounds of debt renegotiations, the cyclical behavior of foreign direct investment flows, and the weakening of concessional aid.

Latin America is *de facto* unable to meet the debt service on loans already contracted. Thus, the question is not whether there will be a moratorium, but rather what form it will take. Up to now the creditor countries and the international financial community have preferred to engage in an orderly process of repeated bilateral renegotiations, where the intervention of international financial institutions imposes a discipline intended to prevent the exacerbation of international payments problems. On the contrary, they consider undesirable both unilateral declarations of moratoria on the part of debtor nations and comprehensive negotiations between blocks of debtor nations and creditors.

Some relief has been afforded by reduced interest rates and the easing of loan conditions in the renegotiation process, as well as by the increased lending capacity of the multilateral financial institutions. Similarly, the Baker Plan acknowledges, for the first time, the connection between expansive adjustment and the possibility of stabilizing the external financing of the debtor countries. Yet, these advances, while significant, are still a long way from achieving the depth which appears to be essential. Strictly speaking, although medium- and long-term adjustments are being undertaken and are paying off on the export supply side, dealing with the Latin American payment crisis will require complementary actions on the part of the international community. In this regard, everything points to the need for an amalgam, in varying proportions, of the following actions by the Western economic powers: full access to the commodities and credit markets, lower interest rates, deferments, reductions and partial cancellations of the repayment of old debts,[4] greater flexibility in the creditor institutions' conditionality rules, and faster and more active industrial redeployment in the First World countries.

SIGNS OF CHANGE IN THE INTERNATIONAL ECONOMY

It is worth exploring the probable circumstances under which the international economy will evolve, to determine Latin America's opportunities more objectively and to evaluate the viability of the rapid advance of the industrialized countries in the direction indicated in the preceding paragraph.

It is undeniable that the last half century has witnessed a gradual but certainly cumulative series of changes that are already substantially altering the physiognomy and functioning of international economic relations. The change in conditions, far from limiting itself to the quantitative plane, is of such magnitude as to affect technological, demographic, institutional, and political or strategic fields.

Up to the 1980s the expansion of international trade easily exceeded production increases. Annual expansion rates of nearly 8 percent were recorded in the 1950s, over 9 percent in the following decade, and 20 percent in the 1970s. For the entire 1950–80 period, the rate of trade expansion was 12.5 percent, more than twice the increases in world production.

There is a significant degree of openness and integration of national units into the international economy, which affects all the countries of the Western World without exception. Take the case of the United States, for example, where exports and imports, which represented approximately 4 percent of the gross national product in the 1930s, rose to 10–12 percent in 1984 (Wallich, 1985).

Furthermore, following the reconstruction of Europe and Japan, and the emergence of the new industrializing countries (NICs), the international division of labor began to change rapidly. The rate of change peaked in the 1970s when declining transportation costs and new technologies permitted the adoption of specific new patterns of industrial organization. Today it is possible to centralize planning, decision making, and control, while at the same time expanding production geographically across national borders. Thus, between 1950 and 1980, the United States and Canada saw their share of world exports decrease from 21.7 to 14.1 percent; Japan, on the other hand, went from 1.4 to 6.5 percent and the countries of Latin America suffered a drop from 12.4 to 5.8 percent (table 7).

Many of the branches of economic activity that sustained world progress in the last three quarters of the century have been on the

TABLE 7

Distribution of International Trade[a]
(Percentages)

	1950	1960	1970	1980	1982
World	100.0	100.0	100.0	100.0	100.0
Developed market economies	61.1	66.7	71.4	62.9	63.3
United States and Canada	21.7	20.4	18.9	14.1	14.9
Europe	33.4	39.9	43.7	40.2	38.7
Japan	1.4	3.2	6.1	6.5	7.5
Socialist countries	8.1	11.6	10.6	8.8	10.3
Developing countries	30.8	21.6	18.0	28.2	26.4
American continent	12.4	6.8	5.6	5.8	5.9
Africa	5.1	4.1	4.0	4.7	3.8
Asia	13.1	9.5	8.1	17.6	16.7

Source: UNCTAD, *Handbook of International Trade and Development Statistics, 1984*, Supplement, New York, 1984.
   a. Exports.

decline, while new, "advanced" sectors, as yet unconsolidated, have surged ahead benefiting from an evolving and therefore unsatisfied demand, (UNIDO, 1983 and 1984). The nature of the technological change in progress has the effect of accelerating the maturation cycle of products and industries, altering both the profile of the leading industries and the worldwide geographic distribution of productive facilities. In the latter instance, as in the case of facilitating the expansion of international trade, the multinational corporations have begun a basic task of coordination which has given them control of 30–40 percent of the trade flows in the Western World.

The energy base of the world's industrial organization is also beginning to change at an accelerated pace, so that it can now be predicted with certainty that fossil fuels will cease to be an essential component of modern production. The current pattern of energy use is on the decline not only because finite, nonrenewable resources are shrinking, but also because such a pattern cannot be duplicated worldwide without causing ecological disasters or exceeding environmental and physical resource limitations (Fajnzylber, 1983).

The opening of economies, the proliferation of interindustrial relations between countries, the transnationalization of trade and production, technological change, and the increased climate of competitiveness and other processes of change that partially explain, why, for three or four decades, trade elasticity, with respect to production increases, has been so great and why a number of cumulative imbalances have developed. Economic and institutional adjustments to the changing international environment pose problems of such magnitude that even the industrial powers are being forced to adopt defensive measures that denote implicit or explicit abandonment of the theories of liberal multilateralism. Trade protectionism, opposition to industrial redeployment between countries, and efforts to revive declining activities are other expressions of the resistance of national companies to the globalization of economies. Therefore, the direction of structural change in the leading Western countries is not limited to competition to invest in new or high technology activities. A great many efforts are being made to promote the conversion of industrial plants, to cut costs and inputs, and to become more flexible in adapting to an intensely competitive environment.

Paradoxically, for the first time in this century strategies postulating international trade as the cornerstone of the future development of mankind have gained widespread acceptance in both the First and the Third Worlds. It is paradoxical because even though underlying economic factors exert pressures favoring the integration of economies, political pragmatism leads individual countries to protect their borders while at the same time attempting to gain access to international markets.[5]

In short, a new international division of labor is beginning to emerge in the world economy which will eventually open up new horizons for the progress of all nations. However, in the current transitional period, changes and uncertainties seem to be demolishing the secure, orderly world of the early postwar decades. In the first place, both the comparative advantages that sustained the old international division of labor and international trade theories has been seriously brought into question. On the one hand, for example, the manufacturing competitiveness arduously achieved by developing countries through the use of labor-intensive techniques could well evaporate as a result of the proliferation of automated production methods (robotization). On the other hand, the electronic control of production could eliminate the predominance of economies of scale and lead to a greater differentiation of supply, clearly benefiting countries with small populations and markets.

At present, comparative advantages are increasingly less dependent on the original endowment of natural resources or the abundance of capital or labor, and much more on a stable world climate that favors coordination and each country's persistent dedication to achieving excellence in specific areas of production (Feinberg, 1983). Moreover, these advantages accrue not so much to the countries themselves, but rather to the multinational corporations involved in each case. And the most relevant criteria governing the decisions of these corporations are not the conditions prevailing in a given economy, but the differences in conditions between economies.

In the second place, the process of integrating industry on a multinational scale, which is being promoted by both the old and the new generations of multinational corporations, is benefiting overall productive efficiency and the *in situ* use of factors. However, there are still no satisfactory answers concerning the distribution of income among the participating countries, nor on formulas to compensate for the loss of economic self-determination, especially in periods of crisis or when the composition of external demand in some countries is adversely affected.[6] An as yet incomplete process of institutional and legal change is underway, revealed by the *de facto* incorporation of the countries into a unified production system lacking an international framework of standards that establish a system of reciprocal guarantees among the participating states.

Along with the tensions that invariably accompany the distribution of international trade benefits, an even more basic question reemerges concerning the distribution of future exportable production among the various countries. The basic problem facing Latin America's economies is the need to establish stable sources of foreign exchange for the future, rather than insisting on better prices for the primary products they already export, the demand for which, in a great many cases, is already shrinking and which run the risk of being displaced by substitutes or competitors with more advanced technology.

The globalization of the economy is specifically associated with the increasing transferability of capital and technology across borders. Today, each of the major industrial powers (United States, Japan, and Europe) has sufficient capacity in place to supply most of the world demand for manufactured goods. The difficult question of distribution is complicated by the successful attempts of more and more Third World countries to create industrial establishments with the dual purpose of substituting imports and competing internationally. This is also complicated by the actions of multinational corporations, which distribute their productive investments in an attempt to take advantage of better markets and geographic differences in production costs in order to displace other established suppliers. In this competitive environment, the advantage is usually held by new producers who benefit from the use of the most advanced technologies and the best locations, or which have a greater capacity to adapt.[7]

It is also possible that surpluses in productive capacity partially explain the declining productivity gains of the world's industrial powers.[8] This, in combination with the influence of the Third World's large reserves of marginal labor, is perhaps associated with the historical phenomenon of the recent increase in "structural unemployment" or the tendencies of value added ratios to contract

(IBRD, 1984, Table 2.2 and UNIDO, 1983, Tables VII–20, 21 and 23). Also at work here are the efforts of the industrialized nations to adapt, either by replacing expensive labor with automated equipment or by opening plants in countries where labor costs are lower.

All things being equal, the adjustment of surplus productive capacity and the consequent intensification of international competition have the effect of halting the heretofore regular growth of the wage bill until a typical Keynesian case of insufficient effective demand is created, in this case on a universal scale.

Some of the problems complicating adjustment of the world's productive structures derive from the coexistence of different price systems, the components of which tend to be standardized at different rates. It can be affirmed that there is a considerably uniform system of prices for most raw materials and primary products.

On a smaller scale, despite the difficulties in standardizing products, international competition reduces the price differences among an increasingly wide range of intermediate, capital, and patented technical goods.

The prices of capital resources, inflated by the integration of financial markets, experience a process analogous to convergence. Loan repayments are subject to a minimum interest rate, set by the major banking centers, to prevent the flight of savings across national borders. In contrast, wages are usually relatively unresponsive to the drop within each economy. Similarly, the international mobility of labor is more restricted than that of any other resource. Consequently, the differences in wages paid to labor are much greater than those in productivity.

The globalization of the economy has repercussions that are expressed in considerable pressures on the labor markets. In the key economies, the cost of labor is best adjusted by replacing it with capital goods or moving production to other countries. However, the rise in structural unemployment is the logical outcome of both approaches.[9] In peripheral areas, cyclical recessions are usually manifested in the deterioration of wages rather than open unemployment, a situation that occurs when the economic crisis reaches major proportions.[10]

As W. A. Lewis has emphasized, the demise of the international division of labor wherein the Third World exports agricultural

products and imports manufactured goods—while the developed
nations do the reverse—proves that such a differentiation of tasks
was sustained by terms of trade unfavorable to agriculture and advantageous to industry. If more than 50 percent of the work force
in the tropics is employed in growing foodstuffs with low productivity, the rest of the work force will earn low wages regardless of
whether agricultural or industrial products are exported (Lewis,
1978). At present, however, imbalances in Third World labor
markets are being transmitted to the industrialized countries because of the mobility of capital and technology in search of cheap
labor.

The world process of price standardization—a basic requirement in the economic calculations of the multinational corporations—has created an increasingly rigid connection between national
economies and the international economy. Apart from general and
geographic fluctuations in employment and wages, price adjustments
are now almost exclusively dependent on exchange rate movements.
Herein lies one of the major causes of the misalignment of the exchange rate parities that in ultimate terms is expressed by the conflict between the demands of national economic self-determination
and the limitations arising from functional integration into a broader
economic system.

On the financial side, integration on a world scale advanced
more than in any other field during the 1970s. With the consolidation of the Euromarket and the penetration of international commercial banks, Latin America's financial flows—savings-expenditure or
savings-investment—gradually shifted outward, except in the case
of Brazil. National financial systems lost ground to foreign banks,
which began to attract funds from Latin American businesses and
individuals and also began to make unusually large loans to public
and private applicants for funds in the region. During this decade,
external financing, most particularly commercial bank financing,
permitted the majority of the countries of Latin America to maintain their economic growth rates and absorb the shocks of the rise
in oil prices and the worldwide recession of 1974–76, though not
without excess and waste. Later, when the debt crisis emerged, external financial flows were disrupted. Latin American funds continued flowing outward, while the incoming flow of loans stopped.
Capital flight in five Latin American countries (Venezuela, Mex-

ico, Argentina, Uruguay, and Brazil) totaled almost $72 billion in the 1979–82 period (see IBRD, 1958).

As a result of the ongoing changes in the international economy, the capability of the industrial powers to contribute to the development of the peripheral countries has been weakened, if only temporarily, because they have been forced to devote most of their energies to competing abroad and making enormous internal adjustments. The reduction in concessional development aid, the difficulties in replenishing the capital of the multilateral financial institutions, and the manipulation of international interest rates are an eloquent expression of these diminished capabilities (ECLAC, 1984; Feinberg, 1983; Haq, 1985). So is the fact that, in addition to the old-style protectionism adopted by the developed countries to compensate for the lack of competitiveness of their agricultural activities, there is now a defensive protectionism caused by the aging of industries reluctant to accede to the reorganization of production on a universal scale and to involvement in foreign trade.

However, the most obvious manifestation of this situation is the fact that, for the first time since the English Industrial Revolution, the leading Western economy is becoming a net importer of capital. Instead of exporting surplus financial resources, it requires international savings to support domestic spending, completely reversing the traditional mechanism of balance-of-payments adjustments.

Finally, it must be realistically admitted that the changes evolving within and among the industrialized nations determine an international agenda, in which the problems of the developing countries are relegated to a secondary position. Before reforming the old way of life between North and South, it will first be necessary to address questions of trade, the division of production, the opening of financial and commodities markets, and/or the financing of the reciprocal trade balances between the countries of the First World (Bergsten and Kraus, 1975). It therefore seems unlikely that the subject of Latin American trade and indebtedness will be dealt with in depth while there is still disagreement on the scope of effectiveness of the GATT, the management of exchange systems, interest rates, the control of capital movements, or the formulas for symmetrically adjusting the persistent balance-of-payments deficits of the major industrialized nations (Cline, 1982).

Even so, the generalized character of the Latin American crisis points to a common, external source, that is, changes in the international economy. Countries with marked differences in size, degree of industrialization, political and administrative organization, or economic development strategies are similarly affected. Strictly speaking, to correct the misalignment of Latin America's export sectors with respect to the dynamics of world demand, a cooperative effort of considerable magnitude will be necessary to reduce the time and the sacrifices required by structural adjustment.

However, for the reasons mentioned, solutions to the crisis will not come spontaneously from outside. To find such solutions, Latin America will have to organize its own forces and initiatives, and even influence the economic policy priorities of the industrial powers. In the new circumstances, economic growth will not come easily. To render the sacrifices of economic reconstruction tolerable without creating irreparable social rifts, the governments will have to mobilize their societies for a national, democratic effort.

TODAY'S POLICY

Adjustments within and among the most developed nations have been producing important *de facto* changes in the principles and evolving patterns of international economic relations. It has not been possible to complete the restructuring of the world monetary and financial system, which began with the Smithsonian Agreement in 1971, because the minimum essential balance has not been achieved in the bases of change in real terms. Although floating exchange rates make international economic relations more flexible, they have not freed national policies from the constraints associated with the integration of markets and production on a universal scale. On the contrary, by failing to produce a proper alignment of parities they have frequently served as a channel for destabilizing capital movements, which is especially damaging to the Third World.[11]

The principles that currently govern international trade are also undergoing considerable change. The most-favored-nation clause, which has been the cornerstone of multilateralism and trade liberalization, is gradually being abandoned in favor of bilateral agreements. The principle of retroactive reciprocity, which is beginning to dominate the trade policy of certain developed countries, so intensifies the inclination toward bilateralism as to undermine the one-way preferential treatment of developing nations that was at the heart of the UNCTAD agreements.[12]

The inertia associated with the proliferation of nontariff barriers and the regulation of trade has been creating an atmosphere increasingly less favorable to the sound multilateral liberalization of world trade flows and fair access of the developing nations (table 8).

Judging from the contents of the Trade and Tariff Act of 1984, U.S. trade policy has already moved considerably away from liberal multilateralism and toward the use of reprisals or bilateral agreements as a basic negotiating weapon.[13] The new policy rejects the assumption that there are competitive markets (where a large number of participants make independent decisions and no one is able to affect market results), and instead embraces the strategies of oligopoly, where the actions of each company, government, or country affects the equilibrium of the market and the behavior of the other participants. This strategic approach may have the merit of more realistically adjusting to an international economy influenced by blocks of nations, large multinational corporations, and growing government interventionism in trade. However, it implies the full use of the negotiating power of the most powerful nations in the world, frequently without attention to considerations of welfare, efficiency, and equity in the distribution of development opportunities.

TABLE 8

Regulated Trade[a]
(Percentages)

	TOTAL REGULATED TRADE		REGULATED TRADE IN MANUFACTURED GOODS	
	1974	1980	1974	1980
European Community	35.8	44.8	0.1	16.1
United States	36.2	45.8	5.6	21.0
Japan	56.1	59.4	0.1	4.3

Sources: Page (1981) and Greenway (1984).
a. Regulated trade is defined as that which is subject to nontariff restrictions.

Furthermore, an aggressive policy of reciprocity will always provoke defensive reactions on a greater or lesser scale, which, taken as a whole, inevitably decrease trade and the benefits that all nations derive from it. As Cline (1982) points out, the successful resistance of countries affected by the forced opening espoused by the U.S. Trade Law will effectively diminish already established trade flows. Similarly, the retroactive use of the criterion of reciprocity, together with the inclusion in national legislation of structured reprisal systems and the application of the criterion of graduation to the preferences granted to the Third World, will make access to the markets uncertain, with dynamic repercussions that are also damaging to the future growth of international trade.

It must be admitted, however, that U.S. trade policy is based on considerations that do have some validity. First, there is the perception—reinforced by the shrinking U.S. share of world trade throughout the postwar period—that many countries take unfair advantage of the increased opening of the U.S. economy to foreign trade. Second, there is a belief that the open intervention of many governments in favor of national companies has permitted unfair commercial penetration into the U.S. market. Third, the adoption of a reprisal system by the U.S. Congress was a way of sidestepping strong domestic political pressures that favored the implementation of outright protectionist measures.[14]

Both on the ideological and the economic planes, the former liberal approach that supported the principles of internationalism and the application of multilateral strategies in world trade has been largely replaced by a more conservative, nationalistic concept. In a way, it reflects the tensions characteristic of a transitional stage in the productive structure of the industrial countries. In principle, industrial redeployment is essential to the creation of a new stable international division of labor that permits the orderly participation of both the developed nations and the Third World countries. First, however, the developed countries consider it essential to consolidate their supremacy in the new key activities to facilitate domestic adjustments and secure new export flows to foreign markets— hence the emphasis of U.S. trade policy on liberalizing the trade in services, high technology products, and the treatment of foreign investment, and its interest in making these areas the focus of a new round of GATT negotiations.

In addition, there is another requirement to be satisfied in the reordering of international economic relations. The rules of conduct imposed first by the gold standard and then by the Bretton Woods agreement must be replaced by others that permit the regulation of trade and international ties in an interdependent world, where the coordination of national policies is more necessary than ever. The chosen route is that of standardization, the doctrinare adoption of the neoclassical pattern that postulates, as its central principle, opening markets and limiting the sphere of influence of the national states in the economic arena. The disciplinary and consensual mechanisms are located in two different spheres. One is provided by the reciprocity measures of U.S. trade policy, which the other developed nations will surely make their own — the other, by the development of an integrated set of rules, only partially consensual, which international organizations such as the International Monetary Fund, the Paris Club, the World Bank, regional banks, and the GATT have been adopting.

There are, of course, points of agreement between the stated goals of U.S. policy and those pursued by the other industrialized or developing nations. However, there are also a number of serious discrepancies, which will hinder *a fortiori* the creation of a new international economic order and which can be resolved only through complex, repetitive processes of adjustment and negotiation.

An illustration of this is the possible working agenda of a new round of multilateral trade negotiations within the framework of the recently negotiated devaluation of the dollar. The United States is promoting such negotiations to introduce the new topics already mentioned in connection with the GATT negotiations. Japan also supports them because it wants to alleviate the intense bilateral pressures it is experiencing. However, like the European Community, Japan views with concern the domestic consequences of opening its protected agricultural and financial markets and being forced to limit the scope if its development policies to the high technology industries. Europe would like Japan to make essential domestic adjustments that would considerably increase its willingness to import, the United States to reduce the pressures aimed at liberalizing agricultural products, and financial agreements to prevent immoderate interest rate hikes, which necessitate the adoption of restrictive macroeconomic policies. Europe does not want to be forced to dispense with selective criteria in negotiating a multilateral code of safeguards.

The countries of Latin America are opposed to extending the thematic scope of the GATT for two basic reasons. On the one hand, they note delays or nonfulfillment of agreements in the great majority of fields that are of interest to them and that correspond to subjects already discussed in previous rounds of negotiations. On the other, they are reluctant to assume new obligations when the burden of the economic crisis and consequent adjustment impose obligations on them that are extremely difficult to fulfill.

For Latin America, the first priority is to finish the work pending: trade in tropical goods has not been liberalized; the multifiber agreement has not been annulled; a multilateral code of safeguards has not been signed; nontariff barriers affecting footwear, clothing, meat, sugar, and steel exports, among others, have not been lifted; valid "stand-still" policies have not been applied; and there has been no return to the principles of multilateralism. It has not been understood that Latin American protectionism is not aimed at restricting the volume of international trade—since foreign purchases are made up to the limit of available foreign exchange—but rather favors the processes of productive modernization. Moreover, "graduation" and bilateralized reciprocity have not been eliminated, nor have numerous other regulated trade measures that render the concessions of the Generalized System of Preferences useless, block industrial redeployment, and introduce enormous doubts about the access of Third World exports to the international markets.

The list of dissatisfactions is impressive, for it contains demands that have been put off time and again in the process of restructuring North-South relations. Even so, Latin America hopes that a series of principles fundamental to the reordering of international economic relations will be recognized. Multilateral action is the best way to correct imbalances in the negotiating power of nations. Attention to the development of backward economies still requires liberal, nonreciprocal concessions on the part of the industrial powers. Multilateral action, preferential treatment, and more intense industrial redeployment are necessary—but insufficient—conditions for enabling the developing areas to achieve a reasonably equitable place in the configuration of the future division of labor. In addition, the obstacles to finding solutions to the current economic crisis in the region demonstrate the imperative need to make an organic connection between international trade policies and financial policies. From this perspective, the external exigencies of adjustment and crossed conditionality—to which financial aid is subjected—are excessive, for by eliminating development possibilities and creating collateral instabilities of a social and political order, they eliminate the very objectives they pursue in terms of financial reorganization, stabilization, and the orderly transformation of structures.

A summary review of the diverging views and interests of the various participants in the restructuring of the international economy is not encouraging. The worldwide integration and technical ubiquity of production make it increasingly difficult to separate the distribution of trade benefits from market mechanisms that recognize no borders. In the era now dawning it will be necessary to learn to make policy coordination the cornerstone of the new international division of labor. In the meantime, it is to be expected that international trade will play a much less prominent role in Latin America's progress than it did in the early postwar decades. The restructuring of North-South relations will be hindered by major obstacles, as a function of both the intrinsic adjustment capacity of the Third World and the aid that the industrial powers can provide for the development of peripheral areas. On the threshold of the emergence of a new international economic order, it is discouraging to note how rich nations and poor nations are becoming increasingly polarized—and, what is worse, how the collective capacity to close this gap, which threatens to plunge the world yet again into profound divisions, is diminishing at an equal rate.

NOTES

1. The World Bank, in reviewing the situation of the developing countries, concluded that "the growth of the gross domestic product in 1980–85 is estimated at a little more than half of that of the 1973–80 period. Exports increased by almost 6 percent but the pressures of persistently high interest payments held the growth of imports to scarcely more than 1 percent per year" (IBRD, 1985).

2. According to the World Bank, "An increase of protectionism sufficient to produce a 10 percent decline in the terms of trade of Latin

America would cost the region as much as the real cost of interest on the aggregate debt" (IBRD, 1985, p. 42).

3. The only solid opportunities for action open to the countries are creating generally favorable conditions for promoting foreign sales, utilizing integration programs as a preparatory mechanism for gaining experience and achieving efficiency in exportable production, deliberately promoting the consolidation or expansion of products that have begun to penetrate foreign markets, and undertaking long-term efforts to achieve competitive excellence in a limited range of goods, even if selected with insufficient criteria.

4. That there are margins for redistributing these charges is convincingly demonstrated by the emergence of a secondary Latin American debt market, where truly substantial discounts are frequently offered. According to A. H. Meltzer (1985, p. 66), the market value of the Latin American debt varies between 70 and 80 percent of the recorded book value of the creditor institutions.

5. Therefore it is not at all inappropriate to speak of neomercantilist trends, even though the historical context is different.

6. The World Bank, noting the phenomena of the emergence of a global economy, indicated that "with increasing frequency the ties are of a financial nature, through changes in the availability of funds and fluctuations in the interest and exchange rates. This was revealed in 1979–80, for example, when the focus of U.S. monetary policy shifted from interest rates to monetary aggregates, the instability of interest rates increased" (IBRD, 1985, p. 5).

7. The process described yields some benefits but also involves significant costs. The benefits derive from the fact that intense competition makes production more efficient and is a spur to technological progress. The costs, however, are linked to the decreased utilization of capacity in place (except in the case of the more competitive new producers), the premature obsolescence of equipment, and the reduction in investment incentives. In addition, widespread surpluses in capacities in place lead to protectionist opposition to industrial redeployment.

8. Even before the economic crisis of 1979, worker productivity in Germany, the United States, and Japan fell from average levels in the 1962–69 period of 5.3, 2.7, and 9.9 percent per year to an average of 4.5, 2.1, and 4.1 percent, respectively, in the 1975–78 period (IBRD, 1984, p. 17).

9. According to data in the *Statistical Yearbooks of the International Labor Organization*, open unemployment in Germany, the United States, and Japan went from 0.9, 3.5, and 1.1 percent in 1969 to 9.1, 9.5, and 2.6 percent, respectively, in 1983.

10. Open unemployment in Latin America remained relatively low in the 1970s and did not begin to increase substantively until the 1980s, when the economic crisis that began in 1979 was already full-blown. By way of example, note that unemployment was barely 2.8 and 4.6 percent in Argentina and Venezuela in 1979, but in 1983 it rose to 4.2 and 9.8 percent, respectively.

11. Changes in international interest rates, exchange rates, and the direction of financial flows not only dominate the volume of trade quantitatively, but also unequivocally affect Latin America's trade policy (SELA, 1985).

12. W. R. Cline points out that "More than thirty bills have been introduced in the Ninety-Seventh Congress calling for U.S. government action to achieve reciprocity in foreign trade, or, as this term is used in these proposals, access to foreign markets comparable to that in the United States. U.S. reciprocity objectives in the past meant seeking reciprocal changes in protection in trade negotiation; the new approach seeks reciprocity in the level of protectionism bilaterally or over a certain range of goods" (Cline, 1982).

13. According to Section 301 of this law, the President of the United States has the power to respond with reprisals (taxes, duties, cancellation of benefits, and other restrictions) to unjustified, irrational, or discriminatory actions by a foreign government which adversely affect or restrict U.S. trade. Reprisals may be taken not only with respect to the goods or services affected by the aggressive action of the foreign government, but also against any good or service.

14. In the background of the debate, of course, are the enormous external deficits of the U.S. economy and the results of a policy — just beginning to be corrected — that led to a 30 percent appreciation of the dollar between 1980 and 1985.

REFERENCES

Bergsten, C.F. and L. B. Krause, Editors. 1975. *World Politics and International Economics.* Washington, D.C.: The Brookings Institution.

Cline, W. R. 1982. *Reciprocity: A New Approach to World Trade Policy?* Washington D.C.: The Institute for International Economics, No. 2, September.

ECLAC. 1984. Políticas de ajuste y renegociación de la deuda externa. *Estudios y Informes*, No. 46, Santiago, Chile.

———— 1985. *Desarrollo y crisis en América Latina y el Caribe* (LC./L.333/Rev.1), Santiago, Chile.

_____ 1986. Síntesis preliminar de la economía latinoamericana, 1985. Santiago, April.

ECLAC/UNIDO. 1985. División Conjunta de Industría y Tecnología, *Informe* No. 1, Santiago, Chile, September.

Fajnzylber, F. 1983. *La industrialización trunca de América Latina*, Mexico City: Editorial Nueva Imagen.

Feinberg, R. E. 1983. *The Intemperate Zone*. New York: W. W. Norton & Co.

Feinberg, R. E., and V. Kallab. Editors. 1981. *Uncertain Future: Commercial Banks and the Third World*.

Greenway, D. 1984. International Trade Policy. In *From Tariffs to the New Protectionism*. New York: Macmillan.

Haq, K. Editor. 1985. *The Lingering Debt Crisis*. Pakistan: North South Roundtable.

IBRD. 1984. *Report on World Development*. Washington.

_____ 1985. *Report on World Development*. Washington, July.

Lewis, W. A. 1978. *The Evolution of the International Economic Order*. New Jersey: Princeton University Press.

Meltzer, A. H. 1985. *Financial Failures and Financial Policies,* The Report of the Technical Committee of the Global Action Institute, New York.

Norr, K. 1975. *The Power of Nations*. New York: Basic Books.

Page, S. B. 1981. The Revival of Protectionism and its Consequences, *Journal of Common Market Studies,* vol 20, No. 1, September.

Prebisch, R. 1981. *Capitalismo periférico*. Mexico City: Fondo de Cultura Económica.

SELA. 1985. *América Latina y el sistema de comercio internacional*, XI Ordinary Meeting of the Latin American Council, Caracas, September.

UNIDO. 1983. *La industría en un numdo de cambio*. New York: United Nations.

_____ 1984. *IV General Conference, World Industrial Restructuring and Redeployment* (LD/Conf.5/3), Vienna, Austria.

Wallich, H.C. 1985. U.S. Monetary Policy in an Interdependent World. In *International Financial Markets and Capital Movements*, Essays in International Finance, No. 157, Princeton, N. J., September.

The Question of Foreign Investments and the Economic Crisis in Latin America

EDUARDO WHITE*

Just fifteen years ago the appearance of a book by Raymon Vernon, *Sovereignty at Bay* (1971), reflected the prevailing international state of mind on the subject of foreign direct investments (FDI). A key aspect of the question was how to ease the mounting tensions between the multinational corporations (MCs), the primary source of said flows, and the national governments, anxious to avoid the excessive economic domination perceived in multinational penetration, the continuation of which was taken for granted.

The tone of the discussion has changed significantly in recent years. Criticism of the MCs seems to have lost considerable force compared with the flood of proposals extolling their virtues and benefits. The analysis has become depersonalized, inasmuch as reference is now made to "private direct investments," just as it was in the 1950s and 1960s before attention was focused on the MCs. The analysis has also become trivialized: FDI tends to be viewed in macroeconomic terms once again, almost as though it were one of the many accounting items of external financing.

This change in tone has not come about because the MCs have lost significance; on the contrary, they have continued to grow, diversifying and increasing their role in the recent past. The sales of the world's 500 largest industrial firms climbed from 23 to 30 percent of the world gross product between 1962 and 1980 (Trajtenberg, 1985). These firms accounted for 80 percent of the interna-

*Director, Center for Development Studies and International Economic Relations (CEDREI), Buenos Aires.

tional production (that is, that of foreign affiliates) in 1980 (Stopford and Dunning, 1983).

Nor is the reduced tension due to the disappearance of the problems identified, nor to a refutation of the critical arguments that prevailed several years ago. At the very least, no new frames of reference or empirical evidence have as yet appeared sufficient to explain or to justify other perspectives. What is certain, though, is that the defensive actions of the developing world in the 1970s seem to have given way today to a much more open attitude, generally more concerned with attracting foreign investment than worrying about control. This is beginning to be revealed by the liberalization of regulatory policies, even in developing countries characterized by highly centralized national policies or economies (China, Ethiopia, Tanzania, etc.). The relaxing of tensions has also allowed the governments of a number of developed countries and certain international organizations to begin speaking openly and to propose initiatives of various types to increase the role of foreign investment in the developing countries.

Nowhere in the world is the recent evolution of the FDI question as significant and complex as it is in the Americas. This is true for several reasons. First, North America has been—and continues to be—the primary source of FDI and the principal headquarters of the MCs; and the South, Latin America, is the leading recipient of FDI in the developing world, especially from the United States. Second, the Latin American counries led the cycle of defensive or reactive policies that spread through the Third World in the past decade. Third, the current government of the United States has shown great interest—not devoid of aggression—in the role of private foreign investment in the developing countries, and especially in Latin America.

The international crisis is undoubtedly the main reason for new attitudes on the subject, and within the crisis the debt problem certainly plays the largest role. In fact, although trends toward relaxing the policies of Latin American countries had already begun before the outbreak of the crisis in the region at the beginning of this decade—because of the increased experience of the governments and greater confidence in their regulatory and negotiating capabilities (White, 1982)—the appearance of the crisis seems to have intensified the process of relaxation, which was prematurely set in motion by the ultra-liberalist experiments attempted by Southern Cone military regimes in the middle of the last decade.

Paradoxically, the new perspectives tend to be founded on an aspect of FDI which, it was widely agreed, was of little significance: its contribution to external financing. The renewed interest in the subject is focused primarily on the possibility or expectation that FDI will replace or complement the limited scope of external bank loans in recent years. In this context, the purpose of this essay is to analyze recent FDI trends in Latin America, with particular reference to U.S. investments, and to discuss future perspectives within the framework of the crisis.

In light of the comprehensive growth of FDI and its performance in Latin America, new factors will be reviewed that influence a reassessment of the subject in terms of both internal changes and external forces. The principal questions currently being asked about the role of regulatory policies in the investment decisions of the MCs will be analyzed, as will the determining factors of the MCs' strategies and the possibilities of using FDI as an alternative for channeling financial resources. Finally, certain conditions and strategies are suggested for formulating constructive policies that will effectively improve the contribution of FDI to the economic recovery of Latin America.

RECENT GROWTH OF FOREIGN INVESTMENTS

The sharp drop in the growth rate of industrialized economies at the start of the international crisis in the early 1970s did not curb international investment. Throughout the past decade the annual growth rate of foreign investment flows from the major source countries was much higher than that of domestic investments. In constant dollars (corrected for inflation), the annual growth rate of the latter in the seven leading economies of the OECD was 1.9 percent between 1974 and 1980, while foreign investments grew about 7 percent per year.

The phenomenon of transnationalization is spreading, and growing numbers of countries and businesses are becoming involved. U.S. companies are losing their hegemony—their share of the total FDI fell from 46 percent to 30 percent in a little over ten years—

while Japan and Germany increased their share of international production, not only in terms of volume but also the number of companies operating abroad: hundreds of small and medium-sized firms
in these countries are entering the international arena (White and
Feldman, 1980). And "Third World multinationals" are beginning
to appear, encouraged in part by the increased experience of local
entrepreneurs and the narrowing of the international technological gap (Wells, 1984; Lall, 1983).

During the past decade foreign investment tended to increase
primarily in the North, particularly in the United States.[1] In the
developing countries as a whole it increased only slightly in real terms
(World Bank, 1985). In any case, Latin America continued to be
the principal target of foreign investments in the developing world,
absorbing 60 percent, almost twice that of Asia. At the beginning
of this decade more than half the stock belonged to U.S. companies,
but they have been gradually losing their share: FDI from the United
States represented almost two-thirds of the total fifteen years ago.
Nevertheless, while U.S. investments in Latin America represent only
14 percent of its total FDI, the region has attracted 60 percent of
the investments placed in developing countries (ECLA, 1984).

FDI from the United States is concentrated in the largest and
most advanced countries of the region. Brazil absorbs approximately
30 percent. Its share, plus those of Argentina and Mexico, represented approximately 60 percent in 1982. Similarly, in terms of sectoral composition, the share of the manufacturing industry (which
accounts for about half) and the financial sector is growing significantly, with petroleum and mining activities on the wane. On the
other hand, during the past decade, FDI was becoming a far less
significant factor in the net flow of external financial resources,
which fell from 39 percent per year in 1971–75 to 21 percent in
1980 (Ffrench-Davis, 1982), with steady increases in the reinvestment of profits (65 percent in 1970–80) (Bitar, 1984).

Up to the end of the past decade, changes noted in the performance of foreign investment reflected the evolving structural changes
in the world economy, especially within the industrialized countries. At the beginning of the 1980s, however, the crisis spread to
the South. The most advanced developing countries, which were
generally maintaining high growth rates, were hit full force by the
sharp increase in interest rates and the stagnation of international

trade. Debt moved to center stage. Since then, foreign investment has been on the decline. After peaking at $17 billion in 1981, the flows fell to $11.9 billion in 1982 and $3.5 billion in 1983 (World Bank, 1985).

The decline in foreign investments is particularly significant in Latin America, where the principal debtor countries are concentrated. The flows fell from $6.375 billion in 1982 to $3.297 billion and $1.874 billion in 1983 and 1984, respectively (see table 1).

The decline in direct investments from the United States is not viewed in relative terms only: the stock from this source, which had been increasing since 1972 at growth rates higher than those of other developing regions, started to fall in 1981, going from $38.8 billion in that year to $28 billion in 1984,[2] while in other developing countries the volume tended to increase (see table 2).

Thus, the stagnation or decline of foreign investments is coupled with the drastic reduction of the net external financing available to continue financing balance of trade deficits and interest payments. Combined with the international trade crisis and increased unemployment in the developing countries, giving rise to growing protectionism, this situation forced the countries to attempt adjustment by drastically cutting imports and curbing internal demand. It being impossible to curtail consumption beyond certain humanly and politically tolerable limits, resources have been deflected from investment expenditures. On the other hand, it is highly unlikely that commercial bank credit will again play a major role in the 1980s

TABLE 1

Annual FDI Flows to Latin America (1977–84)
(Millions of 1980 U.S.$)

PERIOD	LATIN AMERICA (millions of dollars)	BRAZIL (%)	MEXICO (%)	ARGENTINA (%)	OTHERS (Except the Caribbean) (%)
1977–81	5522	43.1	28.6	8.0	20.3
1982	6375	46.3	22.0	3.6	28.1
1983	3297	47.1	14.8	5.6	32.5
1984	1874	51.2	2.1	11.5	35.2

Source: *Balance of Payment Statistics*, IMF

(see Feinberg, Ffrench-Davis, in this volume). Furthermore, the traumatic experience with high, unstable interest rates and the negotiations with the international banking community and the International Monetary Fund has changed the countries' perception of the advantages of financing domestic capital formation through heavy reliance on external credit as a means of avoiding or curbing the oligopolistic power of the multinational corporations (Oman, 1984).

NEW IDEAS AND OLD INTERESTS

In the circumstances described, the pressing need for external capital to complement or replace scarce local resources focuses attention again on foreign direct investment. FDI is beginning to be seen as a possible substitute for, or at least a complement of, external credit. In this new perspective, FDI is perceived as a less costly way of obtaining external resources, according to various lines of reasoning. First, its service would be tied to profitability, which in

TABLE 2

FDI from the United States: Growth of Stock, 1982–1984

	FDI			VARIATION			
	Millions of dollars			Millions of dollars		Percentage	
	1982	1983	1984	1983	1984	1983	1984
Developing Countries	52618	51430	53932	−1189	2502	−2.3	4.9
Oil	16040	16903	18417	864	1514	5.4	9.0
Manufactures	19210	18400	20146	−810	1746	−4.2	9.5
Other Sectors	17369	16126	15368	−1242	−758	−7.2	−4.7
Latin America	32655	29674	28094	−2981	−1580	−9.1	−5.3
Oil	6677	6944	5940	268	−1004	4.0	−14.5
Manufactures	15640	14766	15665	−874	899	−5.6	6.1
Other Sectors	10337	7963	6489	−2374	−1474	−23.0	−18.5

Source: U.S. Department of Commerce, *Survey of Current Business*, August 1985, Vol. 65, No. 8.

turn would depend on the conditions of the local economy and not on predetermined contractual requirements, as is the case with loans, particularly short-term loans. Second, it is argued that FDI has an element of continuity and renewability, given the importance of the reinvestment of profits. Third, it is asserted that FDI flows would not have the procyclical nature of bank loans and, therefore, the former could compensate for fluctuations in the latter. Fourth, FDI would have to be tied to the most careful identification of investment projects. Finally, the undifferentiated and highly integrated nature of financial capital would make it much less vulnerable, in cases of dispute, to the pressures of the recipient countries than industrial capital, which is much more differentiated, even in cases of relatively high concentration (IMF, 1985; UNCTAD, 1984; IDB, 1985; Oman, 1984). However, as discussed in the next section, these expectations do not appear to be solidly grounded in reality.

The new obsession for macroeconomic equilibrium, which tends to reestablish foreign investment as an element of national accounting, is, however, reinforced by another type of perception. One of these is undoubtedly the growing reassessment of the private sector as a factor of development, as a result not only of the current scarcity of public resources but also as a reflection of a certain disillusionment with the effectiveness of state intervention in the recent past.

Yet in addition to these internal changes, there are equally effective external factors contributing to the new interest in foreign investments. The reliance on banks and the IMF's terms of conditionality has clearly restricted the governments' freedom to formulate economic policies and ability to negotiate with multinational corporations. In this context, Latin American governments have been receiving clear "messages" from the governments of a number of creditor countries, certain international organizations, and various sectors of multinational corporations concerning the advantage or necessity of increasing the role of foreign investments through the formulation or revision of certain national policies.

Initiatives of developed countries

The U.S. government has been taking a series of international actions aimed at liberalizing conditions governing the access and handling of its investments abroad. In September 1983 President Reagan issued the "Statement of governmental policy on international investment," which makes the following assertions:

- FDI is the basic factor for international economic development and should be expanded through a free market system;
- FDI is the most appropriate instrument for contributing new resources, given the reduction in bank credits; that interfering with the flow of FDI is negative;
- the principles of national treatment and not discrimination and the most-favored-nation clause should govern foreign investments;
- expropriation can be permitted only in exceptional cases, and in any case, should be subject to "international law" and compensated in a prompt, adequate, and effective manner.

On this basis, the U.S. government is formulating the following unilateral, bilateral and multilateral strategies.

1) The chief example of the first is the New Trade and Tariff Act, which entered into force in January 1985. This law widens the President's powers of coercion and reprisal in trade matters, based on the principle of reciprocity. The President can now withhold the benefits of the Generalized System of Preferences from those "countries that do not offer fair and reasonable access to their markets and basic resources, and that do not provide adequate and effective legal measures enabling foreign countries to assert their exclusive intellectual property rights, such as patents and trademarks." Recipient countries are required to provide unrestricted access for U.S. investments and technologies, with penalties for requiring "performance guarantees" such as the export agreements entered into by foreign companies.[3] These powers have already begun to be exercised in specific cases in Latin America.

2) On the bilateral plane, the most notable example is the negotiation of a series of investment guarantee agreements with various developing countries, especially in Asia and Africa, whereby measures are established to promote and protect U.S. investments based on the principles of the presidential statement. To date, few agreements of this type

have been signed with the implicit targets, the countries of Latin America (UNCTC, 1984).

Similarly, the current government of the United States has strengthened the action of the Overseas Private Investment Corporation (OPIC), a decentralized agency responsible for insuring U.S. investments against certain political risks. The OPIC system functions through bilateral agreements with the governments of the recipient countries, which must accept international arbitration and the subrogation of the U.S. government in the event of disputes with investors. Until recently, the insistence of various countries in the region on the "Calvo Doctrine," which rejects the diplomatic protection of foreign investment, made OPIC action difficult, but this agency has been making significant efforts and in recent years has obtained the support of most of the countries of Latin America.[4]

3) Multilateral action is taken through a series of initiatives with international organizations. Among these, the most significant is the promotion of international negotiations within the GATT to establish a normative framework for services. The ultimate objective is to liberalize the flow of services, apply national treatment to companies in the service sector, and neutralize state monopolies. Areas involved include telecommunications, transportation, banks, insurance, consulting and engineering, tourism, and international data flows. In almost all of these, FDI plays a more important role than it does in traditional trade. Given the growing importance of these areas in the international economy, the obvious superiority of the developed countries, the impact of new technologies on these areas, and the vitality of the sector as a basis for economic development, the developing countries fear that the initiative will lead to a new and perhaps more serious form of dependence, and their reaction has therefore been critical. However, the United States has already obtained the necessary support to include the subject in the forthcoming GATT negotiations.

Concurrently with its active support of the international organizations most responsive to its interests, the U.S. government has been blocking possibilities for approval of certain multilateral instruments in other international organizations. The principal cases are the Code of Conduct on Transnational Corporations (ECOSOC), the Code of Conduct on the Transfer of Technology (UNCTAD), and the revision of the Paris Convention on Patents (WIPO), in which the positions and proposals of the developing countries continue to be resisted by the U.S. delegates, even though they are supported almost unanimously by the rest of the international community and have been made considerably more flexible after several years of negotiation.

On the other hand, the United States government is undoubtedly the major influence behind a series of proposals put forward in various international organizations and financial forums, in which openness to foreign investment and the implementation of privatization and deregulation policies increasingly appear as conditions for obtaining the new resources needed to solve the debt crisis and resume growth. The most widely known expression of these influences is the Baker Plan, proposed by the U.S. Treasury Secretary in Seoul in October 1985.

Proposals of international organizations

The major international organizations involved in financing have begun to present ideas on foreign investment as a means of resolving the crisis. Although their analyses have been moderate in tone and take into account a large number of the problems and criticisms raised earlier, the recommendations are unanimous in pointing out the advantages of "trade systems and open development strategies" as the best ways to maximize the benefits and minimize the costs of FDI. Low tariffs, positive real interest rates, greater stability and continuity in regulations, nondiscrimination with respect to ownership structure, unlimited sectoral access, incentives, and free remittance of profits are recommended as elements of appropriate FDI policies (*IMF*, 1985; World Bank, 1985, IDB, 1985). The most recent World Bank report cites the growing number of members of the International Center for Settlement of Investment Disputes (ICSID), which, after twenty years of Latin American indifference, has aroused the interest of some governments (Costa Rica, Ecuador, Paraguay, and Panama).

But the most significant World Bank initiative is undoubtedly the Multilateral Investment Guarantee Agency (MIGA), created to promote direct investments in the developing countries. The guarantee covers three noncommercial risks: convertibility, expropriation, and war. Distinguishing the new system from various similar proposals that failed in the past is the fact that it offers certain novel characteristics such as parity in recipient and source country voting rights, participation in the capital of the developing countries, and the inclusion of new forms of international investment. From the viewpoint of the developed countries, these features would seem to promise fewer risks of confrontation with the recipient countries. When the initiative appeared, however, it was met with coolness by the principal developing countries, who continued to see in this type of arrangement negative, asymmetrical aspects and the risk of losing autonomy in the formulation of their policies, which would not be offset by the few clear benefits that might result, such as investment incentives.

On the other hand, the International Finance Corporation, affiliated with the World Bank and dedicated to promoting private investment in the developing countries, recently increased its capital; and the IDB has resolved to form the Inter-American Investment Corporation, also to promote private activity in the region, apparently with special emphasis on helping small and medium-sized enterprises to obtain external financing and technology. It appears that this agency would devote special attention to the small Caribbean countries and that its scope would be relatively modest in the short term.

Pressure from the multinationals

In this new international climate the aggressive reactions of certain groups of multinational corporations to some of the sectoral programs of the Latin American governments is not surprising. Two of the most significant cases concern the recent problems encountered by the governments of Brazil and Mexico in the context of national programs for the development of the information science and pharmochemical sectors. The information science program of Brazil, before it was approved in 1984, was explicitly attacked by multinational corporations, particularly IBM, because it was designed to reserve the established market for national capital firms. This program was presented to the Brazilian people as being closely linked to national security — which should have come as no surprise to the United States, considering the growing intervention of its government in the area of controlling the technology of this sector — but this did not prevent President Reagan, in early September 1985, from voicing concern about perceived discrimination in the treatment of U.S. companies. In the case of Mexico, governmental policies in the information science sector gave rise in 1984 to arduous negotiations with foreign companies and representatives of the governments of developed countries. IBM was the key protagonist in these discussions as well. Yet IBM did not have its initial investment proposal rejected even though it did not include local capital participation, which was required as a general condition; rather, in July 1985 the establishment of a wholly owned affiliate was approved in exchange for certain concessions.

The pharmochemical sector has had similar difficulties. Both Brazil and Mexico have insisted on no-patent policies, local development of raw materials, price controls, promotion of generic medicines, and, particularly in the case of Mexico, foreign investment constraints and incentives to national companies. In Brazil, a development program for the sector still has not won approval. In Mexico, the program approved in February 1984 led to legal actions and warnings of disinvestment by almost all the multinational corporations. After the U.S. Departments of State and Commerce became involved threatening among other things not to sign an important trade agreement and to remove Mexican products from the Generalized System of Preferences), the Mexican government introduced significant concessions in the program, including the acceptance of brand names, greater participation by foreign companies, and the promise to reestablish patents.

It should be pointed out, however, that the direct action of multinational corporations is not a generalized phenomenon. Tensions have been limited to certain sectors and businesses characterized by high technology and a traditional aversion to state intervention in intra-company trade. Even in these sectors, the action of the multinationals has not been openly manifested in the recent past. There is no doubt whatever that the economic crisis and the acknowledged loss of the recipient countries' negotiating power have substantially increased the foreign companies' room for maneuver.

THE CURRENT DILEMMAS

Foreign investment policies

In truth there are no sound arguments to support the view that the decline or stagnation of foreign investments is caused by the inadequacy of national policies. To be sure, the regulatory process that spread through the region at the beginning of the past decade introduced significant changes with respect to the formerly predominant "open door" and "laissez-faire" situation. The registration and authorization requirements, the marking off of closed or restricted sectors, the provisions on local participation in ownership, the systems for controlling the transfer of technology, and the limitations on access to long-term credit and on the remittance of profits were not generally well received by foreign investors, and no doubt were not viewed as incentives. However, the truth is that up to the middle of the last decade the performance of foreign investments was relatively good in Latin America, especially in countries such as Brazil, Mexico, and the Andean Group, where the regulatory emphasis was stronger. For example, in the 1971–77 period, with the controversial Decision 24 in full force, the countries of the Andean Group received an increasing flow of foreign investments, estimated at some 7.6 percent per year (Carmona Estanga, 1984). There were no significant conflicts and no dramatic cases of nationalization or disinvestment, except in Chile and Peru in the early 1970s, where it appears that some nationalization processes coincided with more comprehensive strategy changes on the part of the multinational corporations in the fields of mining and oil (Lichtensztein, 1984; Michalet, 1985). Similarly, during the past decade glaring examples of inefficiency or negative effectiveness were observed in the deregulation policies of the foreign investors. The best-documented case is that of Argentina after the military coup in 1976. The experiment with monetary openness, admittedly favorable to the earnings of multinational corporations, coincided with a decline in the industrial output of these corporations of 20 percent in constant values up to 1981 (a higher percentage than the decline experienced by other corporations), causing a reduction in its share of industrial added value and the shutting down of several of the largest foreign subsidiaries (Sourrouille, Kosacoff, and Lucangeli, 1985).

Although the content and methods of enforcing regulatory policies can be debated, no one today who is moderately informed can deny that some type of regulation governing foreign investments was and still is necessary. The above-mentioned IMF analysis admits that "the achievement of development objectives can be significantly affected by the actions of foreign subsidiaries and their parent companies." In summary, this analysis also recognizes:

- the degree of foreign ownership and control is not a problem that has concerned the developing countries only;
- each country must determine these levels on the basis of its needs and objectives;
- foreign investors can not only promote competition and the development of local enterprises, but also may use their superior resources to absorb local enterprises and reduce their number;
- the transfer of technology is carried out in a highly imperfect market where the developing countries often find themselves at a disadvantage in negotiations;
- the "unincorporated" methods of technology transfer can help to lower the recipient countries' costs;
- foreign companies in some developing countries use more capital-intensive techniques than local firms do;
- intra-company trade allows multinational corporations to be less sensitive than local companies to changes in the competitiveness of the recipient countries with respect to other countries;
- intra-company trade creates opportunities for fixing the prices of the transfer of technology and avoiding taxes and exchange controls, etc.

Ignoring some of the excesses of nationalism (more rhetorical than effective) at the beginning of the past decade, the truth is that the regulatory policies of Latin America were aimed at correcting problems such as those just mentioned. It is not easy to evaluate their effectiveness in this regard, although there are significant indicators. Among other aspects, mention can be made of the increased national participation (private and public) of some countries, such as Brazil, in the ownership structure of foreign-capital corporations (Lichtensztein and Trajtenberg, 1985); of the substantial improvement in the balance of trade of the foreign subsidiaries (Lahera, 1985); and of the significant reduction in payments abroad and the restrictive practices associated with technology transfer contracts (UNCTAD, 1980; Carmona Estanga, 1984). On the other hand, the liberalization programs attempted in some countries revealed not only their ineffectiveness in stimulating the flow of foreign capital and technology, but also their connection with poor performance. For example, when Argentina liberalized its policy on technology transfer contracts in 1977, there was an enormous increase in royalty payments abroad in the following years (especially in the case of foreign affiliates), which contrasted with the constant decline of the gross domestic product during these years. This suggested that the increased number and value of the contracts brought about by the opening had little to do with the transfer of technology.

However, it is undeniable that the regulatory policies may have generated new problems, especially with regard to the efficiency of investment projects, the type of market structure created by FDI, and other areas. But it must also be recognized that in the process of evolving, the regulatory policies have acquired a dynamic, adaptable character. Experience in the application of legal systems, the growing professionalism of the competent agencies, and the greater familiarity gained in negotiations with multinational corporations have purged the control policies of certain rigidities and made them more flexible. Principles and concepts initially applied in a highly comprehensive and somewhat dogmatic manner have been gradually adjusted to the sectoral and business characteristics of the various foreign investment projects (White, 1982; UNCTC, 1984). Finally, there do not appear to be sufficiently convincing arguments to show that the existing foreign investment policies are clearly responsible for the reduced flow of investments in Latin America.

The attraction of foreign investments

Very few countries in the world are in a position to influence the determinants of foreign investment decisions. Such decisions depend entirely on the growth of the world economy and, in all cases, on the internal factors of the economies of the major industrialized countries. Interest rates, exchange rates, and international trade are decisive factors, as evidenced by the recent impressive flow of foreign investments into the United States. Similarly, the reduced dynamism of direct investment during the 1970s reflected the greater availability of bank financing and the low real interest rates on bank loans, indicating that the return required by private investors was much greater than that of the said loans (World Bank, 1985). There are also indications that the low interest rates in the world financial market persuaded foreign subsidiaries to finance their capital requirements with external credit instead of transfers from the source countries (IMF, 1985). There is evidence too that in periods of high, unstable real interest rates, multinational corporations hesitate to invest in developing countries because the increased opportunity cost of capital tends to drive up the minimum rate of return and to shorten the amortization period (UNCTAD, 1984).

It is also recognized that decisions to place foreign investments vary according to their objectives: a) those aimed at the goods and services industries to satisfy domestic markets are determined by the size of the markets and are particularly sensitive to import substitution policies, fluctuations in domestic demand, and the facilities for importing inputs; b) those aimed at the export of manufactured goods are influenced above all by lower production costs and the possibilities of international trade; and c) those associated with projects for exploiting natural resources depend, among other factors, on the international prices of commodities.

The reactions of the multinational corporations to the crisis indicate a clear preference for the strategy of exploiting domestic markets, which has traditionally prevailed in Latin America. Other strategies seem to be meeting with serious difficulties. Investments in extraction projects must now contend with the crisis in the commodities markets, and now that the national governments have taken control of the companies' mineral and petroleum wealth, their general tendency is to specialize in related activities such as transportation, marketing, and technical and administrative assistance, through "new forms" of investment with low-risk capital content (Oman, 1984). Investments in export industries are suffering from the slump in international trade, the impact of protectionism, the rise in wages in Southeast Asian countries, and the progress in automation in the source countries, plus the growing resentment of unions over the export of jobs inherent in this type of investment. In contrast, the strategy of penetrating large markets, which today explains the constant intercrossing of investments among industrialized countries, would be the most appropriate in times of crisis, given the possibility of maintaining or increasing sales in national markets where there is a large demand and protectionist trends tend to flare up.

This context would explain the current and projected lack of dynamism in direct investments in Latin America in the coming years. The current deep recession, together with the uncertainty over payment of the debt, the difficulties with imports, and the lack of foreign exchange are the principal disincentive factors. Moreover, it is recognized that in the case of new investments, the interval between the decision to invest and the actual disbursement can be fairly long (Sourrouille, Gatto, and Kosacoff, 1984). Therefore, the possible recovery of the international economy and of the recipient countries would not be reflected immediately by a significant inflow of external resources (UNCTAD, 1984). In the best of cases, a return to the record level of investments recorded in 1981 could not be expected until the end of the decade (IDB, 1985).

It is important to note that opinion surveys of multinational corporations reveal that foreign investment incentives—except for protection against competitive imports—have little or no effect on investment decisions, particularly those aimed at production for the domestic market (Group of Thirty, 1984). In any case, the effects of specific foreign investment incentives are uncertain and lose effectiveness as their complexity and the frequency with which they are modified increases (World Bank, 1985).

In conclusion, it is not easy to identify, at least in terms of explicit policies, appropriate strategies for attracting foreign investments. These alternatives depend primarily on factors beyond the control of the recipient countries and are tied to the performance of the world economy and the changing strategies of the multinational corporations. As the World Bank affirms (1985), a policy favorable to national investors can, in many respects, also be advantageous for foreign investors. Thus, the key issue in the question of foreign investments would appear to be that of defining an economic development strategy and an investment policy. A discussion of this subject clearly exceeds the scope of this paper, but it is important to note this aspect, given the ever-present temptation to rely on foreign investments without a general economic policy and, in particular, without an economic reactivation strategy, which seems to be a prerequisite for dealing with the problem. An example of this incongruous approach is proposing FDI as a solution to the debt crisis.

Foreign investment: substitute for or complement of external credit?

One of the reasons for the renewed interest in foreign investments in the developing countries, especially those that are heavily indebted, is the possibility that the investments may serve as a partial substitute for the external financing of investment requirements. It has already been shown that the prospects of increasing the flow of investments in the coming years are rather poor. Even if such growth occurred, the relative differences in volume between bank loans and FDI are so large — for example, in both Brazil and Mexico the volume of net bank flows was almost two-and-a-half times greater than that of FDI — that a large increase in the base of the latter could not compensate for the decrease in loans (UNCTAD, 1984). Moreover, although possible growth would mean that the ratio between direct investment and external liabilities would fall back to a more reasonable level (IDB, 1985), the proportion of FDI in the total financing of current account deficits and the building of reserves would continue to be low (no more than 15 percent according to IMF estimates for the non-oil-producing developing countries), as would its impact on growth rates since foreign investments finance a small portion of the imports (IMF, 1985).

However, it is worth commenting on the arguments advanced concerning the relationship between loans and foreign investments, and the theoretical possibility that the latter may replace or complement the former. As noted above, the advantages of FDI would consist of the greater adaptation of its service to the economic situation of the recipient country, its greater stability and continuity, its supposedly noncyclical nature, its greater flexibility in the event of failure, etc. Yet there are various problems with these arguments.

In the first place, as compared to new equity capital, reinvested profits represent a much larger proportion of the foreign investment flows. In the 1970–80 period, reinvested profits accounted for 65 percent of the recorded value of U.S. investment in Latin America, while only 35 percent was new capital (Bitar, 1984).

In addition, direct investment is generally included with the subsidiary's other financial requirements that are handled with short- and long-term loans from the parent company or other affiliates, as well as commercial banks (national and foreign) and commercial credits. Approximately three-fourths of all the funds obtained by Latin American affiliates from U.S. companies have been in this form (World Bank, 1985). The external financing of the affiliates is considered external debt, but it frequently depends on the parent company — affiliate relationship. This type of indebtedness reaches considerable proportions; in Brazil in 1979 it totaled some $8.6 billion, or about half of all the stock of foreign direct investment, and 17 percent of all the external financing (IMF, 1985). Thus, the prospects of increasing FDI are closely linked to the possibilities of external financing and debt service, and these questions, in turn, seem to depend primarily on the investment financing strategies of the multinational corporations. During the past decade, the instability of the world economy and the wide fluctuations in interest and exchange rates led the companies to try to minimize the risk of immobility implicit in direct investments through the use of loaned capital, facilitated by the enormous supply of credit in the international financial market. This had the added advantage that the loans guaranteed a minimum flow of income, unaffected by the exchange restrictions applicable to the remittance of profits.

Another phenomenon associated with easy access to financial sources in the past decade was the expansion of the so-called "new forms of international investment" (Oman, 1984), characterized by low or nonexistent risk capital participation by the foreign companies. These forms include minority "joint ventures," licensing and management agreements, plant engineering and assembly contracts, etc. In some sectors they seem to have replaced or supplemented foreign direct investments; in others, they appear to have opened new fields for the participation of foreign companies. This latter characteristic, linked on the one hand to the noted tendency of multinational corporations to minimize risk capital exposure and, on the other, to the policies of many developing countries of increasing their own participation and control in investment projects through the splitting and separate acquisition of resources usually supplied as a foreign direct investment "package," led to the increased use of the new forms of investment.

The implications of this phenomenon for the developing countries are still unclear, although from the financial perspective it is obvious that the new forms may lead to increased external indebtedness and the shifting of some or all of the risks of foreign investment to the recipient country. It also seems clear that the development of the new forms is a response to structural changes, which the policies of the developing countries—sometimes cited as their principal cause—are unable to determine or influence decisively. In fact, although unexpected increases in interest rates may have caused many developing countries to doubt the advantages of the new, as opposed to the old, forms of foreign investment, the new forms seem already to have been incorporated into a "new international division of risks and responsibilities," in which they play a fundamental role along with the governments and groups of developing countries, the multinational corporations, the banks, and the international financial organizations (Oman, 1984).

Another problem with the supposed advantages of FDI is that any analysis of the financial contribution of foreign investment must consider the remittance of profits. It is generally asserted that payments for foreign investment earnings would vary according to the profitability of such investments, which depends on the growth of the local economy and the balance-of-payments situation. There is some evidence in this connection that foreign investment earnings in developing countries are related more to the recipient country's capacity to handle them than to the interest on the external debt. In Latin America, U.S. investment income rose from $3.712 billion in 1977 to $6.968 billion in 1980, only to fall suddenly ($6.143 billion in 1981, $2.706 billion in 1982, $690 million in 1983) (Howenstine, 1984).

Nevertheless, the effect of variations in earnings depends on their distribution between reinvestments and remittances abroad. Thus it has been shown that, while a significant part of the earnings is reinvested, this part varies substantially with changes in economic conditions; in contrast, the dividend payments of the affiliates have been much more stable in recent years. During 1982 and 1983 the earnings of U.S. affiliates fell considerably in Latin America, while remittances of profits did not change significantly. The same trend is observed in royalty payments and other payments for the transfer of technology, part of which is linked to parent company–affiliate transactions. These remittances remained stable in the countries of the region throughout almost all of the past decade, but increased appreciably as the crisis advanced. Between 1977 and 1979 remittances to the United States reached an annual average of $364 million; in 1981–84, the average rose to $589 million (Howenstine, 1984).

In conclusion, remittances of profits would appear to be influenced not only by the profitability of the investment, but also by the strategy of the corporations—primarily the parent companies (Sourrouille, Gatto, and Kosacoff, 1984)—in terms of their liquidity requirements, the adjustment of international interest rates, projections concerning the balance of payments of the local economy, etc. Under these conditions, the theory of the noncyclical nature of FDI does not seem well founded.

In short, the hope of using FDI as a significant source of external financial resources does not seem to have much basis in reality, not does FDI's alleged noncyclical nature. FDI flows have little importance, not only in fixed capital formation in the developing countries—between 1979 and 1981, approximately 1.5 percent in Brazil and Mexico, 5 percent in Chile (IMF, 1985)—but also in financing current account and import deficits, as well as most public sector investment projects. The importance of direct investment as a channel of foreign exchange earnings seems conditioned by the significance of reinvestments, of the external loans associated with investment, and of the "new forms of investment" (which require a large contribution of local resources from the recipient countries), as well as by the difficulties of controlling the remittances of profits.

With respect to the contribution of foreign investment to the developing countries and its role as a possible factor in economic recovery, attention should be focused on other aspects of the phenomenon, which unfortunately do not end with the transfer of capital.

FUTURE PROSPECTS

It seems clear that the role that foreign investments can and ought to play—in both their old and their new forms—is not the one they have again been temporarily assigned (their alleged financial contribution), but rather their capacity to mobilize the productive resources of the Latin American countries, that is, their contribution to the reactivation of the national economies. This role is directly related to the specific potential of the multinational corporations as a channel of technology transfer and as a catalyst in foreign trade. However, the expected contribution of foreign investments can be realized neither within the framework of the current imbalances of the international economy nor under the external restrictions weighing on the Latin American economies, over which the countries of the region have little control.

By definition, foreign investment requires the availability of productive projects. For this, it is essential first to solve the external debt problem and to overcome the recessive effect of the current stabilization and structural adjustment programs. Thus, it is impossible to understand the logic of conditionality proposals in the renegotiation of the debt that simultaneously require policies of recession and policies of investment attraction, despite the fact that the key motivation for investment is the large and growing domestic market.

Latin America urgently needs to update its technological–industrial profile, which, in various sectors, has become outmoded as far as international competition is concerned. The MCs can play a very important role by supplementing domestic efforts through the transfer of technology. Thus, what must become clear to the developing countries is that for Latin America, it is no longer a question of importing technological packages to replace imports, but rather one of learning and assimilating knowledge and participating actively in the changes on the leading edge of technology. Therefore, there is concern about some of the measures and proposals of the United States, such as its insistence on the amendment of the patent laws of the countries of the region, its rejection of the Code of Conduct on the Transfer of Technology, and its program to liberalize the international flow of services. These actions are aimed at protecting the interests of technology exporters and fail to consider the need of the Latin American countries to participate in the processes of innovation.

Given the multinational corporations' significant role in international trade, their activities as exporters and importers can have a crucial effect on the ability of the countries to service the debt.

Thus, it has been noted that the foreign affiliates in various Latin American countries have won a large share of the exports of manufactured goods, especially in the high technology sectors. Nevertheless, the share of these exports in the total sales of the affiliates is still very low, particularly when compared with the Asian countries.[5]

The export decisions of these companies are determined, on the one hand, by the general policies of the parent companies that define the area of influence of each affiliate, and, on the other, by the export policies of the recipient countries. Latin American governments have been attaching growing importance to promoting exports, both generally and through specific measures for coordinating intra-company trade with the foreign affiliates. Judging from the results achieved in Brazil and Mexico, these coordination policies are effective. Nevertheless, efforts to give these policies the necessary depth are currently being hindered by the protectionist policies of the industrialized countries and the stubborn attitudes of the U.S. government with respect to the so-called "export agreements," despite the fact that such agreements are a clear case of applying the concept of protection to infant industry, as the literature and experience of the developed countries unarguably demonstrate.

The difficulties and obstacles raised in the external context are all the more regrettable because, at present, numerous elements are favorable to maximizing the positive contribution of foreign investments on both the international and the domestic planes. Prominent on the international plane, first of all, are the greater transparency and the wide range of options resulting from the larger number of countries and businesses offering international investment opportunities. A particularly interesting phenomenon, especially for intermediately developed countries that have more complementary resources, is the emergence of small and medium-sized companies in industrialized countries such as Japan, Germany, France, and the United States. In the second place, there are currently more options for negotiating the transfer and organization of productive resources through the above-mentioned "new forms of investment," which offer interesting possibilities for designing production plans based on specific objectives, such as the transfer and development of technology, export programs, etc.

Various positive elements also exist on the domestic plane. First, the foreign investment policies have been stripped of ideology.

The Latin American countries have already tried all the possible policies, from direct confrontation to open ports, and have learned that dogmatic approaches of any kind are largely ineffective. A more complete knowledge has been gained of the special characteristics of the multinationals' investment decisions and of the affiliates' operating methods; this knowledge facilitates the discussion of strategies and projects between governments and companies. Regulations tend to be adapted to the individual nature of the different sectors of the MCs, among which considerable differences in objectives and strategies have been observed. This has made it possible, for example, to adjust the general principles of joint ownership, the conditions governing the transfer of technology, and export programs to the characteristics of each specific case. In the second place, the process of productive diversification in various Latin American countries has already created an experienced national corporate sector, even in the activities of international investment and the export of technology, the existence of which offers foreign companies receptive capabilities and an atmosphere of increasingly integrated investments.

It is worth stressing the current contrast between the attitudes of the Latin American countries and the rarefied signals from the North. Curiously, the initiative on policies for investment in Latin America now seems to be more in the hands of the U.S. government than under the control of the governments of the region. The unilateral strategy, aimed at imposing changes or ties by means of reprisals or diplomatic protection, as well as the manipulation of multilateral programs without consulting the countries of the region, not only appears as an excessive form of interventionism, but also reveals nearsightedness with respect to the way in which Latin American societies function, particularly at a time when democratic policies are making headway in the region. But even in cases where the governments may agree with some of the aspects or objectives of foreign claims, the style in which they are articulated inevitably recalls an era thought to be past and tends to have contrary effects or to create resentments not conducive to maintaining lasting economic relations.

In the scenario described, numerous opportunities are appearing for a new series of negotiations in the next few years among source countries, multinational corporations, and recipient countries. An essential requirement for dialogue must be ideological dis-armament. The Latin American countries have already taken impor-tant steps in this direction, and it remains for the competent agencies of the United States government to do likewise. Implicit in this point is the reciprocal agreement not to use policies of reprisal to influence the behavior of governments or businesses.

At the outset, it will be necessary to develop some program of coordination and consultation with the participation of businesses and governments interested in a rational discussion of the specific problems that have arisen recently in certain sectors, such as infor-mation science and pharmochemicals, and certain questions such as patents, export agreements, restricted markets, the sanctions of the U.S. Trade Act, etc. In the recent past, inappropriate procedures and places were chosen for discussing these questions. The old specters of political interference and corruption reared their heads, and negotiations among some countries went on behind the backs of others. In the high technology sectors, where growth potential is great, markets are rapidly expanding, and international competi-tion is growing, equitable formulas should provide a harmonious solution to the major problems (disseminating technology and exploiting markets). A number of regional organizations could host and promote such negotiations, including the OAS and the IDB, or some arrangement could be worked out involving SELA participation.

Furthermore, current circumstances favor the development of new mechanisms, by joint agreement and on a basis of equality, for comprehensively promoting foreign investment and the transfer of technology within the context of specific investment programs and projects, selected by the Latin American countries and negotiated by companies on both sides. To date, most of the Latin American countries have vacillated between a passive attitude—assuming, of course, that foreign companies are interested in investing—and a defensive attitude, concerned more with preventing abuses than max-imizing benefits. The U.S. government has not considered it im-portant to promote investments in Latin America, except through legal and economic policy concessions on the part of the countries of the region. Nevertheless, it seems that the conditions are right for a more positive attitude on both sides. For example, the United States has an extraordinary number of medium-sized companies that have not yet become involved in international production and are suffering from the changes in U.S. industry. These companies could satisfy the demand for technical knowledge in various sectors of the Latin American economy.

A few years ago, Baranson (1981) analyzed several proposals for creating new mechanisms to permit the capitalization of other possibilities through technical assistance and financial aid. Recently, OPIC announced that it was emphasizing foreign investment by small and medium-sized companies (OPIC, 1985). And the International Finance Corporation and the new Investment Corporation of the IDB now offer several prospects for progress in this direction. In any case, this type of approach, based on catalytic elements of a financial-, informational-, and technical-assistance nature, offer better perspectives and should be given priority, instead of continuing to insist on conditionality, reciprocity, guarantees, and investment insurance, which tend to politicize international economic relations. Although it now seems paradoxical, the promotion of foreign investments requires the development of new governmental functions. As an example of the various possible formulas, thought should be given to the creation of coinvestment funds, with the participation of development banks and other public and private financial institutions from the developed countries and Latin America, for the purpose of promoting joint investments. Nacional Financiera de México already has some experience with binational funds of this type, created jointly with a number of European countries. This type of fund could be used to identify viable projects and businesses and to create an atmosphere of genuine reciprocity, security, and common interest in the attraction of new investments. Moreover, such funds could serve as instruments for capitalizing part of the interest on the external debt, and in this way introduce, even if on a modest level, some strategies to place debt in the service of growth.

NOTES

1. The United States is becoming the chief recipient of foreign investments, having absorbed approximately 27 percent of the flows from developed countries by the middle of the past decade. See United Nations Commission on Transnational Corporations (UNCTC), 1984.

2. The suddenness of the drop is due in part to loans obtained by U.S. firms from their affiliates in the Netherlands Antilles. See Howenstine, 1984.

3. Curiously, among the developed countries — and the United States is certainly no exception — cases of imposing "performance requirements" on foreign companies proliferate, probably in a more effective manner than in developing countries.

4. In early 1986 the only countries still outside OPIC were Argentina, Mexico, Peru, and Venezuela.

5. During the 1970s the share of foreign affiliates in exports of manufactured goods varied from 25–30 percent in Argentina, Colombia, and Mexico to 43 percent in Brazil. Nevertheless, the impact of exports on the total sales of the affiliates was low, rising from 6 to 10 percent in Latin America in the 1967–77 period, in comparison with the growth in Asia from 23 to 62 percent in the same period (UNCTC, 1985).

REFERENCES

Baranson, J. 1981. *North-South Technology Transfer: Financing and Institution Building*. Mt. Airy, Md.: Lemond Publications.

Bitar, S. 1984. Corporaciones transnacionales y las nuevas relaciones de América Latina con EE.UU. *Economía de América Latina*, no. 11.

_____. 1985. La inversión extranjera en América Latina. In *El Perú frente al capital extranjero: deuda y inversión*. CEPEI.

Carmona Estanga, P. 1984. Discurso en el Seminario-Taller sobre la inversión extranjera en el Grupo Andino, July 23–25, 1984. Lima, Peru.

Correa, C., S. C. de Zalduendo, and R. Cherol. 1984. *Regulación de la inversión extranjera en América Latina y el Caribe*. Buenos Aires: IDB-INTAL, November.

ECLA. 1984. Las empresas transnacionales y América Latina: situación actual, perspectivas frente a la crisis. Santiago.

Ffrench-Davis, R. 1982. Dueda externa y balanza de pagos en América Latina: tendencias recientes y perspectivas. In *Economic and Social Progress of Latin America*, IDB report.

Group of Thirty. 1984. Foreign Direct Investment 1973–1987, A Survey of International Companies, New York.

Howenstine, N. J. 1984. U.S. Direct Investment Abroad in 1983. *Survey of Current Business*, August.

Instituto Nacional de Technologia Industrial-Secretaria de Ciencia y Tecnica (INTI-SECyT). 1985. Contratos de Importación de Tecnología 1977–83. Buenos Aires, April.

Inter-American Development Bank. 1982. *Economic and Social Progress of Latin America*, report.

_____. 1985. *Economic and Social Progress of Latin America*, report.

International Monetary Fund. 1985. Foreign Private Investment in Developing Countries. *Occasional Paper 33*. Washington, D.C.: January.

Lahera, E. 1985. Las empresas transnacionales y el comercio internacional de América Latina. *Revista de la CEPAL*. no. 25, April.

Lall, S. 1983. *The New Multinationals: The Spread of Third World Enterprises*. Paris: IRM.

Lichtensztein, S. 1984. Experiencias de política económica respecto de las empresas transnacionales en América Latina, Análisis preliminar de tendencias. Buenos Aires: CET.

Lichtensztein, S., and R. Trajtenberg. 1985. Políticas económicas e inversiones extranjeras (Elementos para una discusión del caso argentino). Buenos Aires: CET.

Michalet, C. 1985. *Les multinationales face à la crise*. Paris: IRM.

Oman, C. 1984. *New Forms of International Investment in Developing Countries*. Paris: OECD.

Overseas Private Investment Corporation (OPIC). 1985. *Annual Report*. Washington, D.C.

SELA. 1983. *Las relaciones económicas de América Latina con Estados Unidos, 1982–1983*. Mexico City: Siglo Veintiuno Editores.

_____. 1984. La política económica de Estados Unidos y su impacto en América Latina. SP/C/XD/DT No. 10/Corr. 1. September 17.

Sourrouille, J., F. Gatto, and B. Kosacoff. 1984. *Inversiones extranjeras en América Latina: política económica, decisiones de inversión y comportamiento económico de las filiales*. Buenos Aires: IDB–INTAL, January.

Sourrouille, J., B. Kosacoff, and J. Lucangeli, 1985. *Transnacionalización y política económia en Argentina*. Buenos Aires: Centro Editor de América Latina, CET.

Stopford, J., and J. Dunning. 1983. *Multinationals: Company Performance and Global Trends*. London: Macmillan.

Trajtenberg, R. 1985. Concentración global y transnacionalización. Buenos Aires: CET.

UNCTAD. 1980. The Implementation of Transfer of Technology Regulations: A Preliminary Analysis of the Experience of Latin America, India, and the Philippines. TD/B/C6/55, August.

_____. 1984. The Role of Foreign Direct Investments in the Financing of Development: Current Questions. TD/B/C3/1986, December.

United Nations Commission on Transnational Corporations (UNCTC). 1983. *Transnational Corporations in World Development, Third Survey*. New York.

Comments

SERGIO BITAR*

The papers by David Ibarra and Eduardo White are clear and comprehensive. With respect to Ibarra's analysis, I concur with what he calls "an obsolete external trade structure" (and the decline of traditional products), as well as the need to link the growth of trade to payment of the debt. Furthermore, implicit in his presentation is the political requisite of opening a channel for a concerted social effort, both national and regional, which is a necessary condition for bringing about the suggested changes.

Ibarra's figures show that in the 1980–85 period the volume of Latin American exports grew by 24 percent, while the volume of imports decreased by 36 percent. Both variables indicate a highly significant adjustment effort. And yet, the impact on growth of this enormous sacrifice is minimal because of the erosion in the terms of trade.

White's paper contains several conclusions that coincide with the positions of the Sistema Económico Latinoamericano (SELA) on U.S. foreign investment. Particular mention should be made of the phenomenon of stagnation and decline in foreign direct investment in our region. The most recent figures indicate, that foreign direct investment flows to Latin America were $7.5 billion in 1981, $5.4 billion in 1982, $3.1 billion in 1983, and $2.0 billion in 1984. These figures include the reinvestment of profits.

Latin America's significance for the multinationals and for U.S. foreign direct investment has decreased since the end of the 1970s. Our region, which six or seven years ago represented 15 percent of the total amount of U.S. investment in the world, today attracts

*Director, Centro Latinoamericano de Economia y Política Internacional (CLEPI), Santiago.

175

only about 10 percent. In addition, there is the phenomenon of heavy
concentration in countries such as Mexico and Brazil. The trend
toward a decline in the relative importance of Latin America is being
repeated in trade as well.

White states that it is difficult to identify the factors that attract foreign capital, and points out that many of them are beyond
the region's control. Thus, Ibarra and White arrive at similar conclusions. First, the economic dynamic is essentially a North-North
process. Furthermore, the international economic policies of the industrialized nations result from considerations mainly related to the
interactions among the United States, Europe, and Japan. From this
perspective, the resultant policies concerning us are merely a by-
product of the N-N process. Second, both authors emphasize the
need to concentrate Latin American efforts on managing the variables that are under their control, instead of waiting for the beneficial
effects of possible changes in international conditions. In short, it
is necessary to better define opportunities for direct action, where
our possibility of control is greater, even if the results are less than
optimal. There, at least, we have a chance to take action.

EXTERNAL TRADE

An evaluation must be made of the new legal provisions and
reprisals that the United States has been imposing since 1985, following approval of the Trade Act in October 1984. Recent studies of
the SELA and other institutions emphasize the need to strengthen
Latin America's negotiating capability in Washington and in other
centers where these matters are dealt with. Countries such as Japan,
those of Southeast Asia, and even Brazil are sending vast numbers of
experts to lobby and to monitor judicial and administrative actions
taken by the government or by businesses against foreign exporters.

Also in the area of trade, I believe it essential to innovate, using
unorthodox methods, to increase intra-regional trade in Latin America. New avenues must be explored, particularly when we consider
that regional trade has fallen between 30 and 40 percent in recent
years. A simple recovery of the levels prior to 1980 would represent a significant stimulus to the growth of Latin American trade.
Flexible mechanisms and procedures should be found. The nature

of the Brazilian-Argentinian economic agreements could be extended to other countries.

A second reason for supporting such an effort is that the percentage of manufactures exchanged in Latin American intra-regional trade is higher than the proportion reached in extra-regional trade. Therefore, intra-regional trade has the potential to dynamize productive conversion, improve competitiveness, and speed up industrial renewal in our countries.

A third topic related to trade is that of services. This year, new GATT negotiations have begun, and services are one of the important topics. Although a number of large Latin American countries, such as Brazil, have already outlined some policies, consideration must be given to the possibility that the United States will impose rules that may hinder Latin American goals. At a time when most Latin American countries seem preoccupied with the trade in goods (and fail to see services as a highly critical topic), they may yield to the temptation to settle for some concessions from the developed countries in merchandising in exchange for accepting general procedures in the area of services that may hinder their subsequent development.

Finally, emphasis should be placed on exploring alliances with other Third World countries to open up new markets. Although the impact of this may seem minor in the short term, it is an option worth considering. There are several notable examples in this regard; the pressures exerted by the European Community and the United States on Japan have brought about major policy changes in Japan, leading even to the creation of "Import Promotion Committees." These committees have been visiting countries to promote exports to Japan. Most of Japan's efforts are concentrated in Southeast Asia and are aimed at striking a balance in its relations with the United States and the Middle East. But we have done very little to take advantage of this opening and, in particular, the additional opportunities offered by the Japanese policy for the Pacific Basin.

FOREIGN INVESTMENT

In the area of foreign direct investment I will emphasize four aspects. First, it is worth noting that while the United States is linking its new trade provisions to the subject of foreign direct investment (the trade act contains a number of regulations on multinationals), on the Latin America side these themes are considered separate: there are experts on trade, on multinationals, and on debt, but the problems are not addressed concurrently, or at least are not coordinated into a coherent position. It is a question, then, of a weakness in our negotiating methods, which we ought to correct. The conditions on national treatment, the right of installation, and performance requirements are intimately linked to trade and financing, and we should deal with them in an integrated manner.

Second, the multinationals' financial contribution is below expectations, both in the U.S. and in Latin America. It is possible and necessary to adopt norms that will result in a higher percentage of equity capital as compared to the mere reinvestment of profits or credits obtained by the multinationals, especially in the current phase where the inflows of share capital are so limited.

A third point concerns the impact of U.S. tax reforms on the conduct of the multinationals. A number of measures are being studied. For example, there are provisions that require the multinationals to list their operations on a country-by-country basis to obtain tax deductions in the United States. This may seem a positive effect for us because it would make it more attractive for the multinationals to operate in those countries that grant more tax incentives. However, there are other measures that would tend to equalize the tax treatment of investments within and outside the United States, which would reduce the attractiveness of operations abroad.

Analysis of the new U.S. policies and the behavior of multinational firms reveals that the tax incentive policies of some Latin American countries are ineffective. They ignore the fact that the factors determining the decisions of the multinationals have little to do with the incentives that a small country may grant them. Recent surveys, as well as the information provided by White, indicate that such incentives are low on the multinationals' scale of priorities and that the chief attraction is the size of local markets.

The final aspect concerns investment insurance. OPIC has provided very little insurance in Latin America because one of the conditions it imposes is the acceptance of international arbitration, which numerous Latin American countries reject. White mentions that the U.S. government, through an exchange of letters, has succeeded in getting Ecuador and Colombia to accept international arbitration. Will all the Latin American countries follow suit? Formulating a regional policy on this subject would be useful, for it could lead to the development of an additional negotiating strength that could replace the bilateral mechanism of an exchange of letters currently in use.

THE CONNECTION AMONG TRADE, FOREIGN INVESTMENTS, AND DEBT

The discussion so far points to the conclusion that we have few elements at our disposal to individually correct the current state of affairs. We must therefore be cautious in selecting our tools.

We are being shaken by international events. For example, we must consider the effect of the recent change in oil prices on our ability to negotiate collectively. Apparently, a falling-out is possible because of the contrasting impact on Brazil, Chile, Uruguay, Paraguay, and the Central American countries, where the effect is positive, and on Mexico, Venezuela, Peru, Ecuador, and Bolivia, whose oil or gas exports are adversely affected. If this situation creates differing attitudes toward banks and the renegotiation process, to what extent are we faced with a factor of heterogeneity, which will require us to revise things quickly to avoid divisions?

Additionally, it is probable that the United States, Europe, and Japan view the 1986 GATT negotiations as something more than a simple round of negotiations for incorporating new products and lowering tariffs. They could be seeking a general reorganization of world trade. It is also possible that they will promote an international monetary conference.

Under these circumstances, what does the future hold for us? OECD projections for 1986 indicate only a slight growth in trade. The effect of world growth on our products has declined because of technological changes. If we do not modify our policies, we will have fewer options. To increase them, it seems essential to revise the trade-debt connection. If we act exclusively in the area of finance, we will be almost powerless to place limits on interest rates or to obtain any additional contribution from the multilateral banks. It is in the area of trade that we can take a negotiating stance, linking the net transfer of resources abroad to our foreign trade, to exports. This is one of the areas where we have some power to rely on.

We must also be alert to the "structural adjustment" objectives of the World Bank and the Baker Plan. If new conditionalities on Latin America are taken, this would have a greater impact than we imagine on the development strategies of the region. This was already brought out in the chapters in Section I of this volume, but it bears repeating: In the new conditionalities, there is an implicit development strategy that limits our ability to specialize our productive structure and to introduce the technological innovations necessary for improving international competitiveness. Furthermore, multilateral institutions tend to neglect the negative impacts on employment and distribution of income derived from the application of conditionalities based on liberalization and privatization.

If we look at the possible net flow of financing from the World Bank in the next few years, the question is even more disquieting. These flows represented almost 100 percent of the net inflows of capital in 1985, and, according to Feinberg, the net disbursement could be zero around 1988–89. If, in our moment of greatest weakness, new conditionalities are accepted in exchange for funds that in two years will either dry up or merely trickle in, Latin America would be paying an enormous cost and would receive very little in return.

PART III

Country Studies: Perspectives on External Indebtedness and Internal Development

Brazil's External Debt Outlook, 1986–1990

DIONISIO DÍAS CARNEIRO*

Since late 1980, under the pressure of Brazil's external accounts, the country's economic policy has been conducted with a dual aim: to meet the requirements of completing the adjustment of the economy to the unfavorable circumstances of the international environment, and to persuade creditors that the adjustments already made do in fact help reduce the risk of insolvency. Until the world crisis of 1982, this second aim was met through direct negotiations with the creditor banks. Since the end of 1982 the IMF assumed the role of guarantor of the solvency of debtors and became the most important negotiating partner of the Brazilian government. Inasmuch as the divergence between the two aims will be the larger when analyses behind policy recommendations are based on less accurate information, that divergence reached a maximum during the period when the Fund's supervision was more decisive in setting the course of economic policy, that is, in the dramatic period between late 1982 and early 1984, during which the economy operated almost constantly without any foreign exchange reserves.

In 1985, taking advantage of a better bargaining position made possible by the previous year's reserve buildup, the Brazilian government ignored the Fund's recommendations for the first time in three years and resumed domestic discussion on the course of its economic policy. It made the changes it deemed necessary in its monetary and fiscal policies and, with difficulty, administered the conflicts resulting from the unavoidable wage adjustments that had to occur once labor

---

*Director, Department of Economics, Catholic University of Rio de Janeiro.

activities were released from the constraints of political repression. Interest rates declined gradually, real wages recovered; inflation, though still high, did not accelerate; and the economic expansion that began with the export boom of 1984 continued.

The resumption of private investment, in conjunction with the recovery of employment as the use of productive capacity increased, suggests favorable economic growth prospects for the near future. The weak points of the current recovery are the public sector's financial situation and the high inflation rate. The political difficulties faced by the government in attempting to restore the net tax burden must not be ignored; the precariously stabilized high inflation created continuing tensions for the wage and price adjustment process, threatening to break the inertia with new inflationary shocks. On February 26, 1986, seeking to eliminate the inertial component of inflation, the government decreed a currency reform that abolished indexation of short-term contracts, froze prices, and adjusted wages on the basis of real wage levels in the previous six months.

The crucial problem of the current external debt renegotiation lies in the insistence of creditor banks, represented by an advisory committee, on having the IMF act as guarantor of Brazil's domestic policies.

The purpose of this paper is to present a number of projections for Brazil's foreign debt and to discuss some major questions affecting the performance of the Brazilian economy's external accounts through the end of the decade. In order to provide a suitable perspective for the current Brazilian situation, the first section presents a brief historical background covering the last five years, focusing in particular on changes in short-term policies before and after the IMF intervention so as to permit a critical view of Brazil's recent experience in negotiating policy objectives with the Fund. The second section presents a number of simulations of Brazil's external debt under the current prospects of renewed economic growth. The final section sets forth some conclusions and attempts to identify the main points of divergence between the Brazilian government and the IMF.

BACKGROUND

Early in the present decade, the Figueiredo Administration (1979–85) had great difficulty defining an economic strategy to guide the economy along the narrow path between the dangers of a recessive stabilization policy aimed at controlling inflation and the risks associated with the emergence of a balance-of-payments crisis due to insufficient external financing. The economy's long-term adjustment to the price situation and the availability of financing after the first oil crisis had been the main focus of the Second National Development Plan (1975–79). The Plan's investment program, aimed at increasing the nation's export capacity and reducing its dependence on imported inputs (especially petroleum, basic industrial inputs, and capital goods) was far from completed by the end of the previous administration. Efforts to maintain a high investment rate were subject to growing criticism. Conservative forces in both the government and the opposition repeatedly pointed to the burden that government enterprises' capital expenditures represented for government finance and insisted that these expenditures were the main factor behind the public sector deficit that added to inflation and the external debt.

In December 1980 Brazil's external debt totaled $53.8 billion, of which 71 percent was owed to private banks. The history of this indebtedness can be explained basically by the impact of the two oil shocks, and the long-term strategy followed from the second half of the 1970s for adjusting the economy by changing the output composition and the input use pattern. As the time needed for the investment program to mature passed, interest payments on the accumulated debt accounted for a gradually larger share of the total debt; by 1980 they absorbed about 65 percent of export receipts and represented $6.3 billion, or 49 percent of the current account deficit, which in turn amounted to 5.1 percent of GDP.

The reversal of the economic policy that was intended to adapt the economy to available external financing took place in two stages, leading to the gravest recession in Brazilian economic history since the 1930s. The first stage, extending from the last quarter of 1980 to the last quarter of 1982, was characterized by an emphasis on contractionist monetary policy, through increased domestic interest rates and, to a smaller extent, on fiscal contraction, taking into account the need to continue, insofar as possible, to complete the investment programs begun in the previous decade. The essential objective was to show foreign bankers that both inflation and the current account deficit could be held under control and to make them forget the ill-fated economic experiments of 1979 and 1980.

The foreign debt would continue to grow strictly in line with debt service requirements and with the need to finance priority projects intended specifically to control it in the long term. The high interest rates served not only to control domestic demand, but also to induce the private sector to make new borrowings abroad and to discourage capital flight.

The recessive effects were felt primarily in the industrial sector. In 1981, industrial employment fell by more than 7 percent and output declined by more than 10 percent. By midyear the trade balance showed a surplus for the first time since 1977. A $5 billion increase in the net inflow of foreign loans was more than sufficient to cover the $12 billion current account deficit (table 1) and make it possible to add slightly to reserves. However, the rising interest rates (including spreads) paid on the external debt caused a dangerous increase in interest payments, which already absorbed about 30 percent of total outward payments, compared with about 10 percent at the beginning of the previous decade.

Once imports were brought under control as a result of the induced effects of the industrial recession and the initial effects of the substitution policies, the feasibility of further external borrowing depended on the potential for increasing exports. Since 1975, when the adjustment started, Brazilian exports had been growing

TABLE 1

Brazil: Current Account Deficit and Its Main Components
(1979–85)
(Millions of U.S. $)

YEAR	TRADE BALANCE	RESOURCE BALANCE[a]	NET INTEREST PAYMENTS	CURRENT ACCOUNT DEFICIT
1979	−2827	5205	4185	10742
1980	−2810	5931	6311	12807
1981	1232	1631	9161	11734
1982	780	2808	11353	16311
1983	6470	−4063	9555	6837
1984	13078	−11364	10076	−166
1985	12450	−10576	10400	650

Source: *Boletim do Banco Central.*
a. Surplus of absorption over GDP.

at an average annual rate of 21.8 percent. In 1982, despite continuing restrictive domestic policies and exchange, tax, and credit incentives to exporters, export prices fell by 6 percent and export volume declined by about 9 percent due to the international recession, resulting in a $3 billion decline in proceeds. Despite the drop in imports (from 8 percent to 6.8 percent of GDP) (table 2), the trade balance declined by $400 million. The monetary policy had had only moderate recessionary impact on inflation because of the inertial nature given inflation by the indexation system; a decline of approximately 20 percent in capacity utilization led to a drop of no more than 10 percentage points in annual inflation. This reversal of the gains achieved on the external front added to the difficulties faced by the government in obtaining political support for the stabilization program in an election year.

When the financial world was shaken by the Mexican moratorium, which put an end to the voluntary financing of the Latin American debt, the political constraints on Brazil's economic management were totally changed. The need to convince the domestic public and the country's private creditors of the economy's long-term solvency led to a period during which the domestic public had to be convinced that a unilateral moratorium would not be the best solution. Meanwhile the new negotiating partner abroad became the International Monetary Fund, manager of the painful process of channeling private and multilateral resources toward the

TABLE 2

Selected External Indicators, 1979–85
(Percent)

ITEMS	1979	1980	1981	1982	1983	1984	1985
Exports/GDP	6.4	8.0	8.5	7.1	10.4	12.3	11.8
Imports/GDP	7.6	9.2	8.0	6.8	7.3	6.3	6.1
Debt/Exports	264.0	233.0	231.0	325.0	351.0	304.0	310.0
Debt Service/Exports[a]	70.0	65.0	72.0	97.0	91.0	71.0	78.5
Interest/Exports	27.5	31.3	39.3	56.3	43.6	37.3	40.6
Reserves/Imports	53.6	30.1	34.0	20.6	29.6	86.1	90.8[b]

Sources: *Boletim do Banco Central* and Fundação Centro de Estudos do Comércio Exterior (FUNCEX).

a. Principal repaid or refinanced plus interest/merchandise exports
b. Estimated

Third World's financing needs. This was the beginning of the second phase of the post-1980 adjustment:

On January 6, 1983 Brazil submitted what would turn out to be the first of a series of seven letters of intent to the International Monetary Fund, requesting resources for three years under the Fund's extended financing facility and agreeing to a stabilization policy theoretically oriented toward structural adjustment to reduce its internal and external imbalances during 1983–85. In reality, that letter resulted from a hurried attempt to make the program for containing domestic absorption consistent with the programming of external accounts defined in October of the previous year.

The very design of the program specified in the first letter of intent contained a number of ambiguities that explain at least in part the long path of negotiations that extended through 1983 and 1984.

In the first place, the three-year program was aimed at a "structural adjustment" that was very narrowly defined, considering the long structural adjustment that had already been taking place in the composition of Brazilian expenditure and output since the first oil shock. The idea of bringing about such an adjustment by reducing government investment and accelerating the minidevaluations and domestic price revisions was aimed at increasing exports, but it neglected the fact that exports had declined the year before not because of internal problems of the economy, such as excess absorption, but because of a drop in external demand resulting from the international recession.

Second, the resistance of inflation to the overall demand cuts of the two previous years was insufficient to draw attention to the role of indexation in the dynamics of Brazilian inflation. The internal imbalances, of which inflation and the public deficit were seen as the most evident symptoms, would be fought with the Fund's usual medicine: the performance criteria represented by the ceilings on the nominal expansion of net domestic credit from the Monetary Authorities and of the financing requirements of the nonfinancial public sector.

Third, the targets for public sector financing requirements and net domestic credit of the Monetary Authorities were not only arbitrary, as noted by Bacha (1983), but also inadequate in view of Brazil's economic realities. As pointed out by Marques (1985, p. 30), the first letter of intent underestimated outstanding net domestic credit at the end of 1982 by 46 percent. This underestimate was corrected in the subsequent letters, but this did not prevent the year-end targets from being exceeded in each of the year's four letters of intent (except those of the second letter, which started with more realistic values that, however, were revised in the two subsequent letters). Moreover, a new definition of net domestic credit was used in the third and subsequent letters, in an attempt to take into account the fact that the liabilities of the Monetary Authorities included foreign currency deposits. After this revision of the definition, starting from September 15 (the third letter) the variable adopted (essentially the monetary base plus time deposits with the Monetary Authorities minus external reserves) was still completely inadequate even for the proposed objective of monetary control.[1] Continued discussions between Brazilian government and IMF officials led, beginning with the fifth letter on March 15, 1984, to the inclusion of targets for the monetary base and the money supply, reconciling the IMF's approach and the traditional prescriptions of Brazilian monetarists.

The fiscal policy side probably involved both the largest mistakes and the worst consequences for the level of activity (especially in 1983) and for the lack of coordination in Brazilian economic policy during the period. In the first place, the notion of public sector financing requirements itself had to be revised, as applied to the Brazilian economy, in order for the IMF to take into account the country's state financial complex. The concept adopted in successive arrangements was that of requirements of the nonfinancial public sector, leading to arbitrary classifications of types of debt as between the nonfinancial and financial public sectors in order to calculate an acceptable measure of the public deficit. For example, a change in a state bank's equity participation in a government enterprise would not result in a change in the deficit, but an injection of funds through financing would. Second, the IMF simply ignored the implications of the indexation of government bonds for the impact of inflation on the nominal change in public sector financing requirements.

With the second letter (February 24, 1983)—submitted by the Brazilian government even before the Fund's Executive Board could approve the first one, as a consequence of the major exchange devaluation of February 18—a debate began regarding the unfeasibility of the targets for the nominal public sector deficit and the magnitude of real fiscal contraction implicit in the nominal targets included in the performance criteria.[2] As inflationary pressures arising from the exchange devaluation became combined with a relative price increase favoring agriculture, it gradually became clear that the projected demand containment through fiscal restraint would not prevent an acceleration of inflation during 1983.[3]

In May the agreement with the Fund was suspended because of noncompliance with the fiscal targets. The turbulence caused by expectations of a new discrete devaluation and by difficulties in arranging new external financing fed a climate of uncertainty as the economy operated with negative net reserves and accumulated external payments in arrears.[4] On the economic policy side, the Brazilian government strove to reduce the level of indexation of the economy; it worked on no fewer than four wage policy laws during the year, adopted partial indexation for rents and certain public prices, and tried out a partial indexation for financial assets.

The attempts to reduce wage indexation had a dual purpose. On the one hand, they may well have been the most significant "unwritten conditionality" in Brazil's negotiating experience with the IMF to date. Not until Decree-Law 2045 was signed did it become possible to reach an agreement leading to signature of the third letter of intent (September 15, 1983), after the government centralized foreign exchange operations (Central Bank Resolution 851) to administer outward payments and thus prevent Brazilian borrowings from being declared in default pursuant to U.S. banking legislation. On the other hand, it was hoped that a smaller increase in public sector wages would lead to some reduction in terms of the public deficit.

Fourth and last, the period was characterized by strong exchange speculation. The surge of speculation with the dollar and indexed bonds dominated financial sector activities during practically the entire year, being fed by the opinions of several analysts who recommended a maxidevaluation. The exchange speculation contributed to the rise in interest rates and slackened only between the last quarter of 1983 and the first quarter of 1984. As 1983 came to an end, the gradual recovery of exports (which in December had already risen to 8.5 percent above the 1982 level) and the continued contraction of imports (–20.4 percent)—due to the exchange policy, the substitution of oil imports, and the decline in industrial activity —suggested that the external targets included in the agreement with creditors would be met despite the failures represented by the domestic goals (table 3). Signs of recovery in the U.S. economy supported more optimistic projections regarding world economic performance during the next year and encouraged setting a trade balance target of the order of $9 billion for the following year. The actual results obtained for the external accounts are shown in table 1, which reveals the magnitude of the adjustment in the trade balance, in the balance of real resources (which measures the excess of internal absorption over output), and in the current account of the balance of payments.

The trough of the recession that began in 1980 was reached in 1983, by which time Brazil's per capita income had experienced an overall loss of nearly 12 percent. Industrial output fell by 6 percent a year and industrial employment by 7.3 percent a year during the three years of the recession.

TABLE 3

Composition of Imports, 1979–85
(Millions of U.S. $, with percentages in parentheses)

YEAR	CONSUMER GOODS	INTERMEDIATE GOODS[a]	PETROLEUM	CAPITAL GOODS	TOTAL
1979	1786	12311	6264	3975	18072
(%)	(9.9)	(68.1)	(34.7)	(22.0)	(100.0)
1980	1387	16937	9372	4619	22943
(%)	(6.1)	(73.8)	(40.9)	(20.1)	(100.0)
1981	1106	16698	10604	4257	22061
(%)	(4.9)	(75.8)	(48.1)	(19.3)	(100.0)
1982	1014	14862	9566	3519	19295
(%)	(5.3)	(76.6)	(49.3)	(18.1)	(100.0)
1983	793	12130	7822	2505	15428
(%)	(5.2)	(78.6)	(50.1)	(16.2)	(100.0)
1984	695	11063	6736	2169	13927
(%)	(5.0)	(79.4)	(48.4)	(15.6)	(100.0)
1985	793	9880	5418	2477	13150
(%)	(6.0)	(75.1)	(41.2)	(18.9)	(100.0)

Sources: *Relatório CACEX* and FUNCEX.
a. Including petroleum.

The effect of the efforts of the IMF and the main creditor banks on the flow of private bank resources to the country was not sufficient to bring the external accounts into balance, although the current account deficit target was reached. Only half of the estimated $6.9 billion inflow of private capital was obtained, resulting in a negative net external reserve position of $3.3 billion (table 4).

Beginning with the fourth letter of intent, signed on November 14, 1983, the domestic goals were modified to include the notion of operational result of the public sector, which subtracted monetary and exchange correction payments on the outstanding public debt from the public sector's financing requirements. Using this new criterion, all the quarterly targets were met, except in the last quarter of 1984, when the target was an operational surplus equivalent to 0.5 percent of GDP, in comparison with a 1.9 percent deficit the year before.[5]

"Phase 2" of the Brazilian foreign debt renegotiation started in late 1983, when payments arrears still amounted to approximately $2.3 billion, including $1.3 billion in interest commitments. In com-

TABLE 4

Brazil: Financing of the Balance-of-Payments Deficit
(1982–84)
(Millions of U.S. $)

	1982	1983	1984
1. Refinancing	—	5246	6813[a]
2. Reserve-linked liabilities	4177	776	1796
• Bridge loans from foreign commercial banks	2257	—	—
• BIS	500	−500	—
• IMF compensatory financing	544	2152	1796
• U.S. Treasury	876	−876	—
3. Change in short-term liabilities of Monetary Authorities	—	(194)	(498)
4. Arrears	—	(2340)	(−2301)
5. Balance-of-payments deficit	8828	5737	1441
6. Change in external holdings of Monetary Authorities[b]	4651	−285	−7168

Source: *Relatórios do Banco Central.*
a. Of which US$ 2,089 million from the Paris Club and US$ 4,724 million under Project B
b. "−" equals increase in reserves.

parison with "Phase 1," the new renegotiation stage benefited from the fact that practically all those involved now started from the assumption that the difficulties concerning a normalization of international financial transactions with Brazil would persist for a few years, and this led to the adoption of new maturity horizons and to extension of the necessary reschedulings. In addition, three fronts now became involved in programming Brazil's external accounts: national governments that had granted or guaranteed loans to Brazil in the Paris Club; international financial institutions, including the World Bank and IDB; and private banks. A new version of the four projects of Phase 1 was presented to the private creditors: the New Money Facility Agreement, bringing together some $6.5 billion in new loans from 792 creditor banks; Project 2, or Deposit Facility Agreement, coordinated by Citibank and involving the rollover of $5.4 billion in principal repayments falling due in 1984 to some 554 banks; Project 3, or Trade Facility Agreement, coordinated by Chase Manhattan and involving maintenance of marketing credit lines by 231 creditor banks in a total of $10.3 billion; and Project 4, or Interbank Facility Agreement, coordinated by Bankers Trust and involving approximately $6 billion in interbank market operations and 275 private banks.[6]

Thanks primarily to the gains in the trade balance during the first few months of the year—the first-quarter surplus of $2.5 billion compared favorably with $828 million in the same period of the previous year—there was a substantial improvement in the Monetary Authorities' reserve position. In addition, the positive signs of external adjustment, together with some improvement in tax collections in early 1984, meant that the fifth letter of intent could be negotiated with practically no major conflict. In the second quarter of 1984, for the first time since the signing of the first agreement with the IMF, Brazil complied with all clauses.

By the end of the year the final balance of payments data surpassed even the most optimistic expectations as the trade balance posted a surplus in excess of $13 billion, and it became possible not only to settle outstanding payments arrears but also to accumulate $7.2 billion in net reserves (table 4). With the recovery of the industrial sector—induced by exports, the recovery of private consumption following upon larger wage increases for the middle class, and larger industrial purchases by the agricultural sector, which since the end of the previous year had enjoyed a significant favorable trend in relative prices—the nation's economic activity as a whole also recovered, resulting in GDP growth of roughly 4.5 percent during the year.

The international stimulus made it possible to activate the additional productive capacity that had been created by export production and import substitution projects. The decline of the import ratio in 1984 despite the economic recovery indicated that the structural adjustment of productive capacity was finally ready to bear fruit and contribute to redressing the external accounts of the Brazilian economy.[7]

As the year neared a close, approaches were begun to put together what was known as Phase 3 of the foreign debt renegotiation. Now that the emergency situation had been overcome—even if normalcy had not been restored in international financial intermediation—the aim was to design a debt-rescheduling program for the next few years which would permit doing away with the painful negotiations with hundreds of private banks as had occurred in the two previous years. As the sixth letter of intent was approved in September, there were already clear indications that some of the targets set for the end of the month would not be met and that the country would certainly not comply with the year-end objectives.

All attempts to implement the monetary policy package approved in September were frustrated until the end of the year by the impossibility of drastically cutting monetary and fiscal expansion amidst the internal dissension in the government party, which had won a majority in the electoral college but would later fail to elect the President because it could not find a candidate capable of uniting his own party. On the external front, divergences between the Brazilian government and the representatives of creditor banks as to the rescheduling terms which prevented their reaching a common ground before publication of the year-end monetary and fiscal policy outcome prevented the seventh letter from being approved in January.[8]

Rejection of the seventh letter in January led to the second suspension of the agreement with the Fund. Once the new administration took office on March 15, the traumatic aftermath of the President-elect's death led to a longer-than-expected delay in negotiations with the IMF. As a result, the Phase 3 agreement remained suspended because of the banks' insistence on making a debt re-scheduling conditional on approval of a program with the Fund. Negotiations toward a new agreement with the Fund were still under way at the beginning of 1986.

The next section examines Brazilian economic prospects for the next few years of the 1980s and the sensitivity of the country's external accounts to changes in international conditions.

EXTERNAL DEBT PROJECTIONS

An important aspect of the economic recovery that began in 1984 was that it was achieved without interrupting the fall in the import ratio or compromising the ability to export. These are the most significant signs of the success of the structural adjustment that had been taking place in the Brazilian economy since the first oil shock. When examining the outlook for Brazil's foreign debt, it is important to ask to what extent these favorable signs can be projected into the future.

In the area of import performance, the declining dependence on imported petroleum, in conjunction with the price fall, has been a favorable element. Other imports were also reduced as the major import substitution projects begun in the Geisel administration reached maturity. In aggregate terms, there is evidence of further room to prolong the favorable behavior of the import ratio, provided the exchange policy and the investments encouraged during the period of the exchange crisis are retained.

On the export side, the increase of 1985 was followed by a 5.1 percent decline in 1985, more as a result of demand-side reasons than of the impact of increased capacity utilization. The slowdown of growth in the United States and the rise in protectionism in traditional markets were certainly the most important factors behind the drop in exports. The 1986 trade balance will be sufficient to keep interest payments current, however. If the present policy of investing in the export sector is kept in effect, the main constraints on the growth of foreign exchange availability for the Brazilian economy will be defined by events largely beyond the control of Brazilian economic policy.

From the standpoint of external equilibrium, it may be said

that the country's debt remained under control during the last two years despite the fact that external debt interest payments represented 4.6 percent of GDP and 37 percent of exports in 1986. In spite of the growth of the product, the current account remained practically in balance, reflecting a trade surplus of nearly 6 percent of GDP and an outward transfer of real resources (defined as net exports of goods and services) exceeding 5 percent of GDP.

We may ask how likely it is that the indicators of improvement in the country's external accounts will continue unchanged over coming years, given minimally acceptable output and employment conditions.

In the first place, it is essential, after three years of precarious negotiations on the external debt, that capital payments falling due in coming years be rescheduled. Foreign creditors as well as the Brazilian authorities seem perfectly aware that it will be impossible for the country to generate the current account surpluses necessary to meet principal repayment installments due in coming years. The profiles resulting from the payments extensions granted between mid-1982 and late 1985 only *worsened* the problem of maturity shortening that had been affecting the country since the beginning of the 1980s.[9] Consequently, *from the standpoint of the debt profile*, it may be said that, pending a definitive debt rescheduling agreement with the international banks, today's external debt problem *is graver than in 1982*, when the payments crisis exploded. In addition, *given that there is a consensus* among creditors that a payments rescheduling along the lines of the one negotiated with the Mexican government would be sufficient to push away the ghost of a new Brazilian external payments crisis for the next few years, it may be said that prospects are good for the conclusion of some kind of agreement by 1987.

The banks' current requirement for accepting a formal rescheduling is that Brazil sign a new agreement with the IMF. Present disagreements between the Brazilian government and Fund staff pertain to the economy's domestic adjustment variables, particularly with the conditionalities related to financing needs of the public sector and net domestic credit of the Monetary Authorities, that is, economic policy objectives that directly affect *domestic* macroeconomic variables. However, the experience of recent years suggests that—barring new developments on the international scene that radically change the prevailing rules of the game—the solution will once again be political in nature and may be made easier by the results of the anti-inflation program.

Second, assuming that the present divergences between the Brazilian government and the IMF will be satisfactorily resolved or, alternatively, that a rescheduling of the Brazilian debt will be possible in the next few years without the ritual of an agreement with the Fund, one must inquire into the sensitivity of Brazil's external accounts in the near future to changes in the exogenous variables of the international economy.

Using a simulation model for the Brazilian economy, we made projections for a number of variables illustrating Brazil's external debt for the period 1986–90, namely, the trade balance, current account balance, net interest payments, two ratios indicating the debt path (net debt over merchandise exports and net debt over gross domestic product), and a measure of the domestic effort required by the need to service the debt through net transfers of real resources to the rest of the world (net exports of goods and services as a proportion of domestic product). Debt projections (gross medium- and long-term debt minus reserves) were made in nominal terms, assuming that the dollar inflation rate would be 6 percent in 1986, fall to 5 percent during the next two years, and rise again to 6 percent in the last two years of the simulation period.[10]

For exchange policy, it was assumed that purchasing power parity would be maintained, thus presupposing that the exchange rate will be devalued in proportion to U.S. inflation. Export and import prices were assumed to parallel the inflation of the dollar, bringing to an end the deterioration of the terms of trade, which since 1977 have fallen by about 40 percent including petroleum and 27 percent excluding petroleum. As the slight recovery trend seen in 1984 does not seem to have been confirmed in 1985, we opted for the neutrality hypothesis. Substitution of imported oil continues in accordance with available output projections for the end of the decade. Since investment on prospection and substitution was begun in 1975, in conjunction with policies aimed at energy conservation, Brazil has succeeded in reducing its dependence on oil imports, and it may very well attain self-sufficiency before the end of the 1990s. At the time of the first oil shock, domestic production covered some 20 percent of consumption; this year it is expected to supply nearly

60 percent. Even despite the rising incomes of the last two years, consumption has been falling as petroleum is being replaced by automotive alcohol in individual transportation and by electricity and coal in the generation of industrial heat. Assumptions used in the projections presuppose that domestic oil production will increase by 8 percent a year in the near future. International prices are assumed to parallel the inflation of the dollar from 1986 on. Finally, since the economic recovery begun in 1984, the Brazilian economy has shown that it can make use of the room for growth afforded by the adjustment in the external accounts. In the projections, the level of aggregate demand is maintained so as to allow domestic output growth of 8.3 percent in 1985, falling to 6.6 percent in 1986, and rising to 7 percent in 1987 and 1988, followed by a slight decline in the rate of growth of domestic demand in the closing years of the decade.

The following additional hypotheses were adopted in our base simulation. 1) The average interest applicable to the previous year's net debt equals 13 percent in 1986 and 14 percent in 1987 and then declines to 12 percent in the last years of the decade. This variable, defined as interest payments (including interest on the short-term debt) divided by net debt at the end of the previous year, peaked at 21 percent in 1982 before declining to its present level of roughly 13 percent. 2) The world import volume index was projected to rise by 2 percent in 1986, remain stable in 1987, and increase by 3 percent a year during the last three years of the simulation period. To furnish an idea of this hypothesis, the average expansion of world imports has been declining over the last three five-year periods, from 7.7 percent in 1968–73 to 5.6 percent in 1973–78 and only 1.1 percent in 1978–83. In spite of the strong recovery of trade in 1984, the rate of growth declined in 1985 and may fall even further in 1986. Given the catastrophic consequences that a continued slowdown in world trade until the end of the decade would entail for the Third World's debt, a modest recovery was assumed for the last years of the projection period. It should be noted, however, that this hypothesis means an average growth rate of 2.4 percent in 1985–89, well below the one adopted in available projections contained in official reports of major international institutions.

Table 5 shows the results of the base simulation. Under the hypotheses adopted, net external debt in nominal terms reaches a peak in 1987 and declines to approximately $75 billion in 1990. Product growth rates are consistent with the generation of trade balances in excess of interest payment requirements. The chosen debt indicators—namely, net debt over exports and net debt as a proportion of GDP—improve substantially during the period: net debt over exports, which reached a maximum of 3.5 in 1983, falls to below 2.0 starting in 1989, to approximately the level of the early 1970s. Relative to gross product, it also rises to 27.6 percent in 1986 and then gradually declines to 16 percent by the end of the decade. Finally, projections are shown for transfers of net resources to the rest of the world, measured in terms of net exports of goods and services. As a proportion of the product, they decline from 3.3 percent in 1986 to 2.3 percent at the end of the period, allowing the economy's investment rate to recover gradually in the course of the decade even without a major saving effort.

The other simulations, shown in tables 6 and 7, are variants of the base simulation under more pessimistic assumptions regarding interest rates and world trade performance. Simulation 1 (table 6) investigates the consequences of a 2.5 percentage point rise in

TABLE 5

Base Simulation
(Fourth Quarter, 1985)

	1986	1987	1988	1989	1990
Trade Balance[a]	12.5	12.6	13.6	14.5	15.0
Current Account[a]	-0.9	-1.9	0.2	0.9	1.4
Net Debt (ND)[a]	81.4	82.0	80.3	77.9	74.9
Net Interest[a]	10.6	11.4	9.8	9.6	9.3
Net Debt/Exports	2.8	2.6	2.3	2.0	1.8
ND/GDP[b]	27.6	24.6	21.5	18.3	16.0
NX/GDP[b c]	3.3	2.9	2.7	2.5	2.3

a. in current dollars
b. in percent
c. NX : net exports
   ND : net debt
(See text for explanations)

the interest rate in the first year of the simulation, followed by a return to the levels assumed for the base scenario. Comparing simulation 1 to the base scenario, the immediate consequence would be an increase in the current account deficit to almost $3 billion in 1986 and $2.2 billion in 1987. The net debt peak rises by $2 billion in 1987, and the end-of-period debt increases by some $3 billion. This simulation illustrates circumstances under which Brazil may require marginal amounts of additional borrowing from private creditors in 1986 and 1987, if compensatory facilities are not established with international financial institutions in the event of a renewed rise in international interest rates.

The last simulation explores the effect of conditions less propicious to Brazilian export growth due to an unfavorable international trade performance. Table 7 shows the consequences of a trade expansion path 1 percentage point below the assumption used in the base simulation. In this case, the decline in net debt at the end

TABLE 6

Simulation 1

	1986	1987	1988	1989	1990
Trade Balance	12.5	12.6	13.6	14.5	15.0
Current Account	−2.9	−2.2	−0.0	0.7	1.0
Net Debt	83.4	84.3	82.9	80.8	78.2
Net Interest	12.7	11.7	10.1	10.0	9.7
Net Debt/Exports	2.9	2.7	2.4	2.1	1.9
ND/GDP	28.6	25.7	22.2	19.2	16.5
NX/GDP	3.4	2.9	2.7	2.5	2.3

TABLE 7

Simulation 2 (Lower trade 1986–90)

	1986	1987	1988	1989	1990
Trade Balance	12.3	12.1	12.8	13.5	13.6
Current Account	−1.1	−2.4	−0.5	−0.2	−0.3
Net Debt	81.6	82.6	81.8	80.5	79.2
Net Interest	10.6	11.4	9.9	9.8	9.8
Net Debt/Exports	2.9	2.7	2.4	2.2	2.0
ND/GDP	28.1	25.2	21.9	19.2	16.8
NX/GDP	3.3	2.8	2.5	2.3	2.0

of the period is some $5 billion less than the estimate obtained in the base simulation. Refinancing requirements during the period will be larger because of the smaller trade surpluses; in addition, maintaining the unfavorable debt indicators for a longer period makes it more difficult to bring about a resumption of voluntary lending.

All three simulations show that even under unfavorable trade conditions—provided that minimum conditions of compatibility between interest rates and trade expansion hold, keeping the Third World's external debt from exploding—Brazil's external debt outlook is consistent with a recovery of economic growth without a worsening of the principal indicators.

Last, one should ask about the degree of feasibility of the hypotheses adopted regarding output growth rates to the end of the decade, considering the observed decline in the investment rate since the end of the 1970s. Without going into too much detail, we can state that preliminary estimates indicate that idle capacity was approximately 21 percent in 1984, the base year of the projections. The conservative assumptions that an investment rate of approximately 16 percent of GDP will be maintained through the end of the decade and that the capital-output ratio will be 3.3 lead to the conclusion that the growth rates implicit in the projection scenarios adopted here would imply a capacity utilization increase below 10 percentage points.[11] In other words, the transfer of real resources to the rest of the world at the envisaged levels is consistent with the adopted growth hypotheses from the standpoint of pressures on domestic saving, given the underutilization of productive capacity resulting from the recession of 1981–83.

CONCLUSIONS

Brazil's external debt outlook can be deemed reasonably favorable in that the economic growth projected for the near future is not likely to require further borrowing from private banks, given a minimally favorable development of the world economy. The basic assumptions leading to this conclusion are as follows: 1) the current renegotiation phase will be successfully concluded in 1986, with creditor banks agreeing to debt rollover terms at least similar to those granted to Mexico in December 1984; 2) the country's investment effort will be mobilized in such a way as to permit maintaining export capacity and import substitution; 3) interest and trade terms do not violate the requirements of consistency between the need to service the debt and trade opportunities; and 4) there is no new round of recessive policies in an attempt to control inflation and the government's accounts.

Comparison of policies aimed at absorbing domestic absorption with and without IMF surveillance, emerging from the analysis in the second section of this paper, does not show any superiority for adjustment with surveillance. Given that the principal arguments in favor of IMF surveillance pertain to the needs of the "domestic" adjustment, as the economy's external accounts have been brought under control, special attention was devoted to the role of the "domestic conditionalities" during the period 1983–84. It can be concluded that the successive letters of intent signed with the Fund did not help make economic policy more rational, and that the continuing renegotiation efforts induced strong financial and exchange speculation. The disruption introduced by the uncertainties of the quarterly judgments of compliance with the targets and of the requests for waivers, in conjunction with the significance of the "unwritten conditionalities" such as the ones that led to successive changes in wage policy in 1983, makes it difficult to accept the argument that the Fund's presence contributed to greater "stability" of the economy. The recession was deeper, the relative price adjustments contributed to higher inflation, and the financial market suffered from great instability as a result of the uncertainty generated by the periodic attempts to comply with—or to create the impression of compliance with—inappropriate targets for net domestic credit. The outcome of this uncertainty was a higher financing cost for the government deficit, due to the increase in the risk premiums implicit in the effective interest rates on government securities.

The performance criteria as a whole were devoid of economic sense, as their specification ignored the special characteristics of the government financial sector of the Brazilian economy. Systematic ignorance of the details of the economic policy instruments in Brazil, together with prejudices concerning trade liberalization and the role of the government in promoting long-term adjustment, prevented the diagnosis or the formulation of the criteria from playing a favorable role in improving the very thing in which the creditors were most interested, that is, the debt prospects, and did not contribute to a better understanding of the required domestic adjustment.

Brazil's recent experience with the IMF does not seem favorable, according to the "Williamson criteria" (Williamson, 1983). Under present circumstances, it is difficult to identify the advantages to private creditors of the Fund's intermediation in the renegotiation of Brazil's external debt.

In conclusion, the Brazilian experience illustrates the importance that selective policies for import control and substitution coupled with export promotion had for the adaptation of the Brazilian economy to the constraints of the international economy after the first oil shock. It also stresses the importance of the role of the Brazilian government in promoting this strategy, which succeeded in simultaneously reducing the import ratio and increasing the export ratio. Thanks to the structural change brought about by the investment program of the 1970s, the results of Brazil's external borrowing point toward an economy whose external sector is less fragile and which will be able to resume a path of long-term economic growth with less risk of exchange collapse in comparison with the situation prevailing at the end of the 1970s.

NOTES

The author thanks Sonia Olinto for her help in editing and preparing the simulation in the second section of this paper.

1. See Marques (1985), p. 25.

2. On these subjects, see, for example, Bacha (1983), Carneiro and Modiano (1983), and Werneck (1983).

3. Inflation accelerated from 99.7 percent in 1982 to 211 percent in 1983. For an analysis of the role of the exchange and agricultural shocks in this acceleration, see Modiano (1984).

4. Central Bank Report, 1983.

5. The change in the criterion for measuring the degree of austerity in the management of government finance is a good illustration of the extent to which the IMF surveillance can be "flexible." After a long debate, it became clear that the nominal NFPS targets were ridiculous, given the indexation of the public debt. The Fund agreed to adopt the new criterion but explicitly included the inflation rate as a target and imposed an ex-

tremely restrictive ceiling on the operational surplus. This bypassed the technical difficulties but did not in practice imply a softening of the conditions. Difficulties persisted in relation to the net domestic credit targets, and, as quarterly discussions were held about the measurement of performance, very short-term monitoring became virtually institutionalized during 1984.

6. See *Gazeta Mercantil*, January 31, 1984.

7. For a more detailed look at this adjustment, which took place during the second half of the 1970s, see Carneiro (1985). Some indicators of the effects on external sector variables are shown in table 2.

8. The main divergences had to do with: the duration and amount involved in the rescheduling (as the banks wanted to exclude maturities that had already been extended in Phases 1 and 2, which would imply reducing the amount of payments to be rescheduled from the $51 billion desired by the government to $37 billion; the payment period (16 versus 14 years) and whether or not there should be a grace period; and, lastly, the spread, which Brazil insisted should be the same as adopted in the Mexican renegotiation (1.125 percent above LIBOR). See *Gazeta Mercantil*, December 26, 1984.

9. Especially if the position initially adopted by the creditor banks in the 1984 negotiations should prevail, in other words, that the amounts renewed in Phases 1 and 2 of the adjustment program should not be included in the rescheduling.

10. In 1985, the first year of the simulation, the short-term debt was estimated at approximately $16 billion, total reserves at roughly $12 billion, and net medium- and long-term debt at $77.4 billion.

11. See capital-output ratio estimates in Díaz-Alejandro (1984).

REFERENCES

Bacha, E. 1983. Vicissitudes of Recent Stabilization Attempts in Brazil and the IMF Alternative. In J. Williamson, ed., *IMF Conditionality*. Washington, D.C.: Institute for International Economics.

Central Bank Report. 1983. Various issues.

Carneiro, D.D. 1985. Long-run Adjustment, Debt Crisis, and the Changing Role of Stabilization in Policies in the Brazilian Recent Experience. *Texto para Duscussão No. 109*, Departamento de Economia, PUJ/RJ.

Carneiro, D.D., and E. Modiano. 1983. Inflação e controle do déficit público: análise teórica e algumas simulações para a economia brasileira. *Revista Brasileira de Economia*. Rio de Janeiro, No. 4, December.

Díaz-Alejandro, C.F. 1984. Latin American Debt: I Don't Think We Are in Kansas Anymore. Brookings Papers on Economic Activity, 1:1983.

Marques, M. S. B. 1985. FMI: a experiência brasileira recente. 1 versão (mimeo). Rio de Janeiro: FGV.

Modiano, E. 1984. Salários, preços e câmbios: os multiplicadores dos choques numa economia indexada. *Texto para Discussão No. 70*, Departamento de Economia, PUC/RJ.

Werneck, R. 1983. A armadilha financeira do setor público e as empresas estatais. In A. Mourna de Silva et al, *FMI X Brasil, a Armadilha da recessão*. Sao Paulo: *Gazeta Mercantil*.

Williamson, J. 1983. On Judging the Success of the IMF Policy Advice. In J. Williamson, ed., *IMF Conditionality*. Washington, D.C.: Institute for International Economics.

Comments

RICARDO INFANTE*

According to the information presented, by Dionisio Días Carneiro, conditions were created in Brazil to maintain a "balance-of-payments structural surplus" in the future.[1] The point of my comments is that while the external sector of the economy was structurally adjusted, internal imbalances were created, resulting in an increase in the country's "social debt." To analyze the current situation from this perspective it will be necessary to illustrate briefly how the various agents of production performed during the period of adjustment and economic stabilization between 1980 and 1984.

With respect to the external sector, although overall balance was achieved in current transactions in the past year,[2] the performance of the principal agents involved was widely disparate. In fact, the said overall balance was attained in 1984 with a private sector surplus counterbalanced by a public sector current account deficit of equal magnitude, totaling some $13 billion.[3] Therefore, while it can be argued that the overall economy has a balance-of-payments structural surplus, the same cannot be said of the public sector, which is operating under conditions of external restriction. Moreover, the public sector, which contributes 20 percent of the GDP, accounts for 75 percent of the external debt, so that the ratio of indebtedness in this case amounts to 480 percent of the product.

The *public sector* implemented a series of policies aimed at closing the said external gap. The measures adopted created a genuine spiral between inflation and public deficit. The principal corrective measures consisted in implementing a periodic system of

---

*Expert at the Regional Employment Project for Latin America and the Caribbean (PREALC), Santiago.

devaluations, high real interest rates, and a regressive wage policy in the context of a highly indexed economy.

The increase of real interest rates meant that the impact of the financial costs on the total cost of the *productive enterprises* rose significantly. This phenomenon was only partially offset by a reduction in the weight of operating costs (wages or inputs) and the net profit margins of the productive enterprises.[4] Finally, during the adjustment period, the financial sectors increased their income share, in real terms, to the detriment of other productive agents, that is, the public and private corporate sector.

The impact of the external adjustment policy on the *labor sector* can be visualized through the behavior, on the one hand, of the labor markets and, on the other, by the social spending policy of the government. Various studies[5] show that the said policy led to a process of disintegration in the work force. This was revealed by an increase in open unemployment, a reduction in the volume of employment in the modern sectors, a significant rise in the degree of informalization among the employed, and, finally, an increase in hidden unemployment or the number of "discouraged workers" in the work force.[6] Concomitantly, the policy of wage disindexation led to a reduction in real average wages. This, together with the reduction in modern employment, meant that between 1980 and 1983 total real wages experienced a decline (−16 percent) that exceeded the reduction in domestic income (−3 percent). The foregoing indicates that the income share of modern wage-earners fell by 13 percent because of the increased impact of the financial sector on production. Furthermore, the policy of reducing the fiscal deficit led to decreases, in real terms, in both public employee wages and government social spending.[7]

In short, the social debt increased during the external adjustment period as a result of the disintegration of the work force, the drop in real wages, and the decline in real income in the labor sector, caused by the cutbacks in public social spending. Considering the number of workers either unemployed or earning less than the monthly minimum wage as an approximate measure, the social debt in urban areas rose from 10 million people in 1981 to 11.6 million in 1984.[8] In other words, in 1984 the social debt equalled 31 percent of the urban work force.

On the basis of this information it is argued that upon having achieved a "balance-of-payments structural surplus," Brazil's major challenge in the immediate future will be to reduce its social debt. Progress will be made in this direction only insofar as a development strategy is adopted that promotes structural adjustment of an internal nature, in which the high growth rate called for in Carneiro's paper has a clearly distributive orientation.

NOTES

1. That is, the economic structure was adjusted in order to generate a trade surplus sufficient to cover the financial costs of the external debt.

2. During that year, the country showed a positive trade balance of $13 billion, while payments for the financial costs of the debt and remittances abroad totaled $12.8 billion (Carneiro, in this volume).

3. According to DEPEC/BACEN estimates (1986).

4. According to MTb/OIT 1985b, the financial costs of the public and private enterprises, which represented 6.5 percent of the value of production in 1978, rose to 27.3 percent in 1983. Operating costs (wages and inputs), however, fell from 18.2 percent in the first year to 8.5 percent in the second. Finally, net profit margins declined from 12.6 percent in 1978 to 7 percent in 1983.

5. See Camargo, 1985; Infante, 1985; and Jatobá, 1985.

6. According to MTb/OIT 1985d, modern employment declined by one million jobs between 1980 and 1983. During these years the rate of urban unemployment rose from 4 to 6 percent.

7. According to MTb/OIT 1985c, it is estimated that the decline in average real government wages reached 27 percent between 1980 and 1983. Similarly, aggregate social spending fell by 18 percent in real terms between 1980 and 1984.

8. Estimates based on FIBGE/PNAD 1981 and 1984. Since the work force grew at an annual rate of 3.8 percent, the social debt increased annually during these years by some 5 percent.

REFERENCES

Camargo, J. M. 1985. Politica de renda e ajuste macro-económico. Ministerio de Trabalho, *Mercado de Trabalho*, Brasilia, June.

DEPEC/BACEN. 1986. Evolução da composição sectorial do balanço de pagamentos brasileiro 1980–84 (Texto preliminar). Banco Central do Brazil, Departamento Economico, Brasilia, January.

FGV. 1985. *Conjuntura Económica*. Fundação Getulio Vargas, April.

Fundação Instituto Brasileiro de Geografia e Estadistica (FIBGE). *Pesquisa nacional por amostre de domicilios: Brasil e grandes regiões* (PNAD). Rio de Janeiro, 1981, 1984.

Infante, R. 1985. Brasil: características estructurais dos mercados de trabalho urbanos. ANPEC, *XIII Encontro Nacional de Economía*, vol. 2, Brazil, December.

Jatoba, J. 1985. Desenvolvimento regional, crise e mercados de trabalho: caso brasileiro con especial atenção para o nordeste, 1981–83. (Mimeo) PIMES, Recife.

Ministerio de Trabajo. Secretaria de Empleo y Salarios. Proyecto PNUD/ OIT-BRA/82026 (MTb/OIT) 1985a. Impactos da política de estabilização sobre a situación economica do sector trabalho. *Documento Técnico* No. POL-20, Brasilia.

_____. 1985b. Indicadores de costo e margem de lucro sectorais. Documento Técnico No. ISR-01, Brasilia.

_____. 1985c. Evolução da massa real e parcela salarial do setor organizado do mercado de trabalho: 1980–83. *Documento Técnico* ISR-07, Brasilia.

_____. 1985d. Metodología e estimativas de emprego 1979–83, a partir de Paneis Fixos para pares de años consecutivos de RAIS. *Documento Técnico* SIE-26, Brasilia.

The Costa Rican Experience with the International Debt Crisis

CARLOS MANUEL CASTILLO*

Costa Rica suffered the economic impact of what would come to be known as the International Debt Crisis before the problem came to be recognized as worldwide and structural. Although the crisis is due to global forces beyond the country's control, the impact on Costa Rica was compounded by mistaken economic policies that were the consequence of a failure to recognize the fundamental shift in the world economic order.

From a position of economic stability and prosperity in 1977, Costa Rica began its downward path in 1978 as public foreign debt increased, foreign exchange reserves dwindled, inflation rose up, and the exchange rate spiraled upward. The two factors driving this accelerating decline were 1) on the international level, deterioration in the country's terms of trade, the rise in oil prices, and interest rate instability, and 2) on the domestic level, a government policy of increasingly uncontrolled public spending, and of using domestic and foreign credit to finance the deficits.

The breakdown of the economy occurred in 1981. Inflation reached triple digits and the exchange rate went out of control, devaluing the currency by over 500 percent. Completely out of dollar reserves and with foreign credit cut off, Costa Rica suspended both principal and interest payments on its foreign debt.

Costa Rica's regularly scheduled elections were held in February 1982, and a new government took office in May. A team of well-qualified professionals was appointed to key economic positions —

Former president of the Central Bank and of the National Assembly, San José.

Central Bank, Treasury Ministry, and a newly created, cabinet-level Foreign Debt Portfolio. The distinguishing characteristic of the new economic team's approach was a determination to gain control over the situation and guide the economy toward purposefully defined objectives. This implied vigorous action on several fronts simultaneously. A decision was made in favor of a "shock treatment" approach over gradualism in the implementation of specific measures, while at the same time a commitment was made to protect the weakest groups from the ravages of both the crisis and the measures necessary to cope with it.

Five specific objectives were decided upon as keys to gaining control over the crisis: 1) reorganization, stabilization, and unification of the foreign exchange market; 2) substantial reduction of the government budget deficit; 3) an incomes policy to manage the adjustment of prices and wages; 4) a return to a contractual basis for the servicing of all public sector foreign debt, by means of formally rescheduling debt repayment with all creditors; and 5) negotiation of an agreement with the International Monetary Fund and renewal of funds inflows from multinational entities and friendly governments.

By the end of 1983, the program showed remarkable results: 1) the exchange rate, which devalued over 500 percent between 1980 and 1982, was stabilized—the two-tiered exchange system in force when the current administration took office was eliminated, and the exchange rate was unified at 43 colons to the dollar, after having reached 65 colons to the dollar on the free tier in July 1982; 2) inflation was reduced from 100 percent in 1982 to 8 percent at the end of 1983; 3) the government budget deficit was reduced from 20 percent of GDP in 1982 to 4 percent in 1983; 4) unemployment was reduced from 12 to 8.9 percent, with the minimum wage regaining pre-crisis levels of real purchasing power; and 5) Costa Rica's public sector foreign debt had been renegotiated, was back on a fully contractual basis, and payments under the new terms were current.

In assessing the reasons behind this success, it is necessary to look beyond solely economic considerations, and incorporate political and social aspects into the analysis. Broadly, the success was due to the cooperative forces applied by a vigorous democracy united against a threat to its economic survival. But specific points that contributed to stabilization and recovery can also be cited: 1) the awareness of the people that a grave crisis was at hand and their willingness to endure the harsh measures necessary to cope with it; 2) a timely election before it was too late, and the people's overwhelming electoral mandate to the new economic team; 3) the speedy organization of an economic policy team; 4) the effectiveness of the "shock treatment" approach to the application of specific policy measures; and 5) the policy determination to put a floor under the socially destructive repercussions of the crisis.

Yet despite the success in stabilizing the economy, Costa Rica remains a poorer country than in pre-crisis days, with both lowered living standards and expectations for the majority of its people. Overcoming economic stagnation is proving to be an intractable problem. An agenda for the remainder of the 1980s to build a foundation for sustained social and economic betterment in the 1990s should include proportioning debt service payments to the capabilities of the economy, restructuring and revitalization of private sector companies, a proper industrial policy emphasizing exports, and a diversified market orientation aimed at exports to all world markets.

FROM STABILITY AND PROSPERITY TO INFLATION AND UNEMPLOYMENT

Costa Rica's principal economic indicators were at what would prove to be a healthy peak in early 1978. GDP was growing at close to 10 percent per annum, unemployment stood at 3.5 percent of the labor force, inflation was measured at around 4 percent by the consumer price index, and the colon–dollar exchange rate was stable. Monetary reserves were at an all-time high of $360 million, a level of 129 days' worth of imports based on the previous year's import level. This was the economic picture as Costa Rica emerged from the crises of the 1970s—the money crisis in 1971, oil in 1973–74, food and raw materials in 1974. The policies that allowed the country to overcome these crises were based on creating stability and a favorable atmosphere for private and public investment, and on a program of balancing the rural and urban portions of the economy by means of substantial income transfers. Also, there was substantial outside help from record coffee export prices in 1975 and 1976.

The external underpinnings for continued prosperity began to deteriorate after 1978. The merchandise terms of trade index, from a base of 100 in 1977, declined to 82 in 1978 and 67 in 1981. The second energy crisis hit hard, with an increase in the price of oil of almost 300 percent. Interest rates on loans from foreign banks rose to unprecedented heights, while repayment periods in the international financial markets shortened. A full-fledged international economic crisis was obviously breaking upon Costa Rica, and appropriate measures of adjustment, to be implemented immediately, were called for.

Unfortunately, the policy responses adopted went in exactly the opposite direction of what was called for. Public expenditure continued to increase at a rapid pace, with a decreasing proportion going to capital formation. From 1978 to 1981 the public sector deficit increased from 8.8 to 14.3 percent of GDP, and the percentage of total banking system credit absorbed by the government increased from 27.5 to 44.5 percent. At the same time, government borrowing abroad was stepped up and used increasingly to finance a shift of government expenditure away from productive use and toward debt financing of the public sector budget deficit, at increasing rates of interest and with shortening repayment schedules.

From 1977 to 1981 external public debt increased at an accelerating pace, with loss of control toward the end of this period. In 1977, total foreign debt stood at $877 million, a level equal to 106 percent of that year's exports and to 35 percent of GDP, calculated at the then stable exchange rate of 8.6 colons to the dollar. By 1981 debt had climbed to $2.362 billion, or 234 percent of yearly exports. Because of the instability of the exchange rate in that year, beginning at 14.23 colons to the dollar in January and increasing to 38.27, with a strong upward trend in December, precise calculations of foreign debt in relation to GDP became difficult. And the foreign debt burden became more onerous in terms as well as in amount. Average maturity of contracted debt fell from 15 years to 9 years. Average grace periods decreased from 5.4 to 3.5 years. The average interest rate went from 8.7 to 10.8 percent.

When internal credit sources dried up because of preemption

of local currency bank funds by the government, the private sector was forced to increase foreign borrowing, if available, on similarly less favorable terms. Not surprisingly, capital formation decreased in real terms by 25 percent, in contrast to a growth rate of 8 percent in 1978. And as public economic and monetary policy began to zigzag, adding to the increase in overall uncertainty caused by intensification of the Central American political conflict, a brake was put on production and investment.

These tragically mistaken policy responses were rooted in the erroneous hypothesis that the negative turn of events in the international economy was of a cyclical nature and that, sooner rather than later, all or most of the unfavorable trends would reverse themselves and return to what had been previously conceived as normality. This hypothesis failed to perceive that, this time, the crisis was structural and, therefore, permanent in nature. The fundamental fact was that the accumulation of changes growing out of the monetary, energy, and financial crises of the 1970s amounted to the establishment of new international economic conditions much harsher than the already difficult ones that had prevailed before.

The economy went into a downward spiral from 1978 to 1981. Consumer prices rose by 6, 9, 18, and then 37 percent per annum. Net international monetary reserves dwindled to $160 million, $60 million, –$139 million, and –$185 million, in spite of the continuous heavy inflow of foreign loans.

The breakdown came in mid-1981. Foreign exchange reserves ran out completely, foreign lending to Costa Rica came to an abrupt end, and the country had to suspend payments of both principal and interest on public foreign debt. Massive devaluation of the colon ensued, and the country's ability to normally conduct business abroad became greatly impaired. During the second half of 1981 and the first half of 1982, the exchange rate went completely out of control and rose continually, reaching unprecedented heights and fueling near triple-digit inflation. People despaired of the possibility of regaining control of the economy and, as uncertainty expanded, a widespread fear for Costa Rica's social stability and democratic political system took hold.

In mid-1982, when the new administration took charge of the government, the economic situation was as follows: the exchange rate in the so-called free market had risen over 500 percent, increasing from 8.6 to over 48 colons to the dollar, and soon going up to over 65 to the dollar; the annual rate of inflation had gone over 100 percent; the government budget deficit was approaching 20 percent of GDP; 12 percent of the labor force was unemployed; GDP was on its way to decreasing 9 percent from 1981; and the government had been in arrears for almost a full year on the service of its foreign debt.

THE RETURN TO STABILITY

Objectives and approaches

Determined to control what had become a desperate situation, the newly appointed authorities focused on two fundamental objectives: to eradicate inflation from the domestic economy, and to rejoin the international financial community by putting Costa Rican public external debt service back on a contractual basis. This dual approach was directed to attack, on the one hand, the number one cause of economic instability and, on the other, what was thought to be the principal barrier to access to funds abroad.

Two fundamental decisions were adopted as to how the basic objectives would be pursued, and how their anticipated effects would be managed. First, in recognition that the perceived decisiveness of the government in applying its economic medicine would be critical to success, it was decided to take, wherever possible, a "shock treatment" approach (as opposed to a gradual phasing in) to the implementation of specific fiscal, monetary, and foreign exchange policy decisions. Second, because of social solidarity and political stability considerations, it was decided to seek major economic objectives in such a way as to protect weaker groups from the ravages of the crisis.

Administratively, the authorities adopted a five-pronged plan of attack: internally, 1) to reorganize, stabilize, and finally unify the foreign exchange market; 2) to substantially reduce the government budget deficit; 3) to follow an incomes policy designed to carefully manage the adjustment of prices and wages. Externally, they would 4) reschedule public debt with creditor banks, holders of Central Bank dollar certificates of deposit (issued to cover private sector dollar import debt), and individual governments (bilateral debt), while continuing payments to multilateral credit agencies and holders of government bonds; and 5) negotiate an agreement with the IMF and obtain fresh funds on concessional terms from friendly governments.

Stabilization of the exchange rate

The first step was to gain control over the market for Costa Rica's reserve currency, the U.S. dollar. Under traditional Costa Rican foreign exchange legislation, all citizens and companies have a right to hold dollar assets and have dollar bank accounts, but all dollar proceeds from export sales must be turned over to the Central Bank, which then issues colons to the exporter. Under these groundrules, "free market" dollars have been those held by persons or companies in Costa Rica that were not produced by an export transaction and therefore did not have to be sold to the Central Bank. Under the previous government this distinction had become blurred when the obligation to sell dollars resulting from exports to the Central Bank had been made partial, required for only a proportion of the total export proceeds. When the new government took office, a two-tiered exchange system was in effect. Within this dual system, the first and larger tier was the so-called interbank market, where foreign exchange earned by the Central Bank (the Bank's proportion of export receipts) was traded on a first-come, first-served basis, without limits on the amounts of specific transactions, at a rate fixed by the commercial banks under the guidance of the monetary authority. The second tier was the so-called free market, where foreign exchange that did not legally have to be turned over to the Central Bank was traded at a rate determined by buyers and sellers at commercial banks, "exchange houses," and in the streets of the capital and border towns. When the new administration took over, a primary goal from the very beginning was the eventual elimination of the two-tiered system and unification of the foreign exchange market under a single exchange rate.

The logical basic operational change to gain control of the foreign exchange situation was to once again put the whole market under the Central Bank's control. Legislation was enacted defining with greater precision the supply of foreign exchange that belonged to the free market; making it mandatory for free foreign exchange to be traded only at commercial banks, with purchases of foreign exchange only for transactions on the import trade account of the balance of payments; giving the Central Bank total monopoly power over transactions involving the outflow of currency reserves; and imposing large fines and severe prison terms when violations occurred.

The basic norm with respect to reserve currency transfers abroad was that the Central Bank would authorize transactions at the market rate of exchange, but limited to only those transactions that were "legitimate" (not capital flight) in the judgment of the Bank. Legitimate uses of Central Bank dollar reserves included current account imports, foreign investment income repatriation, personal remittances for purposes such as support of students abroad, tourism, and export-related investments outside the country. Once a working definition of dollars was arrived at, the process of quantification began. An inventory of public foreign debt was begun, and private businesses and persons were asked to register their debts abroad at the Central Bank so that they could qualify for foreign exchange authorizations.

A policy decision was made to make as many physical products as possible eligible for dollars on the interbank market. As this use of reserve funds constituted by far the largest portion of the country's current account dollar needs, success in administering this tier of the exchange market would have a great stabilizing effect on the economy. And, by remitting the majority of nonessential dollar requests to the free tier of the market, a guideline price would emerge there for use in adjusting both tiers.

By eliminating the "exchange houses" and directing all exchange transactions into the banking system, the newly enacted legislation made it possible to do away with significant institutional imperfections that were pushing up the exchange rate in the free market, creating an artificial upward pull on the interbank market rate. Overall order was soon restored in the foreign exchange market by balancing three factors: a determination to adjust the interbank market rate whenever necessary to avoid overvaluation of the colon; the Central Bank's commitment to provide foreign exchange without limit as to the size of each transaction; and a policy of not depriving the owners of "free" market foreign exchange of the real value in national currency of their holdings. The rates of exchange in the two tiers first stabilized and then began to converge. Having broken the massive devaluation spiral, the monetary authorities could now guide the dual exchange rates toward their reunification.

Reducing the government's deficit

Order in the exchange markets could not have been achieved, nor would it have lasted, in the absence of bold and resolute action to remove the main internal source of Costa Rica's monetary disequilibrium: the fiscal deficit. The first step was to bring the Central Bank's credit to the government down as much as possible, with an overall goal of reversing the allocation between the government and private sector access to local funds from its ratio at the time of two-thirds to the government and one-third to private uses. Such a reversal would restore the use of the Central Bank's currency to the traditional distribution of two-thirds to private uses and one-third to the government.

The second step was to introduce substantial — often brutal — increases in public utility rates: electric power, fuel, transportation, telecommunications, and water services. This was unavoidable because in 1982 the main component of the fiscal deficit was not in the central government, but in the decentralized government services and utilities sector. Several of the main utilities, with heavy foreign debt burdens, had avoided rate increases by means of subsidized exchange rates from the Central Bank for imports and debt service. The increases were put into effect, promptly and without hesitation, with the purpose of putting these enterprises back on a pay-as-you-go basis or, if this was not feasible all at once, of reducing subsidies with the goal of eliminating them over time.

The third step was to increase central government revenues. Already authorized by existing legislation, import surcharges were imposed by executive decree. Additional legislation was passed increasing sales and consumption taxes, stretching out the application of taxes on exports, and imposing a temporary surcharge on the income tax.

The fourth step was to reinforce the beneficial effects of increased revenues on the government deficit with measures designed to reduce spending or to slow down its rate of growth. Although increases in the public payroll—wages and employment—limited the effectivenss of these measures, there was success in reducing non-employment-related expenditures such as outlays for nonpersonal services and purchases of materials and supplies.

The combined successes in ordering public finance and stabilizing the foreign exchange market provided the basis for balancing Costa Rica's current account with the outside world and restoring internal price stability. The policies in both areas reinforced each other, with exchange stability making it possible for the public sector to budget with reasonable accuracy, and a progressively more balanced budget relieving government induced pressure on the exchange rate. The compound effect allowed not only the arrest of the upward trend of the fiscal deficit, but also an actual reduction in the gap between public revenues and expenditures. This gap, which in mid-1982 threatened to reach 20 percent of total production by the end of the year, was reduced by the second semester to 9 percent of GDP for the annual period as a whole, and then to 3 percent of GDP in 1983.

Foreign debt rescheduling

Along with avoiding the disintegration of the domestic economy, regaining respectability for Costa Rica as an honorable, law-abiding member of the international financial community was of the essence in mid-1982. More than just the country's ability to do business abroad was at stake. Important issues of national sovereignty were involved. In hindsight, it is easy to forget that Costa Rica was in the forefront of what would soon, but had not yet, become the biggest debt crisis in modern history. The country underwent the risks and perils attending first experiences in this respect, and was among the first small countries to do so. Thus the top priority was for putting public foreign debt back on a contractual basis and resuming payment as soon as possible.

The first step was to develop an organization to accomplish an unprecedented task. Substantive responsibility for external debt renegotiation was placed in a new cabinet portfolio. Administration and negotiation would be the direct responsibility of the Minister-Advisor for External Financing, with the full political weight of the President of Costa Rica behind him and institutional support provided by the Ministry of Finance and the Central Bank. Technical assistance was obtained from the United Nations and from international prviate firms and specialists. A steering committee of banks, made up of twelve members chosen from among the major creditors, was set up to conduct the debt-rescheduling negotiations with the government on behalf of the foreign creditor banks.

Once the Costa Rican government had its team in place and got down to specifics with the banks, the first issue was to define the bases and the principal criteria that would govern the negotiations. Foremost among the many issues involved were 1) definition of the scope of the *pari-passu* principle, that is, equal treatment for all creditors, and which creditors would be "equal," 2) choice of a basis for determining cash available for debt service, and 3) avoidance of destructive premature legal action. After much discussion, agreement was reached to apply *pari-passu* only to banking institutions, thus excluding holders of bonds and floating rate notes, as well as holders of the Central Bank's dollar certificates of deposit. In the same manner, it was also agreed to assess the question of foreign exchange available for debt service on a cash-flow basis and not only on balance-of-payments estimates. An additional important task was, from the beginning, to use all the banks' influence to forestall the proliferation of legal actions against the government, and to obtain the best legal representation to defend the few cases that were filed.

The Costa Rican government, as a gesture of good faith, unilaterally decided to resume repayment to the banks as soon as possible, independent of the state of the rescheduling negotiations. Payment began with a small fixed amount, under a formula that called for expanding that amount in proportion to increases in foreign exchange available from exports and from untied capital inflows. This favorable precedent improved the atmosphere for negotiation of the terms and conditions of the rescheduling. The crux of the negotiation was over how and how fast the country could become "current" in interest payments. The difficulty here was the banks' position that capitalization of interest was unacceptable, against Costa Rica's conclusion that current foreign exchange earnings were altogether insufficient to clear the arrears and at the same time cover minimum import requirements. In the end, the controversy was settled by means of a three-year revolving credit facility for imports provided by the banks, for 80 percent interest in arrears, which came to be referred to as "the revolver."

The next questions concerned the rate of interest to be paid on the rescheduled debt, and what the banks refer to as "terms and conditions." Having resolved the issue of interest in arrears, the negotiations entered an advanced stage. The banks now sought, generally with success, to maximize the amount of Costa Rica's cash going to debt service. It came down to such things as the spread to be charged over market interest for normal operations, that is, spread over LIBOR, and then the myriad fees and items that were added on top of it, for example, penalty interest, agent's fee, management fee, rescheduling fee, etc. Finally, there came the inclusion of numerous covenants to ensure compliance and to prevent the diversion of foreign exchange debt service funds to other uses.

As negotiations went into high gear, the foreign debt crisis erupted in Mexico and spread rapidly to Brazil and Argentina. The immediate effect was Costa Rica's sudden and welcome removal from the international debt spotlight, as the creditor banks suddenly had much bigger problems to worry about. The immediate effect was that Costa Rica's negotiations lost momentum and bogged down. But as time went by, it became clear that the net effect of the bigger debtors' problems was negative for Costa Rica. The banks, suddenly aware of the magnitude of their problem, attached ever-increasing weight to the debt renegotiation precedents that were being set with Costa Rica. Terms and conditions hardened as Costa Rica found standards applied to the negotiation, especially with regard to fees and interest rates, that had very little to do with its own specific situation.

Agreement with the banks was reached in the third quarter of 1983 and finally signed in September of that year. It covered principal in arrears falling due up to December 31, 1984, for a total of $600 million, or 18 percent of total public foreign debt in 1983. The payback period for the rescheduled debt falling due in 1983 was stretched to 8.5 years, at an interest rate of 2.25 percent over LIBOR. The amortization of the remaining rescheduled debt was to be over 7.5 years with an interest rate of 2.125 percent over LIBOR or Prime. Ratification by the legislature was obtained toward the end of 1983. After a year and a half of negotiation, public foreign debt with the international banks was back on a contractual basis.

A complementary step to the agreement with the creditor banks was the renegotiation of Costa Rica's bilateral debt. This was accomplished through the Paris Club in January 1983, right after the Standby Agreement with the IMF was approved by the board toward the end of December 1982. The amount rescheduled was $136 million (principal due up to December 1983), or 23 percent of total bilateral debt in 1983. The payback period was entended over nine years, while rates of interest, as is usual, were left to bilateral agreements, approximately at market levels.

Agreement with the International Monetary Fund

Informal contacts with the Fund were made even before the new administration came into office. However, the salient characteristic of the standby agreement was that it was reached *after* and not before the major foreign exchange and fiscal policy decisions had been made by the government. This shows something that is often ignored in current discussions. Government action to bring order to the exchange markets, to reduce the fiscal deficit, to shrink the current account balance-of-payments deficit, to lower the rate of inflation, and to price public sector services at or near their cost followed from the requirements of the situation and would have had to be enacted even if the Fund did not exist. The experience in this case also shows that the negotiations and the *differenda* with the IMF turned not so much on the direction and content of policy, but on the magnitude and timing of the various measures.

Work towards the agreement with the Fund was carried out during the second semester of 1982. Staff work began in June, and the first stage was completed in late August, when the letter of intent was completed. In mid-December it was approved by the IMF Board, covering the main areas of an economic stabilization program: government revenues and expenditures, wages and prices, management of foreign exchange, foreign borrowing, money supply, and volume of credit.

Interest rates on Costa Rica's currency was the one policy area in which the government and the Fund had the most difficulty in reaching agreement. The Fund insisted on the need to move forthwith on interest rates to bring them close to the rate of inflation and, eventually, achieve positive real returns on colon savings deposits. The government disagreed, taking the position that it would be wrong, in an atmosphere of galloping inflation, to chase the rate of price increases with the rate of interest. Instead, the government proposed to bridge the gap by first reducing inflation and bringing the exchange rate under control, and only then adjusting interest rates to achieve positive real rates as soon as possible. The expectation was that, in the meantime, the so-called "monetary illusion" would maintain stable colon financial savings levels. In the end, the basic annual interest rate was increased moderately, from 21.5 to 25 percent, only to be rolled back a few months later as events confirmed the government's forecasts and expectations.

Obtaining new capital inflows

Capital flight, beginning in the latter part of the 1970s, and the near total cut-off of foreign bank lending in the first half of 1981 contributed substantially to and magnified the proportions of the crisis, depriving Costa Rica of stocks and flows of resources that, if available, would have made the process of adjustment much less painful. To make up for these weaknesses, even if only partially, the government sought to renew and increase the inflow of official capital on concessional terms.

Loans and grants were obtained from several friendly governments. Foremost was the United States, which became by far the largest source. The U.S. provided 18.1 percent of total medium- and long-term inflows in 1982, 36.2 percent in 1983, and 22.5 percent in 1984, for a total amount of $950 million over the three-year period. Significant contributions were also obtained from the U.K., Canada, the Federal Republic of Germany, and Italy, among other countries.

Most of the funds provided by USAID were earmarked for balance-of-payments support. Grants from other countries were used to finance imports of specific goods. Inflows from multilateral credit agencies did not play an important role, as project-related funds could not be used to plug the resource gap, and as public investment was shrinking dramatically.

Financial assistance was thus a significant component of the total effort towards stabilization of the economy. Without it contraction of economic activity would have been greater, and living standards would have fallen even more. Even so, the contribution of external cooperation was, as it should always be, at the margin. The main burden of adjustment was internal. It required an unprecedented sacrifice on the part of the Costa Rican people. This major internal adjustment is confirmed by the figures on net capital inflows derived from the current account balance-of-payments deficit. They indicate that over the period 1981–84 net capital inflows were approximately $300 million per year, a rate 50 percent less than that immediately before the crisis.

Incomes policy during the adjustment process

The essential missing policy element that the new government brought to the management of the crisis was the determination to gain control over the situation and guide it toward purposefully defined objectives. In addition to actions in the fiscal, foreign exchange, and external debt areas, this can be clearly seen in the field of price and wage policies. The basic approach was not to let market forces do the job by themselves, but to manage them in such a way as to avoid the instability and distortions inherent in an imperfect economy. The objective was to make sure that the markets affected the proper adjustments in an orderly fashion. The criteria for what constituted proper adjustment was that changes must not go against the grain of economic reality, and that burdens and sacrifices must be distributed among the various groups more or less in proportion to their economic strength. A sort of interlocking and lagged procedure was followed for this purpose. It was crude, but it was successful.

The government used its discretionary powers to price the various utilities and public services it provides (electricity, telecommunications, fuel, and water). The first step was for each entity to measure the impact of the increase in the exchange rate upon the production costs of its services, and then to determine the rate increases necessary for operating without a deficit. The government then proceeded to implement the various rate increases, usually all at once for a specific service but somewhat staggered globally, with the idea of minimizing and spreading the shock of the rate increases throughout the rest of the price system.

The second step was to adjust support prices (prices paid to farmers by the National Production Board) for food staples, in order to absorb the direct impact of devaluation upon the imported component of their cost structure and the indirect cost increases due to the rise in public utility rates. The propagation of this adjustment down marketing channels—to processors, wholesalers, and retailers—was anticipated within the overall policy. It thus became possible to anticipate the short-term behavior of basic food prices, as well as the amount and timing of wage increases that they would make necessary.

Regulation of prices for other basic items that have a significant impact on the workingman's budget (sugar, edible oils, milk, eggs, beef, poultry, etc.) was under the authority of the Ministry of Economy and Trade. Amounts and implementation schedules were fixed with the criterion of not letting prices lag behind costs, but under careful scrutiny to avoid price abuses. Under the provisions of Public Law 480, food imports from the United States (such as wheat and lard) made it possible to soften the impact of massive devaluation upon the system as a whole. The vast majority of other prices adjusted without regulation, but under monitoring by authorities to help correct significant supply deficiencies in specific cases.

The third step was to adjust wages. Inflation, not productivity, was the guiding criterion during the most critical phase. Policy was conditioned by the fundamental fact that the country was undergoing a substantial lowering of living standards. Major impact to the real income and the well-being of the people could not be avoided. This was true for all resource owners. Those with capital were penalized by the negative interest rates, while labor suffered as long as wages lagged behind inflation.

The downward trend in purchasing power of wages was managed by defining a "basic basket" made up of sixteen staple consumer goods, recording their price increases, and adjusting wages for lost purchasing power in money terms (not percentagewise) every six months. Thus the real wage did not keep up with inflation for the goods not included in the basic basket. Wages lagged behind the rate of price increase as adjustments were made to partially offset, but not to prevent, wage erosion. The result was a drop of 10 percent in the average minimum real wage in 1981, and of 5 percent in 1982. Within this general trend, the thrust of wage policy was skewed to protect real wages in the lower brackets. This was done by concentrating the adjustments disproportionately among these groups. The result was an unqualified success, as the lower wages came through unscathed in real terms from the depths of the crisis.

A "social compensation" program was instituted to deal with the more acute repercussions of unemployment. It consisted of a kind of unemployment compensation scheme, with cash payments to the unemployed in exchange for devoting half their time to public works and seeking more productive jobs when not working under the program. In addition, supplementary income in kind was provided for the unemployed in the form of food staples. The program met with mixed results. Owing in part to its very nature and in part to the country's total lack of experience with the phenomenon of unemployment, a certain amount of inefficiency and abuse must be subtracted from the program's overall success.

The outcome in the short term

After eighteen months of intensive and concentrated action under the foregoing five-pronged policy approach, at the end of 1983 the situation was as follows: there was once again only one foreign exchange rate, with the interbank and free rates having converged at 43 colons to the dollar; inflation was down to an 8 percent per annum rate; the government deficit had been reduced to 4 percent of GDP; unemployment was lower, at 8.9 percent of the labor force; the minimum real wage was approaching its pre-crisis level; the downward trend of GDP had been halted; and the country was in full compliance with its financial obligations abroad. A dramatic change, when compared with the situation the administration faced when it took office, and it had been achieved without disrupting the country's longstanding social and political stability. As someone has said, it occurred "literally without a single store window having been broken in the process."

LESSONS, PROBLEMS, AND FUTURE TASKS

Bringing inflation down from over 100 percent to less than 10 percent per annum within eighteen months, while decreasing unemployment, is an accomplishment that has few precedents. The difficulty in explaining Costa Rica's recovery from the crisis can be the result of an overly technical economist's perspective. It was important for the new administration to bear in mind that the various indicators were only tools to use in diagnosing what was happening, that actions to correct the numbers had to be not only economic, but also political and social. The answers to why and how the recovery was brought about lie in the realm of things political, of a democracy at work in response to an unprecedented threat.

The first step was the development of widespread awareness on the part of the Costa Rican people that a grave problem was at hand and that the immediate and effective action had to be taken. This grew out of the all-pervasive daily experience with galloping inflation. The Costa Rican people had never experienced triple-digit annual price increases, and they correctly sensed that this situation was a threat to even the possibility of continued economic activity.

The second step was to provide the new government with a clear electoral mandate to do what had to be done to break the price and devaluation spirals, stabilize the country, and get it moving again. Fortunately, although the crisis was, at the time, out of control, the election in February 1982 proved timely, and the unqualified mandate was given before it was too late.

The combination of the people's awareness and the government's mandate created the necessary conditions for truly national participation in the task at hand. There was a large reservoir of popular support that expressed itself in a willingness to accept almost any sacrifice in order to regain the stability that the country had lost.

The third step was speedy and effective organization on the part of the authorities. A small, close-knit economic team was chosen, with each member appointed to a key economic policy-making position. Fiscal policy, monetary policy, and external financing were individually put on a sound basis by having each area under a well-qualified professional with extensive public sector experience. Policy coordination was assured by the ability of the heads of each area to work together without friction or contradictions, greatly aided by the fact that their small number allowed excellent communication. The team was given total support from the presidency and allowed to act without political hindrance, but with the full support of the existing government administrative apparatus. It was a very cohesive team that provided the leadership to bring the various economic agencies into coherent action. To make an analogy with the business world, Costa Rica's economic policy was put in the hands of a small, highly qualified and fully empowered ad-hoc task force.

The fourth step was the implementation of specific economic policy measures swiftly and in sufficient magnitude to be fully effective in decisively influencing the situation each action addressed. Shock treatment rather than gradualist measures was called for, due to both the magnitude of the problems and to the people's expectations that strong measures were necessary. This shock approach proved to be of great importance. It prevented problems from dragging on indefinitely without solution, and avoided undue complications, frustrations, and disillusions with seemingly unsuccessful policies. Quite to the contrary, swift and vigorous action carried an element of built-in success. The reservoir of popular support made success highly likely for each individual measure, and each success became a beachhead from which to launch additional attacks toward the objective of restoring stability.

In all major policy decisions, consistency between the statement of purpose and its implementation must be pointed out as an important element for success. This was indispensable in the re-establishment of government credibility. It resulted in a gradual buildup of security of expectations on the part of the people with respect to the behavior of the authorities, an important condition for working together toward nationally shared objectives.

The fifth step was the determination to put a floor under the socially destructive repercussions of the crisis. The criterion of making economic decisions with due regard not only to their intrinsic efficiency, but also to their impact upon people in the lower income levels, was consistently applied.

Of course, not everything went according to the blueprint. There were deficiencies and limitations. And mistakes. These grew out of insufficient information, inadequate balancing of means and/or objectives, and delayed or excessive actions.

Lack of data and the impossibility of obtaining figures on time made it difficult to monitor the behavior of, for example, government expenditures. Thus it was difficult to take opportune action to keep the fiscal deficit within targeted limits. The same was true with respect to the structural connection between the rate of inflation and the volume of credit. Lack of quantification of this relationship resulted in regrettable delay, with the result that credit volume was not adjusted upward until long after the rate of price increase started to recede.

The manner in which the government sought to close the fiscal gap may have also suffered from certain deficiencies. The problem was basically tackled from the revenue side, by increasing taxation, much more than by reducing current expenditures. Although research confirmation is still pending, it is possible that tax policy resulted in income transfers to the government that were excessive in view of the requirements of productive activity, and that as a result the latter shrunk more than would have been the case otherwise.

In addition, cutting expenditures by reducing nonpersonal services and purchases of materials and supplies, and not by eliminating, postponing, or redesigning whole programs, had a weakening effect on the activities of the central government. With large groups of personnel lacking even the elementary means with which to do their work, the administration's ability to contribute directly to economic recovery on the level of the ordinary central government employee was compromised.

Inadequate information and the countervailing action of pressure groups limited the timely adjustment of prices and reduced the effectiveness of price administration. Government experience was that repressing prices proved counterproductive, in the sense that the longer the delay, the larger the increase that had to be made in the end.

People's willingness to accept large sacrifices began to diminish as the process of stabilization advanced. Sometimes this was not grasped by the authorities until it was too late. A case in point was a second-round 90 percent increase in electric power rates, decreed in 1983, to be phased in over a six-month period, on top of a previous, one-shot 100 percent increase. The community went into a payments strike against the second increase, and it had to be rolled back and reworked.

Success with the stabilization program should not in any way detract from the fundamental fact that Costa Rica is today a poorer country than it was before the crisis. Income per person is now down

17 percent from what it was in 1978, and the rate of unemployment remains twice the historical 3 percent of the labor force.

Social development has come to a standstill. The middle class, having suffered the biggest impact of the crisis without compensatory protection, is the most important casualty. In a real sense, Costa Rica is now a country of fewer opportunities for all, but especially for the young, in such areas as employment, housing, and education. And what is worse, overcoming economic stagnation has proved to be an intractable problem so far.

This intractability is the result of three factors. First, external debt service takes a very large proportion of foreign exchange earnings, and deprives the economy of much-needed resources. Second, there are many private sector companies that have been nearly destroyed by inflation and devaluation. Third, old formulas won't work. The road to survival is not in going back to where the country was before the crisis. A new way out must be found.

A thoroughgoing process of economic restructuring defines the agenda for the future. New dimensions must be added to the national economy. Restructuring within a framework of new connections among the state, the private sector, and productive activity will be necessary.

Important items on the agenda are 1) proportioning debt service payments to the capabilities of the economy and obtaining new capital inflows to meet the requirements of recovery and growth; 2) corporate restructuring or industrial conversion of business firms, so that they can do their part in economic reconstruction; 3) developing a new protectionism, based on import tariff reform, tax and credit incentives for exports, and an uncompromising commitment to efficiency gains; and 4) a multiple market orientation, restoring regional cooperation in Central America, taking advantage of unlimited access to the United States market, strengthening investment and trade with the rest of Latin America, and working toward a European Initiative for the Caribbean Basin.

Development of this agenda, together with an unflinching effort to consolidate stability, will lay the foundation, over the remainder of this decade, for a push to once again achieve sustained social and economic development in the 1990s.

TABLE 1

Costa Rica: Summary Statistics

	1980	1981	1982	1983	1984
1. Annual changes in selected economic indicators (%)					
GDP	0.8	-2.3	-7.3	2.3	6.6
Private consumption	-1.8	-8.5	-9.6	6.0	7.0
Public sector consumption	1.5	-5.6	-2.5	-2.9	2.7
Gross capital formation	-9.4	-24.9	-27.8	4.2	16.0
Imports of goods and services	-3.4	-26.3	-18.1	13.6	7.7
Exports of goods and services	-4.3	11.1	-5.5	-1.8	
2. Balance-of-payments indicators (million dollars)					
Merchandise exports (Fob)	1,001	1,003	869	853	956
Merchandise imports (Fob)	1,375	1,092	805	898	995
Income from official loans*	425.8	404.5	234.6	461.1	254.1
Change in international reserves	198	47	138	140	70
Net international reserves	-138	-185.3	-47.3	92.6	162.3
3. Unemployment, wages, and prices					
Rate of open unemployment (%)	5.5	8.7	6.6	5.7	5.0
Average wages (in real terms)	–	1,520	1,220	1,348	1,461
Index of consumer prices (for middle and lower income groups in metropolitan area; 1975=100)	147.4	202.0	384.1	509.4	570.3
4. Government finance					
Structure of central government expenditure (100%)					
(%) Current expenditures	74.7	80.1	80.5	77.8	72.1
(%) Capital expenditures	25.3	19.9	19.5	22.2	27.9
Central government deficit as % of GDP	-9.2	-4.3	-3.3	-3.7	-3.2
Public sector deficit as % of GDP	-11.2	-14.3	-9.0	-3.1	-1.9
Financing of central deficit (100%)					
External financing	13.9	36.2	48.6	35.6	82.6
Internal financing	86.1	63.8	51.4	64.4	17.4
5. Monetary variables (million colons)					
Money	7,104	10,809	18,104	24,609	28,240
Quasi-money	10,455	20,575	31,586	40,124	46,273

*Medium- and long-term loans

Comments

ENNIO RODRÍGUEZ*

I would like to discuss the features of the stabilization program put into practice during the period analyzed by Carlos Manuel Castillo. In particular, I will refer to the unorthodox elements of this program. This seems important to me inasmuch as history tends to be rewritten, and in the new versions the orthodox elements of the program increasingly stand out.

From a perspective not exclusively economic, but political as well, three highly unorthodox elements are worth singling out. They were put into practice before an agreement with the International Monetary Fund was reached and, in some cases, even complicated the protracted negotiations.

The administration that left office in May 1982 had, in accordance with orthodox prescriptions, totally opened the foreign exchange market. A system of floating rates was established, with free access to the foreign exchange market in a highly speculative environment characteristic not only of Costa Rica, but of Central America in general. This situation of uncertainty and capital flight was revealed by pressure on the exchange rate. The acceleration of the rate of inflation to levels close to 100 percent was associated with an intense process of exchange rate devaluation.

The principal measure of the stabilization program was the creation of a monopoly over the foreign exchange market by the Central Bank, with the subordinate participation of the national banking system. This measure was accompanied by strict police surveillance of the black market. The success of these measures is clearly associated with the broad endorsement the new government

*Former minister of External Finance and Debt, San José.

232

received in the election and the positive expectations of success with which it began its administration. This changed the climate of uncertainty.

It is also worth noting that the "shock" treatment to stabilize the level of prices was successful, in part, because an inflationary psychology had not been generated. Inflation was attacked in the year it cropped up.

The diagnosis that led to these measures was unorthodox. It was not a question of inflation caused by excess liquidity in the economy, but rather an inflation of costs because of exchange-rate instability in a very open economy where production costs consequently included a large imported component. Thus, to prevent speculation and capital flight, strict exchange controls and modification of the expectations of those who bought foreign currencies became key elements of the stabilization program.

A second element of great importance was the management of interest rates. The pressure to increase them to real levels was resisted, so that a deeper recession was avoided. In a context free of inflationary psychology (a certain monetary illusion), and in order to reduce inflation in a few months, the government argued that an interest rate of 25 percent would become real very shortly. In fact, the diagnosis of the nature of the inflation was correct, and the recessive and inflationary effects of high interest rates were avoided. At the end of the first year of the adjustment process the rates were positive in real terms.

The third element was the wage policy aimed at avoiding a further deterioration of wages. In particular, the minimum wage (the absolute minimum, as there are several depending on the type of activity) actually increased during this process. This characterized both of the stabilization programs agreed to with the IMF, but it was especially true of the intermediate period (1984). This third element, also highly unorthodox, made the experiment politically viable.

A second topic I will refer to is the harsher treatment the smaller countries received in the renegotiation of their debts, as compared to the large nations. However, this does not mean that the differences are profound and that the large countries found satisfactory solutions to the problem of their external debts.

The financial conditions obtained in renegotiating the debts seem to be associated with the debtor's ability to check the international bank. The basic strategy used is aimed at getting the country to pay interest to the commercial bank, and the financial conditions to new flows or of rescheduling the debts are being defined more by the debtor's political weight than by its economic prospects.

If the financial conditions obtained by the small countries in the first round of negotiations are compared with those of Mexico, it becomes obvious that the former obtained higher interest rates and commissions, shorter grace and repayment periods, and it was more difficult for them to obtain new loans (Bindert, 1985). In the second round of negotiations all the countries obtained better conditions. Nevertheless, the small countries, with a few exceptions, again found themselves in a position less favorable than that of Mexico.

There seems to be a concern that the small countries should not be allowed to set precedents that can then be used by the larger countries. From the perspective of the international bank, the small countries are marginal in this regard; it is the large countries that really concern the bankers. Thus, the marginal concessions obtained by the large countries do not necessarily constitute a precedent for the small countries. Nevertheless, a similar pattern of payback periods and interest rates has tended to emerge for all of the countries.

In a recent study, John Williamson (1985) found some evidence that in their negotiations with the International Monetary Fund, the small countries tend to encounter a harsher conditionality than the large countries do. Given the technical neutrality of this institution, there should be no evidence of this type. The greater political weight of the large countries, and perhaps their greater organization and more detailed plans, tend to result in less conditionality in comparison with the other debtors.

The gravity of the small debtors' situation becomes apparent when the principal initiatives of both the creditors and the debtors are examined. The countries that participated in the Consensus of Cartagena are, for the most part, the continent's large debtors; entire regions such as Central America are absent.

Moreover, the Baker Plan contains a list of countries very similar to that of the Cartagena group. It looks again as though the small debtors have been shunted aside.

This lack of attention to the small countries seems to support the theory that the prevailing viewpoint in the process of renegotiating external debts has been that of the international bank and its fear of the consequences of nonpayment by the large debtors. This is inconsistent with the importance that bilateral agencies have given to regions such as Central America when other criteria such as geopolitics are introduced.

A final thought to which I will make reference is the conditionality associated with the sources of new money. Costa Rica sidestepped the burden of its high debt service largely through the external financing it was able to arrange. Thus, the Baker Plan seems to indicate that the route of high conditionality, which Costa Rica was the first to take, is what lies in store for those who seek access to external financing in the future.

Costa Rica's experience suggests that there has been a certain amount of coordination where conditionality is concerned. The Agency for International Development focused on public enterprises, the World Bank on the tariff structure, and the IMF on the monetary and fiscal variables. In its analysis of projects, however, the Inter-American Development Bank has allowed the economic authorities a certain measure of freedom. In the move toward greater conditionality, it is not surprising to see the pressures exerted to include this bank within the network of crossed conditionality.

Conditionality poses a basic philosophical problem as it is based on the assumption that the market is better at allocating resources in every case. Countries opting for the route of conditionality have little choice but to proceed within a program where market forces play a major role.

A second aspect worth noting is the difficulty of managing crossed-conditionality programs. Commercial banks tend to be the most inflexible where conditionality is concerned, so that disbursements and the rescheduling of maturities tend to be tied to the fulfillment of all the other programs (IMF contingency, World Bank structural adjustment). The IMF includes in its objectives certain capital inflows associated with fulfilling the conditions of all the other programs. The World Bank operates with a certain degree of autonomy, but a structural adjustment loan cannot be negotiated without an existing contingency agreement. Finally, the AID works with an ad-hoc conditionality, which can be more or less flexible in certain circumstances. The difficulty of crossed conditionality emerges in the complicated negotiations that become necessary because the program operates only if all its components advance simultaneously. But enormous difficulties also arise later in executing the programs. In all probability, some of the goals or conditions may not be fulfilled, but because of the way crossed conditionality works, this affects all the other programs. Thus it frequently occurs that a difficulty in one program makes it necessary to renegotiate all of the international agreements.

A third aspect of conditionality is the economic sector's enormous role in the government. Practically all areas of government are affected by some conditionality. The economic ministry tends to be the center of a large part of the administration, but it is a center governed in turn by fairly rigid external parameters.

In conclusion, I must say that I agree with Castillo that Costa Rica has achieved a relatively low-cost adjustment, and that this was made possible, in large part, by the external financing it was able to obtain. Nevertheless, the cost has been to advance along the difficult route of conditionality. Looking ahead, the doubt remains whether it will be possible to continue obtaining the large amounts of external financing that will be needed to service the growing debt.

REFERENCES

Bindert, Christine. (1985). "Small Debtors, Big Problems." Paper presented in the seminar, *The External Debt of Small Latin American Countries*, San José, December.

Williamson, John. (1985). "IMF Conditionality in Small Countries." Paper presented in the seminar, *The External Debt of Small Latin American Countries*, San José, December.

Comments

GERT ROSENTHAL*

I find little to disagree with in Castillo's version of events. Castillo was, after all, one of the actors in the "drama" he describes. And certainly not an indifferent actor. Coincidentally, during the years 1974–78, when he played a distinguished role in the government, all of the economic indicators evolved in a highly satisfactory manner. The crisis he describes began in 1978 and lasted until 1982, when he again joined the select group of people that he himself describes, with some modesty, as "a team of highly qualified professionals." Thus, the author has a certain tendency to exaggerate the role of "appropriate" economic policies in the successes of the initial 1974–78 period (growth with stability) and of the recent 1982–86 period (correcting the threatening imbalances and stabilizing the economy), and to minimize the role of contingent factors such as the boom in coffee prices in 1976–77 and the significant amount of financial resources obtained from bilateral sources in the more recent period. Taking the opposite tack, perhaps the role of "inappropriate" policies during the 1979–82 crisis period is exaggerated, with a tendency to underestimate the importance of the external factors that contributed to the problem.

In any case, any disagreements I might have with what is described, with respect to both the sequence of events and their interpretation, are questions of nuance and thus I do not wish to dwell on them. The data the author provides are indisputable, and I would agree that the "management" of the Costa Rican economy in the 1974–78 and 1982–86 periods was qualitatively superior to that of the intervening years.

---

*Deputy Executive Secretary for Economic and Social Development, U.N. Economic Commission on Latin America and the Caribbean, Santiago.

In considering how helpful this paper is as a "case study" to enrich our knowledge of the origin, scope, and consequences of the crisis, the author himself warns us of the peculiar features of the Costa Rican experience and, implicitly at least, suggests that this experience has little or no relevance elsewhere. Nevertheless, the Costa Rican experience was fairly typical of the experience of small economies dependent on agricultural exports and particularly hard hit by the crisis. It should be remembered that the economies in question are quite open to international trade (Costa Rica's import ratio necessarily hovers around 35 percent of GDP), are producers of basic products, have a poorly diversified export structure, and, to make matters worse, are highly dependent on imported energy. Thus, what happened in Costa Rica in 1978 is typical, with differences of degree and perhaps of timing, of the experiences of other small economies in the region. First, the sudden drop in the level of exports, due primarily to the erosion in the terms of trade; next, the search for external credit to compensate for this drop and perhaps to finance a higher level of public expenditures aimed at maintaining a minimum level of economic activity; and then the "snowball" effect caused by higher interest rates and the constant shortening of the payback periods of the said external financing. Throughout this process Castillo underestimates the significant role that the constant flight of capital played in the genesis of the crisis (deposits by Costa Rican citizens in U.S. commercial banks climbed from $200 to $530 million between 1979 and 1984), but the "anatomy" of the deterioration of the Costa Rican economy is indeed typical. What is not so typical is the "formula" used by the authorities to deal with the crisis, which the author himself describes as a "shock" adjustment policy.

Castillo implicitly offers Costa Rica as a successful case of adjustment, evidently worth imitating. To this end, he draws a number of "lessons," but in my opinion, fails to address the most relevant questions. These should include, among others, the following: a) Is adjustment possible without causing a deep recession? Or, in other words, how feasible is an expansive adjustment? b) Is it practicable to achieve sudden stabilization with a "shock" policy? If so, at what cost? c) Is it feasible, as Castillo claims, to protect the poorest segments of the population from the effects of an adjustment and stabilization policy? d) Finally, how important are noneconomic factors in the development of an economic adjustment program?

The answer to the first question is that expansive adjustment is feasible, within certain limits (let us not forget that the per capita GDP in Costa Rican fell 17 percent between 1978 and 1985), provided that the country has enough foreign exchange to allow it to spread the adjustment over time and among sectors and social groups. Much of the explanation for the relative "success" of the Costa Rican adjustment/stabilization program is found in the massive support received from the international community, particularly the principal bilateral source. Castillo points out that the country received the significant sum of almost $1 billion in three years: more than the value of total exports in one year! Thus, the first relevant lesson of the Costa Rican experience is obvious: adjustment is greatly facilitated if sufficient foreign exchange is available to permit a minimum of international liquidity while austerity policies are in effect. This situation also permitted the Costa Rican authorities to follow a less "prudent" wage policy than would normally be required in a conventional adjustment program. Beginning in 1982, real wages, instead of shrinking, actually increased. This, in turn, made it possible to keep restrictions on overall domestic demand within tolerable limits (private consumption fell markedly in 1982 but grew in 1983 and 1984).

The second conclusion I would draw from the Costa Rican example is that stabilization is easier in countries with temporary inflation, where a "psychology of inflation" or inertial inflation has not taken hold. The high levels of inflation experienced in the country originated in an increasing of costs, caused by the increase in import prices following a substantial devaluation of the colon. Once the currency stabilized, it was relatively easy to reestablish normal price stability.

The third important lesson — and here I agree with Castillo — is that an adequate, coherent "menu" of economic policies is important. The search for ways to avoid adjustment, or, in other words, to rescale the economy to the decline already recorded in national income due to the deterioration of conditions in the international economy, has been disastrous for Latin America. This does not mean that we must subscribe to certain orthodox policies, but that there are certain painful realities that we must face courageously and decisively, even if it means following the formula Castillo describes ("shock" policy) or others along the lines of the "Plan Austral." Finally, I believe that he is quite correct in insisting on the noneconomic aspects of any adjustment program. The cooperation of the people, the harmful (or favorable) effect of expectations, and the leadership a government can provide in the coordination of specific actions are all important factors—in Costa Rica, in Argentina, or in any other country.

Finally, there is one key question that Castillo unfortunately does not address, and it is perhaps the most relevant of all. It consists of determining whether, after three years of adjustment, the Costa Rican economy has reached a plateau where renewed growth is possible. Unfortunately, the experience of this small Central American country does not offer any concrete evidence that this is the case, at least not so far. The final verdict on the relative success of the Costa Rican adjustment is still pending.

Domestic Crisis and Foreign Debt in Peru

RICHARD C. WEBB*

President García's announcement that Peru would limit debt service to 10 percent of its exports has received a great deal of international attention. Less attention has been paid to the economic and social crisis that led to that decision.

While few question the government when it states that Peru cannot in fact pay more, there are varying views of the cause of this situation. Creditors tend to blame the crisis on overspending and overborrowing, while their critics stress the domestic costs of adjustment necessary to allow repayment. There is some truth in both of these views, but each focuses on only one of the players in a story that involves several actors. Leading parts have also been played by external events and by ineffective management. The former—world recession and a climatic disaster—are easier to understand and quantify. It is more difficult, but more useful, to judge how much of the crisis could have been avoided by different policies.

This paper discusses the relationship between Peru's repayment difficulties and its domestic crisis by examining the growth of the debt burden, the steps on the road to what some consider is a partial default, and the efforts to adjust. It concludes with an opinion on what Peru's future debt policy should be.

GROWTH OF THE DEBT BURDEN

Peru's external debt has grown from $3.7 billion in 1970 to $13.7 billion in 1985, and presently, it amounts to 97 percent of

*Former president of the Central Reserve Bank, Lima.

241

GDP. Yet overborrowing is the least accurate explanation of Peru's crisis for two reasons.

The first is that, in real terms, the external debt has not grown significantly in the last fifteen years. In fact, it has grown less than the population. Measured in constant dollars, each Peruvian owes less today than he owed in 1970, and also less than he owed six years ago, just prior to the Belaunde government (see table 1). The foreign debt per person was $783 in 1970; it peaked at $969 in 1977, and today stands at $735. In nominal terms, the rate of borrowing was highest at the beginning of this fifteen-year period: the debt grew by 70 percent over the first five years (1970–75), by 53 percent in the next five years, and by 43 percent (or 13 percent in real terms) in the last five years. Peru has, of course, overborrowed as it is now unable to repay, but the crisis cannot be attributed to a recent surge of borrowing. To the extent that the debt is too high, the die was cast before 1970.

The second reason is that "overborrowing" suggests decisions — an active search for new money. In fact, a large part of the debt came about passively, when Peru, at various periods, was unable to make payments. This is particularly true of the last ten years. Since 1975, refinancing credits, including drawings of the IMF, have totaled $6.7 billion, equivalent to 49 percent of the external debt in 1985. Fully half the debt could be called involuntary borrowing. In fact, $4 billion consists of refinancing credits and arrears during the last three years, in other words, after the onset of the present crisis in early 1983. To a large extent, Peru's debt is a consequence rather than a cause of the breakdown.

The payment crisis arises not so much from increased debt as it does from higher interest rates and a reduced capacity to pay, as may be seen in table 1.

TABLE 1

(Constant U.S. $ per capita)

YEAR	DEBT	INTEREST	GDP	EXPORTS
1975	100	100	100	100
1985	88	290	82	90

Source: Central Reserve Bank

If we compare today with 1975, each Peruvian owes 12 per-cent less, in constant dollars, but pays almost three times more interest. One reason is that less of the debt is now owed to soft-loan sources: the amount owed to government agencies and international organizations fell from 43 percent of the total debt in the early 1970s to 29 percent in the last three years. At the same time, a rising proportion of the debt is paying penalty margins as a result of massive refinancings and arrears, particularly since 1983. Third, world interest rates have risen. As a percentage of exports, interest payments doubled between 1975 and 1985, from 22.5 percent to 42.7 percent; as a proportion of GDP, the ratio rose from 2.2 percent to 8.7 percent.

As the interest burden per dollar of debt was going up, Peru's capacity to pay was falling. The economy and balance of payments have been weakening almost continuously since the mid-1970s, with a deceptive interruption in 1979–80. By 1985, output per person was 18 percent below its peak in 1976, and exports were 10 percent below. From 1975 on, the downward slide in output was accompanied and reinforced by considerable financial instability. Inflation jumped from under 20 percent to 60 percent during the 1970s, and into triple digit figures after 1982. The exchange rate and domestic interest rates fluctuated considerably in real terms. Private investment fell and capital flight increased.

One of the many policy failures that explain the economy's decline is the poor use that has been made of foreign credit. In particular, very little was spent in ways that would strengthen the balance of payments. Only one-third of loan disbursements to the public sector between 1970 and 1985 was invested: the rest was obtained for food and defense imports and for balance-of-payments and budget support, including recent arrears. Furthermore, most of the amount that was invested ended up either in unproductive, typically large-scale and capital-intensive projects, or in social infrastructure, such as housing and schools. Less than 10 percent of loan proceeds was invested in export or industrial activities.

The danger of a breakdown in debt servicing was heightened as the problem became increasingly fiscal in nature. Since 1970, the external debt was being gradually but continually converted from a private to a public burden. The proportion of total debt owed by the government rose from 27 percent in 1970 to 83 percent in 1985. It grew, in real terms, at a compound rate of 10 percent per year, while the private debt was falling even in nominal terms. This trend was aggravated after 1980 by the fact that government revenues suffered proportionately more than GNP from the declining economy, particularly in the 1983 collapse. In per capita terms, tax revenues that year were 29 percent below their level in 1975.

The result was a sharp payments squeeze on the government. Interest on the public debt rose from 9 percent of tax revenues in 1975 to 31 percent in 1984. If principal owed to the international organizations is included, because it cannot be refinanced, minimum service on the public debt rises to 36 percent of tax revenues in 1984, to 46 percent in 1985, and to over 50 percent in 1986. A payments crisis became inevitable for fiscal reasons alone.

Overborrowing by the government plays a part in that crisis, but much is due to higher interest rates and to the collapse of the tax base. Furthermore, half of the public sector's external debt had arisen from refinancing credits and arrears, rather than from direct spending decisions: credit became a substitute for lost revenues rather than a way of increasing spending. In the short span covered by 1983–85, for instance, recession caused a total loss of tax revenues equal to $3.9 billion, while refinancing credits totaled $4 billion. During that period, borrowing from abroad provided exactly one-third of total resources spent by the government. By contrast, during the five years just before the crisis, 1978 to 1982, foreign credits had financed only 13 percent of government spending. Paradoxically, the payments crisis followed immediately on several years of relatively low borrowing.

BRIEF HISTORY OF THE CRISIS

In July 1983 Peru was able to borrow $450 million from a consortium of 287 banks. Just two years later Peruvian public sector debt was classified as "value impaired" by the U.S. Interagency Country Exposure Review Committee, and U.S. banks were required to write down 10 percent of the book value of those loans. A few weeks ago President García stated that Peru would pay "when it chose and when it could."

Peru and its creditors have been through this roller coaster ride before. Peru defaulted on its debts to private banks in 1826, 1876, and 1931. Payments crises arose in 1967 and 1977 but were resolved through a combination of austerity, refinancing and export boom. The main ingredients in all these experiences were the same: an export cycle, governments eager to borrow, unproductive use of credit, and banks surprisingly willing to lend again.

The immediate precedent for the current crisis was the 1977–79 period, and its history influenced policy throughout the following years. What stands out about that period is the particularly successful turnaround in the balance of payments achieved by the happy coincidence of an energetically applied austerity program and an export price boom. One effect of this outcome was to obscure the continuing deterioration of the economy and the need for structural reforms. A second effect was to reinforce the monetarist belief that economic problems were fundamentally a matter of financial discipline and could therefore be solved quickly through belt-tightening. Peru was held up as a model by the IMF. During the following years, primary attention was given to fiscal and monetary policies, while devaluation (in real terms) was given little importance and controls were dismissed. When the next crisis began, in 1983, it was a long time before nonmonetarist solutions were sought. Another side effect was to dispel worries raised by emerging debt service difficulties: because balance-of-payments deficits were the result of fiscal and monetary looseness, fiscal discipline would assure future payments capacity.

The first alarm to signal the coming crisis had an ironic origin. The external situation had recovered so thoroughly by early 1981 that Peru decided to prepay $275 million of previous refinancing credits. This would lower the average cost of the debt, as well as improve the country's credit standing. The sudden drop in reserves coincided with other signals of a weakening balance of payments and led to some loss of confidence. For the next two years export prices slid almost continuously, devaluation increased, and the Central Bank lost net reserves.

As 1982 ended, however, and despite the prolonged domestic and world recession, there was nothing to suggest the extraordinary collapse that the Peruvian economy was about to suffer. Indeed,

world growth was expected to pick up and interest rates were falling, providing a basis for optimism. As late as March 1983, the
IMF was projecting the following percentage changes for the year:

GDP	+ 0.9
Exports	+ 8.8
Tax revenue	− 5.7
Inflation	55

Actual changes during 1983 turned out to be as follows:

GDP	− 11.6
Exports	− 14.0
Tax revenue	− 31.0
Inflation	125

The delay in seeing this economic disaster led to an inadequate policy
response—the patient was treated for a severe cold when, in fact
he was, at that very moment, being run over.

From the point of view of debt servicing, the situation was
expected to be tight even on the basis of the original figures. In the
first days of the year it had been decided that $880 million in refi-
nancing and fresh money would be needed from the banks, in addition to a rollover of short term credits. In practice, debt relief obtained during the year was $1.6 billion, or twice the targeted
amount. The balance of payments was further buttressed by a 27
percent, or $1 billion fall in imports, twice as much as had been
programmed. The negative shocks, however, turned out to be even
larger: exports fell $500 million below their projected level; the
financial panic set off by the Mexican collapse led banks to withdraw
$739 million in trade credits; and capital flight drained another $600
million. The net effect was a $700 million loss of reserves, a larger
external public debt, and a severely weakened basis for facing future
payments.

Payment capacity was hit by the 11.6 percent fall in GDP, the
loss of reserves, the fall in exports, and the loss by the government
of almost one-third of its tax revenues. As a proportion of those
revenues, interest on the public external debt doubled, jumping from
15 percent in 1982 to 31 percent in 1984. At the same time, prospects for a recovery of pre-1983 levels of output and foreign exchange were constrained by the inability to import more, and by
the financial disorder and uncertainty created by the jump into triple-

digit inflation. Production was further hampered by a financial squeeze on private enterprise, as lower sales led to increased indebtedness, while credit was tightened to reduce capital flight and inflation. During the first nine months of the year liquidity fell 28 percent: growth in nominal liquidity reached 42 percent, but prices rose by 96 percent under the impact of faster devaluation and hikes in gasoline and other government-controlled prices.

The formal relationship with creditors began to break down in 1983, when Peru was unable to meet the IMF program targets for June. The Fund's targets had been based on the unrealistic March projections and were in need of reformulation. Neither bureaucratic procedures nor official mindsets were flexible enough to adapt to such a radical contrast between official views and reality even though, by June, the severe damage inflicted on the Peruvian economy by El Niño was general knowledge. (It may be noted in passing that by November the Fund was estimating a 6 percent drop in GDP, still only half the actual loss of output that year.)

By mid-year a crucial agreement with the banks had not yet been signed, but Peru used accounting loopholes to delay the day of reckoning with the Fund and signed an eleventh-hour agreement with the banks in August. As the contract contained a clause requiring Peru to be in good standing with the Fund, it was technically void at the time of signing. This situation continued until a new agreement was drawn up with the Fund in early 1984.

Before that new agreement was signed, a policy debate within the government had questioned the advisability of an IMF program, citing the standard objections—the primacy of output recovery, the role of credit as a productive input, and the feedback from devaluation and energy prices to inflation. In the end, these objections were overruled and negotiations with the Fund were completed. A go-it-alone course would have meant the loss of official and commercial bank loans as well as difficult-to-foresee diplomatic waves during President Belaunde's last year in office.

The life span of the new IMF agreement was as short as that of the last. But again, two months were enough to obtain fresh money from both the IMF and the banks (though the amounts in this case were small—$130 million in all). Also, the agreements, however shortlived, served to keep up appearances. Peru was again seen talking to its creditors and renewing its vows.

This attempt at normality ended in July when the government
ran out of cash. Efforts to balance the budget had been drastic since
1982: public sector wages and investment had both been cut by over
25 percent in real terms; food subsidies had been slashed; and military purchases had been held to less than a quarter of their pre-1983
level. Severe as these cuts were, they did not make up for the collapse of tax revenues, plus the doubling of interest due on the external debt. In the 1984 budget, interest due abroad absorbed 32
percent of tax revenues.

Fresh money from banks was conditioned on an IMF agreement, and this was ruled out by the size of the deficit. The central
bank refused to lend. Additional fiscal measures were ruled out by
the government. Starting in August, the shortfall was made up by
postponing debt payments.

For the next twelve months, until the change of government,
a "best effort" policy was followed, with the government making
ad hoc payments according to its monthly cash position, maintaining an ongoing dialogue with the Fund and other creditors, and taking additional fiscal measures. By maintaining a low profile and,
again, keeping-up appearances, Peru gained a considerable measure
of *de facto* acceptance of its inability to pay.

As is well known, new policy guidelines were announced by
President García in his July 1985 inaugural speech: the 10 percent
limit and a rejection of IMF agreements. In the course of the next
seven months it also became clear that debt policy was now to be
carried out with a high profile, that the usual discreet contacts with
creditors were to be minimized, and that the 10 percent was to be
allocated giving preference to the international organizations and
to creditors willing to maintain a flow of new money.

Thus far, the government's debt policy has meant smaller payments and some growth in reserves, despite the fact that, by some
definitions, debt service is closer to 20 percent. The government
has excluded payment in kind (mostly to East European creditors)
as well as interest on private medium-term debt and on all short-
term loans from its definition of the 10 percent. Banks have reacted
by quietly writing down part of their Peruvian portfolio and with-
drawing some $50 million of the $250 million in outstanding trade
credits. The only reaction that comes close to being a political act
has been the "value impaired" classification of Peruvian debt by

U.S. bank regulators. On August 15, the IMF declared Peru "ineligible" for further drawings on the Fund's general resources. The government's major concern, however, is that banks could attempt to collect through the courts and resort to asset and trade embargoes that would complicate and increase the cost of exporting and importing in Peru.

DEBT AND ADJUSTMENT

Looking back, foreign credit has served two quite different and equally important roles: as a supplement to domestic savings, and as a cushion against short-run fluctuations. The traditional purpose and standard justification for borrowing by developing countries has been the first—to supplement domestic savings and raise the investment level. Since the private sector in Peru substantially reduced its use of external savings over the last fifteen years, the investment-boosting objective was entirely carried out by the public sector. If one assumes that every dollar borrowed abroad by the government contributed to investment, exactly half of all public investment since 1970 would have been financed by external savings. If one assumes, more plausibly, that foreign borrowing has permitted a proportional increase in all expenditure items, and has also resulted in a lower tax effort than would have been the case, the addition to public investment is much lower, on the order of 10 percent, or about 0.7 percent of GDP. The contribution to the national investment level is even lower if the low productivity of much of that investment is considered.

Whatever the end result of public borrowing on each item in the fiscal accounts, the immediate purpose of much of that credit has been the second role, to cushion the fiscal accounts and the balance of payments against unexpected fluctuations, usually caused by export prices. Without easy access to foreign credit, Peru would have had to absorb fluctuations on its own, making frequent adjustments in taxes, spending levels, and in foreign exchange availability for imports and other needs. As it was, changes in those variables were frequent before 1982, but the extent of adjustment would have been greater without external credit.

A reliance on credit for stabilization purposes makes a country vulnerable to any limitation in access, the more so because continuous borrowing is required to offset rising interest payments. A sudden withdrawal will have the effect of an exogenous shock, and the impact will be especially severe if it coincides with another shock. This, of course, is what occurred in 1983, following the Mexican collapse. Normal access was cut off during the most severe crisis suffered by the Peruvian economy in a century, partly as a result of a major natural disaster. The blow was aggravated by the fact that banks went further than limiting access—$739 million in existing short-term trade credits were withdrawn in less than a year, an external shock that, in itself, exceeded the impact of any previous downturn in two decades of trade cycle. Furthermore, the sudden crisis thus created was used by banks to raise interest rate margins and improve their security by requiring a government guarantee on $900 million of short-term working capital loans to the private sector in Peru.

Peru is still trying to emerge from the multiple shock it suffered in 1983. The following statistics measure the social and economic setback.

Per Capita Indicators	1985 Index (1982 = 100)
GDP	87
Exogenous GDP	90
Endogenous GDP	83
Wage (modern sector)	65
Wage (informal sector)	79
Exports	88
Imports	42
Investment	61
Farm output per farm worker	96
Measures of Fiscal Adjustment	(1982 = 100)
Government wage	67
Total public investment	67
Food subsidies	7
Police & Defense budget	73
Current expenses (excluding interest)	82

Source: Estimates based on Central Reserve Bank national accounts and government account data. Wage series from National Institute of Statistics.

The data show across-the-board economic contraction and adjustment. The social impact has not necessarily been regressive. Indeed, both farm productivity and informal sector wages suggest that the contraction has hit middle groups more than families in the lowest deciles. But the welfare significance of income loss at the lowest levels is greater.

The causes of this collapse, and of the failure to recover in the last two years, are not easy to unravel. One element is the initial weakness of the economy. Greatly increased state intervention in the economy, affecting labor and land markets in particular, six to seven years of financial instability, capital flight, and falling savings ratios, two years of declining export prices, and six years of stagnation lay behind the economy when it was hit by the combination of weather, export, and credit shocks in 1983. A patient in normal health would probably have sunk less and recovered faster.

The size of the shocks, however, was impressive. Peru's terms of trade and per capita exports were at their lowest level in two decades and foreign exchange scarcity was increased by credit withdrawals. During 1983, damage by freak weather conditions that ran the gamut from floods to landslides to drought and disappearance of fish caused an estimated 5.4 percent loss in GDP that year. Most output in weather-affected sectors bounced back in 1984, but sectors affected indirectly, through various transmission mechanisms, remained depressed, as may be seen in the above indices for exogenous and endogenous GDP.

In an April 1984 press release on the Peruvian standby arrangement, the IMF was definite in its opinion as to the cause of Peru's ills: "The major factor behind the imbalances in the Peruvian economy during 1982 and 1983 was the large deficit of the nonfinancial public sector." Real government spending, however, had fallen by 10 percent in 1983 and was reduced a further 7 percent in 1984. The deficit remained large because output and tax revenues were falling just as fast, while sharply rising interest payments abroad were contributing to offset fiscal efforts. Idle capacity and unemployment grew rapidly during 1983 as overall demand was reduced by public expenditure cuts and by capital flight created by rising inflation and generalized uncertainty. Efforts to increase the fiscal take by raising gasoline and other controlled prices, along with a faster daily devaluation rate, pushed inflation into three-digit levels for the first time. The economy seemed to be caught in a series of vicious circles in which further adjustment efforts had both positive and negative effects, exacting a high price in both inflation and recession, and in political erosion, for marginal fiscal and balance-of-payments improvements. Certainly, by late 1984, the severity of adjustment efforts, measured in the figures cited above, could not prevent the eventual breakdown of normal debt service. The approach to adjustment proved to be highly inefficient in cost-benefit terms.

A more selective approach to adjustment would probably have been more effective. In particular, a more direct attack on the balance-of-payments deficit, combining greater devaluation with import and capital controls, would have reduced the burden on the recessive income-adjustment mechanisms, including the sharp reduction of government expenditures. Industrial policy could have been even more selective, supporting activities that could generate exports or save on imports using idle capacity, and also providing quicker and more supervised financial support where the threat of bankruptcy was causing output reduction. These suggestions add up to a heroic agenda for a country with a particularly weak administrative base and little experience in such efforts. Also, direct interventions cause distortions, corruption, and inefficiency. Nevertheless, it is hard to accept that those costs could have been larger than the massive output reduction, unemployment, and impoverishment that actually occurred. The second ingredient of a more effective program would have been political, since the real difficulty of any adjustment program is getting the patient to take the medicine.

Throughout this period the IMF was prescribing necessary ingredients of adjustment, particularly on the fiscal side. At the same time, IMF involvement hindered, and in some cases vetoed, moves toward greater selectivity and toward the accommodation required to obtain political acceptance. A case in point was the rejection of a two-tiered exchange rate that would have provided a more politically palatable method of devaluation. The grounds for rejection were IMF general principles for the world financial system rather than an evaluation of this tactic from a Peruvian point of view. Other examples of the way in which Fund involvement complicated and impeded the design of a program better tailored to the situation were the continual advocacy of import liberalization, in the midst of a severe balance-of-payments shock, and the rejection of price controls as a supporting instrument in an anti-inflationary program. The alternative, of course, was to rely entirely on recession.

THE ROLE OF EXTERNAL DEBT

External credit has both helped and complicated economic management in Peru. Over the last fifteen years, it helped to raise the investment rate and, until recently, acted as a stabilizer in the face of cyclical fluctuations. Neither of these contributions, though, has been of major importance to Peru's development during that period. The addition to investment was probably minimal and certainly reduced the average productivity of investment. The stabilizing role could have been fulfilled, to some extent at least, by maintaining a higher level of international reserves. Certainly, this alternative would have imposed a more sparing use of resources for stabilizing purposes. Finally, past reliance on credit has contributed to the exceptionally difficult and deep crisis that Peru is facing today. Devaluation was postponed, and efforts to raise domestic savings were less aggressive than they would have been if credit had been less available. And the current crisis would not have been aggravated by the perverse reaction of creditors, nor its solution complicated by the inflexibilities and prejudices of institutions and persons whose principal concern is the protection of a general system rather than Peru.

My personal view is that Peru will benefit by not being able to borrow abroad for the next decade or two. For the present, commercial banks have shut their doors to Latin American debtors except to finance interest payments to themselves, and Peru's debt policy will prolong its exclusion from the international credit market. The resource loss, however, will not be large if we judge by the fact that the net resource transfer (net capital inflow minus interest) has been negative for six of the last nine years, and is unlikely to become positive for a good number of years, even with impeccable debtor behavior. Despite the limitation of the 10 percent rule, Peru will remit $500 million more in interest and debt payments than it will receive from lenders this year.

On the other hand, Peru stands to gain a degree of self-reliance that would be healthy from both economic and political points of view.

PART IV

Panel on Strategies for Confronting the Crisis

Panel

JOSEPH RAMOS*

The external debt crisis requires action on two levels: 1) policies for renegotiating the debt and 2) national policies for restoring external equilibrium. The debate is about which policies. The positions can be schematically summarized by stating that creditors propose renegotiation on a case-by-case basis, with general and similar conditionality, while debtors advocate general renegotiation (a "political" solution) with conditionality on a case-by-case basis (taking the different national situations into account). Although how the renegotiation is resolved will largely determine the final outcome of the crisis, national policies (the subject of this panel discussion) are not without importance. To understand this, it is sufficient to note the marked difference in the costs and successes of the adjustment between the different countries of the region. Thus, my comments will be focused on determining 1) why the adjustment has been so costly, and 2) what policy implications there are for making a less recessive or more expansive adjustment possible.

To be sure, the adjustment has costs. Correcting an external imbalance implies having fewer goods and services at home in order to make more available for export. In other words, the standard of living of countries making such an adjustment declines (or grows more slowly). However, production need not fall. On the contrary, an efficient adjustment would increase exports and substitute imports; domestic demand would fall (absorption), but not production. Nevertheless, because of the adjustment, per capita produc-

---

*Senior Economist, Division of Economic Development, Economic Commission on Latin America and the Caribbean (ECLAC), Santiago.

tion in the region will be almost 10 percent lower in 1985 than it was in 1980.

There are two major reasons for the highly recessive nature of the adjustment: its enormous size and its unusual rapidity. First of all, prior to 1982 the net flow of capital to the region was such that it covered not only 100 percent of the interest payments, but also permitted a level of imports 20 percent higher than the value of exports. In 1982, this net transfer of resources went from being positive (by the said 20 percent) to negative by 25 percent; which is to say that the decline in the inflow of capital was such that, once interest had been paid, only enough foreign exchange remained to import the equivalent of 75 percent of the value of exports. In other words, the change was equivalent to an erosion in the terms of trade of almost 40 percent (75/120), not to mention the possible erosion of the balance of trade. In fact, the countries had to adjust not only to the permanent erosion of their external accounts (that is, changes in the price of oil and overindebtedness), but also to temporary erosion (higher international interest rate and cyclical capital movements). There was, then, a forced *over*adjustment.

Second, the adjustment was inefficient and recessive because it had to be made so quickly. There is no such thing as an efficient "shock" adjustment. An efficient adjustment implies not only a drop in demand, which can be as quick as the circumstances require, but also a reallocation of resources—from non-tradables to exports and import substitution—which is necessarily a slower process. In fact, an efficient adjustment usually requires real changes and not just changes in the nominal values of the variables. This is in clear contrast to a price stabilization policy. An efficient "shock" stabilization policy is possible because an anti-inflationary policy basically requires nothing more than changes in the nominal values of the variables. And this can occur rapidly, both in theory (a more or less simultaneous slowdown of all values) and in practice (for example, Brazil in 1986 and Costa Rica at the end of 1983).

In other words, there are several essential differences between a price stabilization policy and a policy for adjusting to an external imbalance. First, a stabilization policy has no unavoidable costs; an adjustment policy does. Second, a stabilization policy can be postponed as long as desired (inflation can be adjusted to and made tolerable through indexation); but not an adjustment policy, which becomes inevitable once reserves have been depleted. Third, a stabilization policy can be administered as a "shock" and still be efficient (moreover, it is doubtful whether three- or four-digit inflation can be efficiently dealt with gradually); but an adjustment policy must be gradual to be efficient.[1]

The implications of the above are obvious. On the one hand, the aggregate imbalance to which the region must adjust is basically that originating in the permanent erosion of its external accounts, but not that arising from temporary maladjustments. To be sure, determining what is permanent and what is temporary is not easy; obviously, this is a subject for discussion in renegotiating the debt.[2] On the other hand, a gradual approach is essential to efficient adjustment. Brazil is a prime example of this. Its adjustment was only slightly recessive because not only did imports fall because of the reduction in demand (and, typically, production), they were replaced by domestic production. Both the increased substitution of imports and the equally remarkable growth of exports were the results of a significant investment in these items in prior years. Efficient adjustment, then, requires that both investment and demand be reallocated if the external gap is to be closed. Resources must be transferred from nontradable to tradable sectors, instead of simply reducing imports at the cost of a recession (the typical recessive adjustment).

That is the optimal adjustment. What is to be done, however, if the debt incurred in previous years was not well or sufficiently invested in anticipation of a possible crisis such as the present one? In other words, what is to be done if there is not enough time for a gradual adjustment based on a reallocation of investment? The most efficient adjustment possible in such circumstances would have to be based not so much on a reallocation of investment, but rather, because it will have to be more rapid, primarily on the reallocation and better utilization of installed capacity.

Analysis of the recent experience of the region in this regard provides three suggestions for minimizing the recessive cost of an adjustment based primarily on installed capacity rather than investment.

1) Equalize the cost of saving and of generating foreign exchange through the use of switching policies and absorption policies. Precisely because it can be predicted that absorption policies will

work faster than switching policies, the temporary use of excessive
switching policies will be justified. In fact, in its adjustment, the
region pursued both switching and absorption policies. However,
because of the short amount of time available to correct the external accounts, the principal impact—of even the switching policies
(for example, devaluation)—was to reduce demand. In other words,
the income effect (reducing demand even further) prevailed, rather
than the price effect (substituting internal for external production,
and internal for external demand). In very approximate terms, we
estimate that to improve the balance of trade by $100 billion in
three years, the region sacrificed in the neighborhood of $250 billion
in lost production.[3] In other words, two and a half dollars of
domestic production were sacrificed to save one dollar of foreign
exchange. This suggests that any combination of tariff surcharges
or special export subsidies that will save or generate one dollar of
foreign exchange at a cost less than the said amount of lost production would be preferable to the adjustment policy pursued. Of
course, a devaluation of this magnitude is out of the question; rather,
since it is a temporary problem, it is a question of strengthening
the substitution or immediate price effect, instead of the income
effect, and making products with a greater short-term price elasticity
the focus of incentives. In fact, excessive switching incentives would
be temporary, for although reallocation by way of a generalized
devaluation works more slowly than reducing demand, it works
in the end. Once their full effects have been felt, excessive switching
incentives would be unnecessary.

2) The incentives (or costs) of saving foreign exchange through
import substitution or of generating it by promoting exports should
be equalized. Given the current incentive structure in the region—
high tariffs and few special export incentives—it would be difficult
not to conclude that additional policies promoting exports will bear
more fruit (foreign exchange) than those promoting even further
import substitution. Basically, the idea would be to begin exporting many tradables that are not at present being traded internationally (the bulk coming from the import substitution industries), making incentives for export production (which are currently few) equal
to the current strong incentives for the domestic market (at the expense, of course, of non-traded items which are nontradable).

3) Reductions in consumer spending should be favored over

decreases in investment spending. The emphasis of most of the adjustment programs of the region on reducing expenditures regardless of whether they are investment or consumer-oriented has been extremely shortsighted. In fact, the type of spending that was cut the most in the region between 1981 and 1984 was investment spending, by 22 percent. Although the cutback in machinery purchases reduced imports, it was at the cost of diminishing the capacity for future growth. Similarly, the cutback in public works and housing expenditures reduced construction by 20 percent in these three years, without the resources thus freed being used to expand the production of tradables. In fact, an adjustment that lowers the production of nontradables without reorienting this production and installed capacity toward tradables is inefficient.

Nevertheless, even if these three suggestions were followed, it would only be possible to *reduce* the recessive cost of the typical adjustment carried out in the region, not eliminate it. This is so because an efficient adjustment will be based, above all, on a reallocation of investment, which requires time. Moreover, it will be efficient only if it is limited to correcting the permanent imbalance in the external accounts and not, as has unfortunately been the case in recent years, if it also attempts to correct the temporary imbalances in these accounts. Since both the rapidity of the adjustment and the amount of effort expended will depend on the availability of external resources, the effectiveness of national adjustment policies — even the best designed — will be determined in large measure by the success achieved in arriving at a reasonable renegotiation of the external debt.

NOTES

1. Note in this regard that the recommendations of the IMF tend to reverse this conclusion: they are too shock-oriented when it comes to adjustment and more gradual than necessary when it comes to stabilization (for example, the unorthodox shocks in Argentina, Brazil, and Peru far exceeded the initial goals of the IMF).

2. It is necessary at least to insist on the principle of achieving a rollover of the debt in real terms and not just in nominal terms, as is currently the case. In fact, a nominal rollover, with inflation in the creditor

countries, implies repaying the debt in real terms. Repayment of this type hardly seems appropriate at a time like this, at least with the real international interest rates remain abnormally high, the prices of basic products are abnormally low, and the international economy is unpredictable.

3. The overall improvement in the balance of trade between 1981 and 1984 was $100 billion. In this same period, the aggregate loss of production was 6 percent. Adding to this the fact that production would have grown some 5 percent per year, the aggregate loss was 36 percent of the region's GDP, or approximately $250 billion.

Panel

FRED JASPERSEN*

In March 1986 a significant change was announced by the banking regulators in the United States regarding how they would handle debt which commercial banks had rescheduled. The following is from a press release:

> In a major policy change, the federal banking regulators in the United States adopted a controversial plan to encourage banks to restructure problem loans. It is thought that these changes will eventually be extended to all types of problem loans. They allow banks to use more liberal accounting methods for rescheduled problem loans and to modify reporting and disclosure requirements so that banks are not penalized for restructuring such loans. An easing of capital-asset ratio requirements is included in the new regulations. The new policy will permit the commercial banks to be more flexible in rescheduling problem loans. The changes should benefit both the heavy debtor countries and the banks themselves.[1]

My first point concerns how this is related to the Baker Initiative. One of the criticisms that the commercial banks have had of the Baker Initiative is that at the same time Baker was encouraging the banks to lend more, banking regulators were tightening capital asset requirements and other controls, thereby discouraging the banks from putting together appropriate work-out programs for the debtor countries. I think the correct interpretation of this most recent change is that it provides evidence that it is not correct to think of the Baker Initiative as a plan but rather as a process, a process that will evolve over time.

---

*Senior Economist, World Bank, Washington.

An interesting question that can be raised about the new regulations is: How will deferred interest payments be treated by the banking regulators? Unfortunately, no one has the answer to that question yet. As experience is gained with the recent changes, it is possible that the regulators will find ways to give the banks more flexibility in deferring interest payments.

It is significant that the recent changes have not been presented in the U.S. as something that helps the heavy debtor countries in Latin America and elsewhere even though it may have this effect. Rather, it has been explained as something that helps banks cope with weak portfolios stemming from agricultural and energy loans within the United States. In the United States, the most common perception of the Latin American debt problem is that the banks and the countries got themselves into this mess and they should get themselves out of it without society having to bear the cost of these wrong decisions. This view receives even more support in an environment in which Congress is attempting to reduce the fiscal deficit and lower interest rates. In short, the LDC debt problem is not an issue that generates a great deal of sympathy in the United States. An issue that is understood more fully is that of the impact of weak agricultural prices on the financial position of family-farm units in the United States. This is a much more popular issue. In announcing the most recent changes, the banking regulators in the U.S. have chosen to emphasize their domestic impact, but it is possible that they will have a positive impact on the Latin American debt problem as well.[2] I mention this because it is, I believe, indicative of how a government deals with politically unpopular issues in a democracy.

Debtor countries have complained about the list of countries to which the Baker Initiative will apply and the amounts of money envisaged. However, there is no question that both the amounts of money and the countries that are being referred to are not the limits, but rather are indicative.

In what direction will the Baker Initiative evolve? First and foremost, this will be determined by the heavily indebted countries themselves. More specifically, it will be determined by the policy reform effort, by the pace of recovery, and by the payment capacity of the heavily indebted countries. It will also be determined by conditions in the world economy. Any sudden change that adversely affects the heavy debtor countries would most likely be reflected in modifications in the way the Baker Initiative is implemented. This initiative is, in short, a flexible framework or process for addressing the debt problem.

The second point I would like to make relates to the prospects for recovery in the Latin American countries. For the purpose of discussing this, these countries can be grouped into three categories. In the first group are countries (like Colombia) that really do not have a debt problem and that are going relatively well. These countries have had problems in raising new money and need special assistance in raising financing. The World Bank is playing a catalytic role in mobilizing external resources for these countries.

A second group is the heavily indebted countries that have adopted growth-enhancing adjustment policies and have been successful in initiating the recovery process (for example, Brazil). For this group of countries, debt-increasing solutions appear to be appropriate. Their exports are growing rapidly enough (they are reallocating resources toward tradable goods production) that they will increasingly be able to service an external debt that expands at a slower pace than exports. They also need multiyear rescheduling agreements and medium-term work-out programs. Finally, they will require assistance in attracting new money for some time to come. What distinguishes this group is that debt-increasing solutions are appropriate.

The third group is those countries whose burden is so heavy, the prospects for their exports so grim, and the structures of their economies so rigid that debt-increasing solutions are not appropriate, except for debt on extremely concessional terms. This third group of countries does need something that is not being provided at present. Not only do these countries require increased concessional flows, but their old debt must be restructured so that it is supportive of the recovery process and of strengthening their external positions so that, at some point in the future, their creditworthiness is restored. I think that these things will eventually happen. They will occur, I believe, because they are so obviously in the interest of all parties involved.

I have two final points that I would like to touch on briefly. One relates to what the World Bank's response has been to the debt crisis; the other is conditionality.

It was agreed at this conference that the World Bank did not initially assume a significant role to alleviate the Latin American debt crisis. However, in the fiscal year 1984–85, it increased its lending to Latin America by 50 percent over that of the preceding two years. It did this, in part through a special action program that accelerated disbursements by increasing cost sharing. Additionally, quick disbursing loans were introduced to support policy reform in key areas. In 1985 there was a slowdown in structural adjustment lending (SAL), as mentioned by Foxley, but there was an offsetting increase in sector lending. The net result was a substantial increase in quick disbursing loans.

What are the prospects for continued World Bank lending to Latin America? The World Bank is currently planning for an additional 50 percent increase in its lending to Latin America over the next several years. Under these circumstances, the Bank would have very large net disbursements and positive net transfers in Latin America's favor. But I would not want to overstate the role the World Bank can play in this process. Even under the best of circumstances, the Bank can provide only a small amount of the total financing that is needed.

Finally, I would like to touch on the World Bank's conditionality. Why should the Bank attach conditions to its lending? To answer this, another question must also be asked: What are the World Bank's objectives in expanding its policy-based lending? There are two: one is to transfer resources in support of economic recovery in the heavily indebted countries; the other is to help the borrowing countries permanently strengthen their external positions so that, at some point in the future, they will have greater access to capital markets. The World Bank views conditionality as ensuring that the policy environment is conducive to productive use of the resources it lends.

While it is easy to put down on paper a theoretical framework of how adjustment and recovery can take place simultaneously, in practice it may be difficult to design and implement. The World Bank is well aware of this. It is also aware that the answers to the question of how best this can be achieved can be found only in the specifics of each country. Furthermore, the actual policy solutions have to come from each country itself. Experts within each country are the most important source of what the adjustment program should consist of and thereby of the World Bank's conditionality. Definition of this is achieved through a process of dialogue. A number of questions are addressed in this dialogue, such as: Is it desirable to increase investment? How can this be achieved? How can public investment be increased? What public-sector savings targets are required to achieve this? Which investment projects should be given the highest priority? Should projects that are halfway completed be given priority over new projects? How can the poorest groups in society be protected from the impact of adjustment? How will the programs strengthen the country's external position in the future? And, finally, what is the appropriate time frame for adjustment? The World Bank does not have standard answers to these questions. Clearly, they must be answered by the country itself.

In concluding, I would like to look at the experience of the World Bank's recent structural adjustment lending. I do not want to make this specific to any country, but there are a number to which it applies. Such loans frequently have a number of areas of focus. The first is promotion of exports; the World Bank has been particularly concerned with the design and implementation of mechanisms that would expand exports from medium- and small-scale producers. This may entail marketing mechanisms, quality-control arrangements, insurance schemes, and technical assistance. A second focus of structural adjustment lending is how to increase investment. Here the issue becomes identifying the source of resources for increasing investment and the incentive systems that need to be in place for this to occur. A third area of focus is efficiency. How can public-sector investment programs be designed so that only the highest priority investments are undertaken? How can state enterprises be made more efficient? What structural changes and policies are required to make export and import substitutes more competitive? A fourth focus of such loans is institutionalization of development policy formulation and implementation, ranging from external debt policy to tax and trade policy planning.

There have been a number of criticisms of World Bank conditionality expressed at this conference. Most of these have been assertions that such conditionality has a heavy ideological content (for example, privatization for privatization's sake, deregulation of the economy, etc.) which is inappropriate for the conditions prevailing in Latin America. While it is true that some SALs have supported such policy action, the World Bank's participation in the formulation of such programs is not ideological. Each country is taken as a unique case; there is no universal solution that applies equally to all countries. There is, for example, no policy conditionality consistently attached to quick disbursing loans requiring that special direct foreign investment incentives or privatization schemes be implemented. This does not mean, for example, that in trying to identify resources for expanding investment the finances of public enterprises are not assessed. If it is found that some public enterprises are extremely inefficient and generate large deficits and that there is little chance of turning this situation around as long as that enterprise remains in the public sector, then it is quite possible that privatization or liquidation would be identified as worthwhile adjustment action. That does not mean that these ways of dealing with the problem would be pursued as ends in themselves, but rather that they are a means to an end, in this case, expanding savings and investment.

NOTES

1. From general press coverage, week of March 15, 1986.
2. While it is not yet clear that this will be applied to LDC debt, a number of "regulator watchers" believe it will.

Panel

WILLY VAN RYCKEGHEM*

As a result of the external debt crisis and the virtual paralysis of voluntary commercial bank financing, Latin America has encountered grave financial problems which, for the majority of the countries, have severely limited the capacity for sustained growth in the coming years. This situation will be improved by the drop in interest rates, which will substantially reduce debt service, thus providing a greater volume of foreign exchange and domestic savings, which will be utilized for capital formation and the creation of employment. While the drop in interest rates has a favorable impact on most economies, this is not the case in the oil-producing countries because of the decline of hydrocarbon prices, the net effect of which is negative for the region as a whole. Estimates made on a country-by-country basis show that Latin America will need an annual average of net external financing of approximately $22 billion in order to grow at a minimum rate of 4 percent per year. However, it does not seem possible to obtain the required amount for the following reason: the Baker Plan, which seeks the reactivation of commercial bank credits and increased financing by international financial institutions, calls for only $40 billion to be granted to the fifteen largest debtor countries over a three-year period. This will have two important effects: (a) a scarcity of capital for financing new investments and (b) the predominance of loans from multilateral sources over other sources of external financing. Therefore, the financing strategy of the international multilateral banks will be a key factor for the type of investments planned by the countries.

*Chief, Division of Country Studies, Inter-American Development Bank, Washington, D.C.

If, as expected, capital availability is scarce, it would be essential to formulate a development policy to improve the efficiency of both existing and new investments. Available information indicates that there are numerous ways to improve this strategy. An estimate of the percentage of GDP investments necessary for 4 percent growth in a selected group of countries is given below:

Argentina:	21%	Venezuela:	28%
Brazil:	18%	Guatemala:	14%
Chile:	15%	El Salvador:	14%
Colombia:	20%	Honduras:	20%
Mexico:	21%	Costa Rica:	27%
Peru:	19%	Nicaragua:	25%

The percentages vary from 14 percent for El Salvador to 28 percent for Venezuela. This range partially reflects the structural differences between the countries as well as considerable variations in the productive use of capital. Assuming that the net external financing required for the region is $22 billion per year, this is less than 2 percent of the total GDP. Therefore, a better utilization of new investments can easily compensate for the lack of external financial resources. Larger increases in production would be possible with either the same level of investment, or a slightly higher percentage of investment for various countries.

The short-term strategy will consist of increasing production through the accelerated use of existing capital and raising productivity and efficiency in the use of capital. Special attention must be given to completing high-priority projects that are already in progress and that have the desired characteristics of efficient import savings and the generation of employment, especially those utilizing external financing.

In the medium term, financial constraints will force the countries to increase their efficiency in the programming of investments, especially in the public sector. The need for continual adjustment in the public sector will hinder a healthy recovery in the government investment program, and it is highly likely that the sector's role will be limited to satisfying critical social needs and maintaining the infrastructure, which, if ignored, would lead to a costly erosion of overall productive capacity in the long term.

Finally, taking into account the disproportionate share of the adjustment burden that has fallen on the low income segments of the population—in the form of reduced real wages, high unemployment rates, and lower levels of social services—special efforts will be necessary to address the problem of equity, in terms of both the tax system and the impact of public sector spending strategies.

The strategy has important implications for the development of the different sections:

1) Agriculture

The chief objective of the agricultural sector will be to slow or to reverse the trend of the late 1970s, when the volume of agricultural imports increased at a much faster rate than the volume of agricultural exports. The principal elements of this sector's development strategy must be the completion of projects in progress and the more intensive utilization of installed productive capacities. Increased production can be achieved through the wider application of yield-increasing technologies and better quality inputs, and the establishment of incentives to promote their use.

2) Mining sector

Since the late 1970s, the mining sector in Latin America has lost a substantial degree of the dynamism it had previously exhibited, reflecting a possible secular decline in the role of the sector. In view of the current constraints on obtaining external resources, it is hoped that renewed emphasis will be placed on increasing the efficiency of existing investments, reducing market risks, and forging closer ties with the national and regional economies.

3) Manufacturing sector

The basic elements for orienting sectoral policy and strategy in the medium term are:

- Promoting greater productivity and efficiency in the sector to increase competitiveness in the international markets.
- Exerting renewed efforts to intensify the substitution of imports of producers' goods carefully selected for the regional market, the international competitiveness of which can be developed.

- Intensifying and improving export promotion activities and paying greater attention to market research, quality control, product design and efficient administration procedures.

Finally, since the recovery of regional demand will depend in large measure on the dynamism of the growth of the OECD countries, much could be done independently to improve the conditions of intraregional trade, particularly through the gradual elimination of protectionist practices.

4) Energy sector

The medium-term strategy for the energy sector will be largely focused on increasing efficiency in the generation, distribution, and use of energy in order to halt increases in industrial production costs and to alleviate the strains on the countries' balances of payments. The principal elements of this strategy will include the following:

- Consolidating the hydroelectric development achieved to date by replacing hydrocarbons with water power and enlarging the transmission infrastructure, with a view to optimizing utilization of the generating capacity established in recent years.
- Implementing measures to improve efficiency in the sector, including the continual adjustment of energy prices and upgrading the industry's antiquated equipment and transportation.

Human resources

In a world undergoing rapid change, a field of primary importance to long-term economic development will be the training and management of human resources. Although a certain loss of talent has already occurred, a major challenge for governments will be to adapt the existing educational and training infrastructure to the perceived needs for new abilities and to the scarcity of factors. It will be necessary, in particular, to devise strategies to accelerate the absorption of new technology; to develop and promote techniques for the intensive, but efficient use of labor in small and medium-sized companies in the key sectors; to formulate organizational and administrative procedures for efficient economic activity with a high employment content; and to find a way to include in production the substantial segments of the population that are currently unemployed and malnourished. Without new approaches to development, it will be difficult for the region to achieve reasonable growth rates in a manner that is fair and assures social stability.

Panel

RICARDO FFRENCH-DAVIS*

The issue of conditionality is currently of great interest. It has impacted strongly on the Latin American nations and threatens to continue doing so forcefully. This said, it must be acknowledged that there is a lack of systematization and political consistency in the alternative proposals circulating in Latin America in reaction to the prevailing orthodox approach of institutions such as the IMF and the major creditors.

Throughout Latin America there is a feeling that adjustment to the external debt crisis has been particularly costly for the countries of the region. In response to this, the North argues that the costs have been largely due to the continuing "biases" of the Latin American governments. This statement of the problem is synthesized into a set of reforms that the latter should implement: liberalize international trade, facilitate the inflow of direct foreign investment, privatize public enterprises, and, in general, expand the role of the market. This set of reforms is the basis of the "new conditionality" being imposed on the debtor countries.

Although there have been remarkable inefficiencies in state intervention in past decades, it seems to me that the proposed solution is extremely simplistic, fails to interpret correctly the recent economic history of the semi-industrialized nations, and ignores the conditions for formulating economic policy in societies with incipient processes of democratization.

My purpose here is to reiterate the importance of a systematic effort to adequately address the economic and political aspects of designing a constructive conditionality, one that effectively opens

---

*Vice President of CIEPLAN, Santiago.

the way for the national development of the debtor countries. Next, I want to discuss some of the aspects essential to a national development strategy, which an "alternative conditionality" must necessarily take into account.

FORMULATING A CONSTRUCTIVE APPROACH: AN AD HOC COMMITTEE

In dealing with the issue of conditionality, it is essential that a constructive, rather than merely critical, approach be taken. Progress must be made toward an "alternative" conditionality. The question is to avoid the polar solutions of nationalizing or privatizing everything, of liberalizing or regulating indiscriminately. The coexistence of liberalizing elements and regulatory elements must be reconciled. Thus, the subject of an alternative conditionality undoubtedly requires a great deal of reflection and a broad cooperation of open minds.

One way to ensure adequate reflection is to form a qualified, representative, high-level ad hoc group to deal seriously with the subject of conditionality. Anyone who believes in an Inter-American Dialogue must firmly oppose the unilateral imposition of a crossed conditionality, which may be even more damaging than that imposed by the IMF, and seek a form of conditionality that is agreed upon among parties and respectful of national sovereignty. Today, the opposite direction is being taken.

REPETITION OF A FAILED APPROACH

The monetary approach to the balance of payments has been widespread since the early 1970s, especially in the southern cone of Latin America. This approach was based on the perception of a high degree of direct and indirect substitutability between factors and between products. Thus, it is assumed that a change in the volume of capital movements affected aggregate demand (and, consequently, domestic spending), but the productive apparatus continued operating at full capacity, so that there was no negative impact on the utilization of installed capacity. Although it recognized the existence of some obstacles blocking the reallocation of resources, the model postulated that the process of adjusting national economies to changes in capital movements posed no serious threat to productive activity.

The balance-of-payments monetary approach was what gave theoretical support to the idea that the real exchange rate could not be changed by the authorities and that lifting restrictions on foreign indebtedness was a "good deal." The processes that many Latin American nations experienced with varying degrees of intensity during this period illustrated the predominance of this polar model, which was presented as indisputable.

We are living in the second phase today. In several countries, and very markedly in the case of Chile, those who praise the orthodoxy of the balance-of-payments monetary approach today advocate the same general theoretical approach, but with the addition of massive devaluations as the principal adjustment mechanism.

Faced with the prospects of a continued scarcity of external funds, it seems to me that much more is required than the use of exchange-rate policy. To reduce the underutilization of available resources, so well documented in the articles in this volume, it is necessary to apply policies that permit improving the ratio between the net flow of funds and the growth of GDP, which is determined by the income elasticity of imports and exports. Besides the exchange rate, there are other direct and indirect policies that should be used to affect this ratio. There are difficulties, undoubtedly. As Joseph Ramos states, if a set of convergent conditions arises there may be an abrupt change in inflation; with respect to "real ratios," it is more difficult. Demand structures, which are affected by habits, marketing channels, and a number of other factors, are more difficult to adjust. The possibility of changing the production structures seems even more complicated. However, each of these ratios is adjustable, depending on the combination of economic mechanisms used.

It happens, then, that what we need today is to learn, and to be allowed, to use economic policy tools, recognizing and taking into account the structural elements so that they can be reconciled with the use of indirect mechanisms (exchange rate, interest rates, duties, public tariffs, etc.) as well as the application of direct measures (government purchasing power, agricultural and industrial development plans, public investments, preferential access to investment loans, etc.), to advance the objectives of easing the scarcity of foreign exchange and stepping up economic activity. I believe it essential that this combination of policies be explored in greater detail.

TOWARD A MORE EFFICIENT ADJUSTMENT

The adjustments of the Latin American economies have been difficult and costly, and they reveal a dramatic change from a situation of large surpluses of external resources to one of extreme scarcity. Mitigating the impact of this change will obviously require action on the external front, to reduce significantly the volume of negative transfers of funds. Nevertheless, we know that the possible success of such action will not take us back to the situation of plentiful funds that prevailed prior to 1982. Consequently, a structural adjustment was — and still is — necessary. How can it be made more efficient?

The structural adjustments of our economies pose great difficulties and will continue being costly, even if especially well executed. Therefore, a greater abundance of liquid resources would yield a particularly high rate of social return, as the figures presented below demonstrate. Hence the importance of altering the relationship with commercial banks and of assuring that larger contributions from multilateral institutions and official sources represent an effective net transfer to our countries and not a larger payment to banks.

During recent years, however, Latin America has been transferring a remarkable volume of resources to its creditors. In rounded figures, a conservative estimate shows that the $30 billion transferred in 1985 also implied production losses of another $40 billion (the $30 billion in payments required a $70 billion decline in aggregate demand). Thus, the "social" cost of every dollar transferred abroad was between $2 and $2.5 dollars. This order of magnitude of the cost of the debt-led adjustment is obviously excessive, as Ramos pointed out in this panel. This means that there is ample room for suboptimal (second or third best) policies leading to a manifestly improved national welfare.

The indiscriminate opening of markets accentuates the cost

of adjustment because it fails to recognize that the capability of response of the various demand and production sectors is different, and also because indiscriminate liberalization tends to provide confused signals to markets and to discourage productive investment, as shown by the experiences of the 1970s in the Southern Cone and until now in Chile.

The orthodox monetarist recipe of moving indiscriminately toward free trade, of systematically selling public enterprises, and of emphasizing the passivity of the state to guarantee its "neutrality" in the market contributes, in my opinion, to an increase in the inflexibility of the ratio between external resources and the GDP. When external funds are scarce, aggregate demand must be more sharply curbed, and the effects of reallocation weaken in the presence of more passive policies. This leads to a significant rate of underutilization of existing resources and tends to result in reduced capital formation. All these aspects interact, in the short- and medium-term, to produce weak and inefficient development.

SELECTIVITY AND PRAGMATISM: SOME EXAMPLES

As an alternative to this approach favoring state passivity and neutrality, there is another involving state participation of a selective nature. In this case it is a question of promoting the existence of an active but very selective state, aware of both its capacity to act and its limitations, that applies equally selective policies (of relative prices and of direct action on the demand and production structures).

There is no doubt that the exchange rate or the interest rates can yield positive results if they are handled with common sense (setting real interest rates at moderately positive levels, for example), but the use of these mechanisms alone is insufficient because they exert equal force on all sectors, independently of their specific capacity to respond. Here is where it is necessary to consider a combination of both structural elements and economic policy tools in what could be termed "neo-structuralism."

One of the selective policies I would like to mention has to do with import tariffs. The extremes of arbitrary interventionism and across-the-board liberalization must be avoided. Excluding the exchange rate, tariffs represent the variable most closely linked to foreign trade. Concerning the question of how to manage them, there is the conventional approach of liberalizing imports as a means of promoting exports. The orthodox idea that this is the way to ensure a better allocation of resources is based on the search for symmetry or neutrality between export promotion and import substitution, which is achieved with a tariff of zero.

I believe that symmetry is very important, but in a different sense. In the sense of free trade it is erroneous and noncompensatory. What is the right answer? To treat unequals as unequals and equals as equals. Product A, which is exported and is essentially equal to that sold in the domestic market deserves similar treatment with respect to the elements expressing such equality: composition of value added, labor intensity, and degree of incipiency or "infant industry." Thus, it should receive similar effective protection whether sold in the domestic market or abroad. Clearly, this approach involves a radical change from the policies widely applied in the 1950s and to a lesser degree today, of preferential treatment for the domestic market and blatant nonprotection of exporters.

This symmetry, however, is very different from that of free trade. A should receive equal incentives or disincentives in both markets, but they could differ from those granted to B or C according to the characteristics of their production processes and the prospects of acquiring comparative advantage. The issue here is compensatory symmetry: if products A and B are different in terms of value added, or the employment they generate or their contribution to the country's technological development, A and B should be treated differently, but without falling into the error of indiscriminately promoting import substitution at any cost, irrespective of what happens in external markets. This is a selective, differentiated tariff approach designed to equalize social costs and benefits in a dynamic manner.

The existence of large, underutilized installed capacities raises the additional problem of how best to utilize this abundant supply of resources in the short term. A primary concern in this regard is the need to determine which of these resources should be utilized more intensively now, given their availability or the structural difficulties posed by shifting them from one sector to another.

Utilizing installed capacity is one way of intensifying the use of labor, so that a given amount of locked-up capital provides more jobs. Resolving this question implies complementing the schedule of medium-term incentives (aimed at transforming and expanding the productive structure) with short-term incentives (the objective of which is the proper use of existing resources). This distinction is essential. Both the public and the private sectors must be able to distinguish between stable, longer-term policies and those that will be implemented in the current crisis, on a decreasing scale that is very clearly delimited with respect to time. The aim of this combination is to produce real effects in the functioning of the market, so that the existing capacity is utilized more intensively, without deflecting resources to strengthen a type of installed capacity that then becomes dysfunctional for development.

An additional example of this type of selectivity is the role of the transnational corporations. It is true, as Eduardo White states, that the transnationals will not solve the financial difficulties of Latin America. Current projections indicate that their capital contributions will help to fill between a tenth and a fifth of the external gap. Consequently, the importance of direct foreign investment lies in other attributes: the experience of some semi-industrialized countries indicates that positive results are possible when the transnational firms contribute to gaining access to markets for exports and to technology. These companies, in exchange for exploiting domestic markets, make an effective contribution by facilitating access to new markets abroad. Again, this is a selective task, involving markets with access that is in some way restricted.

An active industrial policy is also required because "correct" price ratios (influenced by exchange rates and tariffs, among other things), while necessary, are not sufficient in a scenario as distorted as the current one is. Industrial policy must show the direction to be taken, so that resources can be oriented toward certain key sectors or strategies capable of promoting the development of private enterprises. This is a case where public policy and its institutions are essential for raising the rate of utilization of resources and increasing their volume (investment). The market fulfills a function of great importance, but it is not capable, by itself, of efficiently correcting structural problems and recessive conditions. And these are both determining factors at present.

The convergence of strategic elements, designed and applied

in a centralized manner, with the proper use of mechanisms for selectively and coherently orienting the price system, would contribute to the greater use of productive resources and, ultimately, to the creation of a favorable investment climate. In recessive markets, where per capita production has fallen as much as 15 percent in four years, the productive investment climate is negative. In this situation, the limited private resources and initiative, instead of being oriented toward the creation of new productive capacity, will tend to be focused on the acquisition of public enterprises that are being privatized. The recovery of investment levels requires the coordination of public and private management. From this perspective, blind antistatism can become the worst enemy of public sector efficiency and of a strong private sector, particularly when it is dogmatic and its sole aim is to reduce the role of the State in the national economy. It would be unfortunate if the conditionality imposed on the debtor countries were to aggravate such tendencies. The right direction is generally the opposite one.